STATE POLITICS AND PANCHAYATS IN INDIA

Centre de Sciences Humaines (Centre for Social Sciences and Humanities): Created in New Delhi in 1989 the CSH, is part of network of research centres of the French Ministry of Foreign Affairs. The Centre's research work is primarily oriented towards the study of issues concerning the contemporary dynamics of development in India and South Asia. The activities of the Centre are focused on four main themes, namely: Economic growth and sustainable development, International and regional relations, Institutional structures and political constructions of identity and Urban dynamics.

(Centre de Sciences Humaines, 2, Aurangzeb Road, New Delhi 110011, India, Tel: (91 11) 23 01 62 59/23 01 41 73, Fax: (91 11) 23 01 84 80, E-mail: public@csh-delhi.com, Website: http://www.csh-delhi.com)

Institut Français de Pondichéry (French Institute of Pondicherry): Created in 1955, the IFP is a multidisciplinary research and advanced educational institute. Major research works are focusing on Sanskrit and Tamil languages and literatures—in close collaboration with the *Ecole Française d'Extrême-Orient*—ecosystems, biodiversity and sustainability, dynamics of population and socio-economic development.

(Institut Français de Pondichéry, 11, Saint Louis Street, P.B. 33 Pondicherry 605001, Tel: (91 413) 23 34 170/23 34 168, Telex: 469 224 FRAN-In, Fax: (91 413) 23 39 534, E-mail: ifpdir@ifpindia.org, Website: http://www.ifpindia.org.)

State Politics and Panchayats in India

BUDDHADEB GHOSH • GIRISH KUMAR

MANOHAR

CENTRE DE SCIENCES HUMAINES

First published 2019

ISBN 81-7304-487-2

Published by
Ajay Kumar Jain *for*
Manohar Publishers & Distributors
4753/23 Ansari Road, Daryaganj
New Delhi 110 002

Printed at
Lordson Publishers Pvt. Ltd.
Delhi 110 007

Contents

Preface

The idea of the present work germinated in 1995–6 when both of us were involved in a major research project of the Institute of Social Sciences (ISS) on the status of panchayati raj in eight states of India. We noticed that the support given to the panchayati raj institutions by different states and by different regimes within a single state was uneven. Obviously, this was not a startling discovery, but it roused our curiosity and led us to look into the political variables determining the fate of local government institutions. We decided to study the nature of state level politics and its linkage with the policy on decentralization in a particular state. Four states were selected for this purpose. In two of them, namely Maharashtra and Gujarat, panchayats have been allowed to function uninterruptedly since early 1960s. The third state was West Bengal where panchayats have been receiving continuous support of the state government since 1978. The fourth state was Bihar, which lagged behind all the states of India in establishing these grass roots institutions. What factors prompt a certain regime to take a pro-panchayat stance? Conversely, under what circumstances an opposite policy is adopted? Answers to these questions have been sought through the case studies of these four states.

Basic research on the subject-matter of this book was done in 1996 when both of us drifted to other assignments. For almost five long years we could not find time to take this project to its logical conclusion. During the preceding couple of years, one of us (Kumar) gave seminars and lectures on some aspects of the subject at the Centre for Social Studies, Surat; Department of Politics & Public Administration, Pune University; and L.B.S. National Academy of Administration, Mussoorie. Encouraging feedback received at these academic centres revived our interest in the work. We decided to revise and update our work, but soon found the task quite arduous, as new developments had taken place in all the four states, which required to be chronicled and analysed. Besides, the gaps and loose ends that had remained in the initial stage also necessitated further research. We are happy that we could overcome the obstacles without hassles, thanks to the support we received from our respective Institutes, namely, ISS and Centre de Sciences Humaines (CSH).

We wish to express our deep gratitude to Dr. Frédéric Grare, Director, CSH, without whose encouragement and support this publication would not have been possible. He showed keen interest in the work and encouraged us to publish. We are also grateful to Dr. George Mathew, Director, ISS, for his unflinching support to this endeavour. Our sincere thanks are due to Professor Ghanshyam Shah, Professor Mohit Bhattacharyya, Mr. Satyanarain and Mr. Shashi Bhushan for commenting on parts of the manuscript or for discussion. Last, but not least, we owe a word of special appreciation to Mr. B.N. Varma whose editorial interventions have benefited us immensely.

BUDDHADEB GHOSH
GIRISH KUMAR

Introduction

Panchayati Raj in the Vortex of Politics

After Independence, several attempts were made in India to organize panchayats as institutions of self-government in the rural areas. The initial impulse to develop the institution of the panchayat came from Gandhiji. During the freedom struggle, he had pleaded for panchayat raj or a system of governance under which village panchayats would discharge those functions as could be discharged at the village level, leaving the rest to the institutions of the state.[1] At the time of constitution-making, some Gandhian members of the Constituent Assembly raised the issue of structuring Indian polity on the basis of panchayats, as envisaged in the concept of panchayat raj. But others silenced them.[2] Ultimately, a compromise was reached by inserting a provision regarding organization of village panchayat in Part IV, of the Constitution. This part is known as the directive principles of state policy, and is non-enforceable: the central and state governments took practically no notice of it. But, the idea did not die. It came back again and again.

The idea of constituting representative institutions at the level of the community was keenly felt a decade after Independence, when the centrally driven community development programme failed to enlist people's participation. A study team led by Balwantrai Mehta, which was reviewing the programme, came out with the suggestion of setting up three-tier panchayat system in 1957. 'So long as we do not discover or create', the Mehta team argued, 'a representative and democratic institution, . . . invest it with adequate power and assign to it appropriate finances, we will never be able to evoke local interest and excite local initiative in the field of development' (GOI 1957: 5).

Though driven by the urge to seek rural people's support and participation in a programme designed by the central government, the Balwantrai Mehta Report did give a spurt to panchayats at the three levels of village, block and district in various states. Jawaharlal Nehru gave total support to the new institution, christening it panchayati raj. However, the honeymoon period of panchayati raj was short. After the demise of Nehru in 1964, the institution stagnated and then declined in almost all the states. Only the states of Maharashtra and Gujarat retained the institution.

Another committee, headed by Asoka Mehta, once again revived the concept of panchayati raj in 1978. Several states of the country (notably West Bengal, Karnataka and Andhra Pradesh) welcomed the idea and encouraged the growth and empowerment of the institution. Yet support to these second generation panchayats (as they are popularly known in contrast to the first generation panchayats which came in the wake of Balwantrai Mehta team report) did not last long, except for the panchayats of West Bengal.

The third wave in institutionalizing panchayats came during the period 1986–9, when an initiative was taken by Rajiv Gandhi, as Prime Minister. He took keen interest in understanding the problems of district administration. He toured extensively in rural areas, met district magistrates in a series of workshops, and came to the conclusion that the administration in the district was 'unresponsive, inefficient, unsympathetic, often callous, sometimes even cruel to them whom they are meant to serve'. He thought that the remedy lay in the institutionalization of local democracy, as he felt that 'democracy [had] not functioned at the grassroots'.[3] Rajiv Gandhi tried to institutionalize panchayats throughout the country and for this purpose introduced an amendment to the Constitution. However, the 64th Constitution Amendment Bill introduced by him failed to be passed by the Rajya Sabha and his attempt to give constitutional status to this grass roots institution failed.

Later governments, however, pursued the effort initiated by Rajiv Gandhi. Ultimately, in December 1992, during the Congress regime headed by Narasimha Rao, the panchayats and municipalities received constitutional status through what are now known as 73rd and 74th Amendments.

Constitutionalizing Panchayats

Constitutionalization of panchayats was the fourth phase of the career of the institution. It has made a sea change in the status of panchayats. Earlier, the individual states had absolute power to establish panchayats and hold elections to them. The Constitution has made it mandatory for all states to set-up three-tier (in smaller states, two-tier) panchayats, and to hold direct elections to all the tiers at the regular interval of five years. In respect of devolution of power and resources to panchayat, however, the Constitution has laid down only the basic principles by way of declaring it as an institution of self-government and providing an illustrative list of functions that can devolve to it. The respective states were given exclusive power to determine the nature of power, functions and resources to be devolved to the panchayats.

The Constitution Amendment generated much hope among the votaries of decentralization. They saw in it emergence of a 'third stratum' of governance below the state level (Mukarji 1993). Yet, no evidence is still available to indicate that the country is moving towards a system of decentralized governance with panchayats (and municipalities) as governments at the third stratum. Instances of violation of the constitutional provision, either in letter or in spirit or both, are many. Elections have not been held regularly, functional and financial devolution of power and responsibility has not taken place, the gram sabha has not been empowered, and the power of panchayats to prepare development plans has not been given recognition. While some states like Kerala and Madhya Pradesh have been trying to give concrete expression to decentralization as envisaged in the Constitution Amendment, most states have failed to capture its spirit. Thus, even after finding its place in the enforceable part of the Constitution, panchayats still remain to be institutionalized firmly.

States and the Panchayats

Experience shows that institutionalization of the panchayat depends almost entirely on the state government. This was the position in the pre-constitution-amendment phase, and this happens to be the position, to a large extent, even now. True, under the present constitutional provisions, the creation of panchayats and elections to them are mandatory. This is an improvement over the earlier position when the state governments had the absolute authority to postpone local body election for indefinite periods. But, despite the existence of the mandatory provisions, some state governments found excuses to bypass the mandate whenever they apprehended that election results could go against them. Besides, even after following the mandatory constitutional provisions, the panchayats may be denied powers or resources, because matters relating to the devolution of powers and resources to the panchayats have been left in the hands of the respective state assemblies/governments. Hence, the question as to whether panchayats will emerge as the third stratum of governance is largely dependent upon the willingness and the capacity of the respective state governments to promote decentralization.

The states have not been uniform in showing enthusiasm for the panchayati raj institution. Again, within a single state, one regime may support the institution, another adopts an opposite policy. There are numerous instances all over India when panchayats have flourished during certain regimes and lost their vitality or remained moribund during another.

Yet, there are instances of success as well. For example, there is a continuity of the institution since early 1960s in the states of Gujarat and Maharashtra. This is remarkable, indeed, given the fact that no other first-generation panchayat could enjoy such a long lease of life. Similarly, the institution has received sustained support from the Left Front government of West Bengal since 1978. In all three cases, we find that the respective states were self-motivated to retain it. No constitutional mandate was necessary for these states to ensure survival of the institution. Again in the post-constitution-amendment phase, the institution has received enthusiastic support in the states of Kerala and Madhya Pradesh, while others do little other than fulfilling the mandatory provisions of the constitution. As mentioned earlier, some states had even failed to honour the minimum requirement of holding regular elections to the rural local bodies. In the above context it becomes worthwhile to investigate why do the policies and attitudes of the states and different regimes within a state differ so widely, when all regimes operating within India's political system regard democracy as a universal value.

Investigating the causes of decline of the first-generation panchayats, the Asoka Mehta Committee identified three factors, that went against the growth of the institution. First, there was resistance from the bureaucracy. The bureaucracy did not take kindly to the idea of transfer of powers to the panchayats and of being controlled by the elected representatives at the district level and below. Secondly, MLAs and MPs were equally unhappy with the emergence of parallel centres of power. They resisted the growth of these grass roots institutions. Finally, with the death of Jawaharlal Nehru in 1964, the panchayati raj system lost one of its ablest supporters and a forceful ideologue.

Such an explanation of the failure of the panchayati raj system is not adequate. If it were valid, how would one explain the continuity of the institution in the states of Maharashtra, Gujarat and West Bengal? Again, why did certain regimes in Kerala and Madhya Pradesh take bold steps to deepen decentralization, while implementing the provisions of the 73rd Constitution Amendment? Conversely, why do certain states fail to honour even the mandatory provisions of the Constitution? Clearly factors other than those attributed by the Asoka Mehta Committee were instrumental in the rise and fall of panchayati raj institutions.

In the search for such causal factors, it will be necessary to remember that panchayat has so far been an endowment from above—a gift of the developmental state to the people. There has been no popular movement worth its name, demanding local democracy and devolution of power to the elected rural local government institutions. Hence, if a state decides to decentralize its powers and responsibilities through the democratically elected local government institutions, it has to be treated as a demonstration of its political will. When a state takes an anti-decentralization stance, there are reasons to suspect that there are political compulsions behind it. What are the factors that contribute towards generation of the 'political will' to carry forward the decentralization agenda? What type of political situations prompt a regime to take actions on the opposite direction? These are the questions, which will be addressed in the present study in order to understand the causes behind the rise or decline of the institution of panchayats.

Conceptual Framework

The questions posed for studying the policies and actions of the individual states towards panchayati raj suggest that essentially we shall be investigating certain political facts. This will be done in two ways. First, the history of the panchayati raj institutions of the states will be traced in the background of the major political events. However, to describe what has happened is not the major objective of the study. The second, and more ambitious, objective is to seek answers to the question '*why* what happened did actually happen in that manner' (Kaviraj 2000: 1). In other words, the objective is to identify the political factors that prompted different regimes to take actions that led to the rise or stagnation or decline of the panchayati raj institutions.

The term 'regime' is used in the literature in different ways. Sometimes it is applied to denote broad distinctions in the type of rule, such as 'democratic' or 'authoritarian' forms of rule. It is also used to denote a particular government to distinguish it from other governments within the same form of rule (Harris 1999). It is in the latter sense that the term 'regime' has been used in the present study. It refers to the government headed by a particular political party or a particular combination of parties or a particular charismatic leader having overwhelming influence over the party in power. (For example, the Congress regime is distinguished from the Left Front regime or the Laloo Yadav regime.)

There are various ways to study and to advance explanatory

hypotheses on political facts. One can go to the social system or the economic system to explains them. We have avoided that course. We shall not seek societal or economic explanations of the political events under examination,. even though such explanations have great usefulness in understanding reality. Our limited objective is to trace the political variables in explaining the pro-panchayat or anti-panchayat policies/actions of different regimes in the states being studied. In other words, the attempt will be to investigate *under what conditions* (1) a regime wants panchayati raj institutions to survive, and (2) to what limit are they allowed to be empowered in terms of autonomy over functions and control over resources. We also investiagate under what conditions regimes in power try to keep the panchayat in moribund or weak conditions.

It will be noted that the nature of these questions is based on the assumption that political actors controlling state power are autonomous decision-makers. This assumption has been made for analytical purposes. It is further assumed that the extent of autonomy that the political actors enjoy in taking decisions and implementing them is limited by their capacity to govern. Following Atul Kohli (1991), it is assumed that the capacity of a regime to govern (or governability) is shaped largely by three factors: (i) stability of the support from the coalition of the social groups to keep the regime in power, (ii) effectiveness of the regime in power in implementing programmes considered as important by the government; and (iii) capacity 'to accommodate political conflict without violence'.

This framework helps address the basic question that has been chosen for this study, namely, under what condition a regime takes a pro-panchayat stance. For example, let us look more closely at the issue of effectiveness of the government or its capacity to implement programmes effectively. In order to be effective, the political leaders have to have the capacity to make decisions as also to carry them through (Kohli 1991). In order to acquire this capacity, the ruling party has to obtain support of large segments of people. One way to do this is to build a strong party organization by coopting the local-level influential persons to the party and to receive support of the common people through these influential people, who also might be given the power to distribute patronage. The Congress party in West Bengal had adopted this strategy during the first two decades of Independence. The other way is to have a well-knit party organization that can build a coalition of multiple social groups and garner popular support through persuasion and organized propaganda for a radical programme initiated by the government. The Maharashtra government under Y.B. Chavan adopted this strategy in the 1960s. If the leadership at the top derives its political strength from the organizational network of the party, chances are that it will not be afraid of creating alternative power centres in the form of panchayats. Rather such power-centres may be welcome in certain circumstances to satisfy the aspirations of the elite of certain social groups whose support the party in power requires. Besides, with a network of party organizations at the level of district and below, it may not be difficult to capture elected bodies. Control over these bodies in its turn provides the opportunity for widening and deepening the zone of influence of the party. Hence, it may be hypothesized that the more a political party desires to expand its zone of influence over multiple social groups through party organization in order to create a durable coalition, the more it will promote the institution of the panchayat. This would provide the regime with not only a distinct political advantage, but also enhance its legitimacy and broaden the base of the party.

Panchayats are also useful when it is necessary to provide stability to the coalition of support groups a party seeks to build up. An important characteristic of the panchayat is that it brings the state nearer the people. Indian state is a developmental state with many economic development and redistributive programmes. Some of these programmes may get transferred to the panchayats. Control over such institution generates considerable political power through distribution of patronage, which in turn can help a political party widen and stabilize its social support. Hence, if the political strength of a party in power is desired from the institutionalization of party organization, it is likely that it would lend support to the institutionalization of the panchayat also, because the latter would facilitate the process of the former.

Many local problems and grievances can be resolved at the local level before they snowball into major administrative problems. Thus panchayats have great shock absorbing capacity. By utilizing this institution a party ruling a state can increase its own capacity to resolve conflict through non-violent means. However, a regime may be expected to take this route to enhance its governability only if it also has a well-knit party organization in the villages through which overall control over the panchayats can be exercised.

Every political party has to have an ideology. The influence of ideology on the party workers/supporters may be strong in some parties (as among the Left parties) or very weak (for example, Rashtriya Janata Dal or AIADMK). But even in the case of the latter, the party has to articulate some ideological statements in order to earn its legitimacy. In the present study, it has been hypothesized that the willingness of the political parties to translate their ideologies into action, while in power, is severely limited by the mobilization strategy they undertake in order to build a durable coalition of their support groups.

States Selected for the Study

The set of hypotheses drawn above is tested in the case studies of four states, namely, Maharashtra, Gujarat, West Bengal and Bihar. Among these four states, Bihar has remained a non-starter in respect of institutionalization of panchayats. In West Bengal, after thirty years of neglect, a fairly successful system of rural local government has been put in position since the coalition of Left parties came to power in 1977. Maharashtra and Gujarat are the only states where the first-generation panchayats were not destroyed. They have enjoyed practically uninterrupted existence since early 1960s.

Maharashtra

In Maharashtra, the Congress party led by Y.B. Chavan set for itself the task of expanding the reach of the party with a network of organizations over the state. This needed mobilization of people belonging to the most dominant caste cluster of the state, namely, the Marathas and Kunbis, who are spread over throughout the state and constitute one-third of the population. They had already rallied behind the Congress in the 1930s, and by the 1960s, with their sheer numerical strength, had outnumbered the upper-caste people in the party. After the creation of Maharashtra as a unilingual state of the Marathi speaking people, the problem before the party was to accommodate the political aspirations of the rising rural elite belonging to the dominant caste cluster of Maratha and Kunbi.

Chavan handled the situation with great political sagacity. He understood that it was necessary to create 'opportunity structures' to facilitate the process of social and political mobility of the elite. The institutions appropriate for this were perceived to be co-operatives and the new panchayati raj institutions.

The cooperatives were already in place. With the growth of the cooperative movement in the western part of the country since the 1920s, the Marathas (like the Patidars of the present state of Gujarat) had acquired organizational and managerial skills and the ability to deal with the bureaucracy of cooperative banks and the government. They had ambitions for playing larger roles in the power structures. In order to allow this to happen, Chavan gave a pro-rural lift to the cooperatives. First, he shifted the apex body of cooperative organizations from the city of Bombay to Pune. He also had the city-based directors of these organizations replaced by committed party loyalists, mostly Marathas. Second, he expanded the cooperative organizations by opening branches at the taluka and village levels.

But this was not sufficient to accommodate the ambitions of the Maratha elite. In the early 1960s, the report of the Balwantrai study team provided scope for opening another 'opportunity structure' in the rural areas in the form of panchayat. The Chavan-led Congress could foresee that these grass roots organizations provided an opportunity to the local leaders of the party to taste political power and to distribute patronage. The party lost no time to utilize the opportunity and gave full support to the new institution. Later events showed that it helped the party strengthen its base in the rural areas.

The panchayati raj institutions (PRI) helped the state leadership of the party to provide the office-bearers of the local party units with positions of authority. Such positions were valuable, as through the execution of developmental schemes, panchayats could establish themselves as important institutions of the state. With the elevation of district committee office-bearers of the party to the positions of chairpersons of zilla or taluka panchayats, other aspiring members of the party found an opportunity to move up the party hierarchy. The scope for upward mobility created an image of openness. To bolster this image, people belonging to the OBC and the Scheduled Castes were also accommodated, though in less important positions, in the PRIs. In order to keep the panchayats under control of the party, a system of indirect election of chairpersons of PRIs was introduced and the party regulated the selection of candidates for these key positions.

Thus, it was the network of the party organization, with linkages with other 'opportunity structures' (among which panchayats occupied a pivotal position), that helped sustain the system. And it paid rich dividends to the party. So long as this system functioned, PRIs received all-out support from the state government.

From the 1970s, Indira Gandhi tried to introduce her own brand of politics in the state. Termed as 'plebiscitary politics' by Rudolph and Rudolph (1990), this kind of politics discarded the strategy of Chavan-led Maharashtra Congress. Under the latter, a strategy of developing and sustaining the network of party organizations all over the state, created 'opportunity structures' to facilitate the growth of the party and to develop an image of openness and pluralism in the polity. Even though substantive political power under the system remained in the hands of the dominant caste, the system proved to be successful because the regime sought to derive its strength from a well-knit party organization. It is this that became a casualty under the 'plebiscitary politics' of Ms. Gandhi. The Congress party would now draw its strength not from its organization, but from the leader. The leader would approach the voter directly, and the party in its turn would depend upon her charisma to lead it to electoral victory. The plebiscitary campaign would be based on popular issues and slogans such as *Garibi Hatao*.

It is during this period that erosion of the powers of PRIs took place. Under the 'twenty-point programme', various development and welfare measures were introduced by the central government in order to create a pro-poor image. The responsibility of implementation of these schemes was given to the state bureaucracy, bypassing the panchayats. Towards the end of the 1970s district planning and development committees (DPDC) were constituted and consequently the zilla parishads (ZPs) lost some of their important functions to the district bureaucracy. Yet, the faction of the Congress consisting of the old elite pluralists retained control of PRIs and wielded sufficient political power. It was not easy to kill the institution, but nothing was done to strengthen it.

In a different situation, the Shiv Sena–BJP led government that came to power in 1995, also gave a shabby treatment to the PRIs, despite the fact that the 73rd Constitution Amendment was in operation. The dominant partner of the coalition ministry, the Shiv Sena, is a highly centralized party where powers are concentrated in the hands of its supreme leader. It was not possible for this party to allow local institutions to function autonomously through local level leaders. The Shiv Sena pursues its own brand of 'plebiscitary politics', and in the process has weakened the 'opportunity structures' through which the Congress had operated, without providing a stable alternative. Instead of revitalizing the PRIs after the introduction of the provisions of 73rd Constitution Amendment, the BJP-Shiv Sena ministry took steps to empower the district bureaucracy at their expense. All these steps were taken to cut the base of the Congress, which was still controlling the majority of local level institutions. But in the process it caused more harm to these institutions than to the Congress party.

Another coalition government took the reins of the state after the 1999 assembly election. Apart from several smaller parties that formed the coalition, its major partners are the Congress and the Nationalist Congress Party (NCP). The latter came into existence following a split in the Congress party shortly before the 1999 election. Both the Congress and the NCP fought the last assembly elections separately but no party could gain enough seats to form government on its own strength. Thus, out of sheer compulsion, they joined hands together. In any case, this is an uneasy coalition. The social base of both the Congress and NCP is the same. In order to outbid each other, they have to play all kinds of political gimmicks. This trend was all the more visible during and after the zilla parishad and panchayat samiti elections held in February 2002. They fought panchayat elections separately, but once the results were out showing the division of votes between them, both the Congress and NCP chose to come together to bring maximum number of these institutions under their respective control. In their bid to capture all the levers of power, they did not even hesitate to forge linkages with the opposition. Owing to such opportunistic wheeling-dealing, the government was about to fall in June 2002. Although the government survived no confidence motion, the major coalition partners made it clear that in order to remain in power they could go to any extent. For panchayats, the present Congress-NCP regime is in no way better than the previous BJP-Sena coalition.

Gujarat

The political history of the state of Gujarat presents another example of the instrumental value of the institution of panchayats for the ruling party: expanding the social base of the party and facilitating consensual ways of resolving conflicts between competing social forces. Gujarat, besides, is a state where Gandhian ideology and the influence of leaders championing this ideology had, to a large extent, determined political idioms of the Congress, which was in power until the end of the 1980s. All this meant that panchayati raj institutions had a fair deal from the state leadership. Later, pursuit of the 'plebiscitary politics' of Indira Gandhi destroyed this tradition, and the institution began to lose its vitality.

In Gujarat, as in Maharashtra, the traditional dominant castes, namely, the Brahmins and Banias in association with the Patidars, formed the social base of the Congress party. The Patidars belonged to the middle caste and were inferior to the Brahmins and Banias in the social hierarchy. But they were resourceful, as they had landed assets as well as business interests supplemented by the wealth that migrant Patidars ploughed back to their native villages. As they were numerically large and had a hold in the countryside, Patidars had to be co-opted by the Congress party if it were to expand its base. Panchayats became an instrument to achieve this goal.

Thus in the 1960s, the strategy of the Congress was to maintain a balance among the elite of rural Gujarat and to enlist its support. To meet the aspirations of the Brahmins, Banias and the Patidars, sufficient 'opportunity structures' were needed. Like Maharashtra, cooperatives were in place. Panchayats provided additional outlets. Hence, there was no hesitation in giving support to the panchayati raj institutions as recommended by the Balwantrai Mehta study team.

In the case of Gujarat's Congress politics, ideology also played its part. Gandhiji's ideas had earned respectability in the state and many of its prominent Congress leaders were Gandhian. This created a favourable climate for the growth of panchayats. Two celebrated ideologues of panchayati raj, Balwantrai Mehta and Asoka Mehta, hailed from Gujarat. The former was also Chief Minister in the 1960s. Morarji Desai, another luminary of Congress at the national level, was Gandhian and he wielded much influence in the politics of the state. So long as the pre-Independence leaders held the party reins, Gandhian ideas influenced the political idioms and helped the leaders to earn legitimacy in the eyes of the people and workers of the party. Thus there was a political ambience that valued commitment to panchayati raj, and could give birth to a lobby championing its cause. Gujarat was one of the few states where the State Panchayat Parishad and State Panchayat Council, the former an advisory body and the latter a statutory body, played an active role in advising the panchayats, coordinating their activities and running training programmes for the panchayat leaders. The setting up of several expert committees to review the functioning of PRIs, the introduction of social justice committees at all levels of PRIs as well as devolution of 100 per cent land revenue to these bodies are some of the examples that testify to the commitment of the state leadership to the panchayats.

The 1972 assembly election saw massive victory for the Congress (I), of which Indira Gandhi was the supreme leader. As mentioned earlier, she had no concern for strengthening the party organization, and, as such, the instrumental value of PRIs in enhancing the capacity of the regime to govern was of no importance to her. Besides, ideologically she had scant respect for decentralization. Despite these negative factors, the state leadership showed its concern for PRIs, thanks to the strong pro-panchayat lobby created during the earlier regime. An expert committee was set-up immediately after the Assembly election to suggest reforms of PRIs. Even though the panchayat election was postponed in 1973 on the ground that the said committee had not completed its work, it goes to the credit of the then legislators that they pressed for elections, even during the Emergency period.

In the 1980s, Ms. Gandhi's followers came to dominate Congress politics in the state, displacing the traditional leaders. In the logic of 'plebiscitary politics' that they pursued following their supreme leader, there was no place for the concept of decentralization. On the contrary, they tried to resolve conflicts through centralization of political power and the use of force. Their strategy was to raise populist slogans and to pay lip service to the programme of distributive justice. (The 'twenty-point programme' of Ms. Gandhi's government is an example of the latter.) Ideology, sustained political and social work through party organization, local government institutions, and the cooperatives took a back seat. This type of politics saw the entry of leaders for whom pursuit of power was the only objective. They were not prepared to go through the rigours of political work and lacked the patience and perseverance to gradually move up the political ladder. It is during this period that one can notice a steady decline in the institutions of panchayati raj. With the constitution of a District Planning and Development Board, and the District Rural Development Agency with substantive powers conferred on them, the wings of the PRIs were clipped. Gradually, the hands of the bureaucracy were strengthened, weakening further the local government institutions in the process.

Later, by delaying panchayat elections for no apparent reason, along with uncontrolled factionalism—an inevitable result of 'plebiscitary politics'—the Congress party provided the basis for its defeat in the 1995 assembly election. The BJP, that came to power, followed in the footsteps of its predecessor and the state witnessed centralization of power in the hands of the Chief Minister, resulting in great political instability. Panchayats, naturally, had a raw deal during this period. Even for holding panchayat and municipal elections the High Court had to issue instructions. Keshubhai Patel was subsequently replaced by Narendra Modi who did not treat panchayats differently either. When the state was passing through a phase of an unprecedented crisis triggered by communal carnage, the gram panchayat elections were held, not in the entire state but in a few hundred villages. Clearly, the move was aimed at cashing on the polarization of votes on communal lines than strengthening the village level PRIs. Indeed, the polarization of voters on communal lines paid rich dividends as the BJP bagged more than two-thirds of seats in the assembly election held in December 2002. This unprecedented victory of the BJP, third in a row since 1995, has confirmed that in an assembly election issues pertaining to good governance, including decentralization could be brushed aside with the might of a resurgent Hindutva wave.

West Bengal

For an adequate understanding of the fortune of West Bengal's rural local governments, the nature of the politics of the state needs to be studied in three parts.

The first part consists of the period from 1947 to 1967, when the Congress ruled the state uninterruptedly. The social base of the party during this period was restricted to the elite, the landed gentry, professionals and traders. Unlike many other states, the force of caste identities was never strong in West Bengal for political mobilization, even though it remains a fact that the elite sections came mostly from the upper or intermediate castes.

Because of their social, economic or professional background, they were influential persons locally. The strategy of the Congress was to co-opt them and to secure electoral support of the masses through them. The elites were accommodated in the local party units, and in other power structures like union boards, district or school boards, municipalities, the governing bodies of educational institutions, cooperative societies, various government committees and the like. Unlike Maharashtra or Gujarat, the need was not felt in West Bengal to create more 'opportunity structures' in the form of three-tier panchayati raj system to satisfy the aspirations of the locally influential people, partly because of the existence of village local self-government institutions in the state from the British days. Even though these institutions were constantly starved of funds, their chairpersons or other office-bearers had social prestige and considerable influence over the local bureaucracy to enable them to distribute patronage. Probably the other reason was the absence in significant number of groups, like the Marathas of Maharashtra or Patidars of Gujarat who had the skill as well as ambition to move upwards in social or political hierarchy. Whatever may be the reason, the Congress strategy of building a network of party organizations through co-option of locally influential people was working well for the party. No need was felt to create new structures by reforming existing local government institutions. The prevailing ideology of the state government, which had a positive urban bias, did have little sympathy for village democracy. Since the party continued to get electoral support for three consecutive Assembly elections, there was no demand from the party to change the government policy.

A change in the panchayat policy was noticeable after 1962, when B.C. Roy, the first Chief Minister, died, and P.C. Sen replaced him. Sen, a Gandhian, tried to give shape to the recommendations of the Balwantrai Mehta study team. Accordingly, a panchayati raj system was put in place on 2 October 1964, dismantling the old union boards and district boards. During two years that followed, Sen's government passed through a severe crisis, owing to drought, food shortages and political disturbances. Before the Congress went out of power in the assembly election of 1967, Sen could not find time to nurture the new PRIs he created.

The decade 1967–77 may be considered the second part of the political history of West Bengal. During this period, the state went through chaos for the first five years and thereafter a rule by Congress (I) which introduced a kind of politics under which centralization of power became a sort of creed. The first United Front ministry that replaced the Congress regime in 1967 had, immediately after assuming power, superseded the block and district level panchayats, because these were relatively powerful bodies controlled by the Congress. Neither the first nor the second United Front ministries could, however, last long. The state saw two other short-lived ministries, intermingled with spells of President's rule between 1967 and 1972. This was also the period of the rise of Naxalite movement. In a chaotic situation like, this all development work was stalled. In 1972, the Congress (I) came to power. This was a new Congress, under the leadership of Indira Gandhi. PRIs had a raw deal from this party. A comprehensive legislation to set-up a three-tier panchayat system was enacted by the new regime in 1973, but it did not find time to hold election under this Act for the next four years of its rule. In 1977, when the party went out of power, the panchayati raj system was decaying. The intermediate and district panchayats were under supersession and, with election pending in the lower tiers for about fifteen years or more, the lowest tiers were practically defunct.

The period beginning 1977 is the most remarkable in the history of panchayati raj in West Bengal. The institution was revived at a time when it was going through a period of decline elsewhere. In two other states, Andhra Pradesh and Karnataka, where the institution was given a new lease of life following the Asoka Mehta Committee Report of 1978, it could not be sustained for long. On the contrary, ever since the first panchayat election in June 1978, West Bengal's panchayats have grown from strength to strength and today they are firmly rooted and regarded as a vital agency for rural development in the state. The credit for the success of these grass roots organizations must go to the Left Front government, particularly its dominant partner CPI(M), which has been in charge of the state government since 1977, winning six consecutive assembly elections. Institutionalization of panchayats is generally considered one of the most significant achievements of the CPI(M)-led rule.

What prompted the CPI(M) to give such high priority to the panchayats? In its classical form, the ideology of the party has little respect for the institutions of liberal democracy. For it, the party is supreme and it is the only agent of social change. But after assumption of power, the CPI(M) decided to adopt a pro-panchayat policy, ideologically justified on the grounds that the panchayats would be an instrument for building mass movements against 'age-old exploitation'. Later developments showed that these institutions did not develop as a nodal point of mobilization for conducting the class struggle. Rather, they began to play a pivotal role in rural development management. Hence the reasons behind CPI(M)'s support for the rural local government institutions have to be located not in its ideology, but in the compulsions of electoral politics. It is necessary to remember that the principle of organization of the CPI(M) is 'democratic centralism' which, as experience shows, creates an ethos of centralism. The authority-structure of the party is also hierarchic. It was somewhat unusual for the party to throw its full weight behind decentralization. It is instructive to note that in the election manifesto of the Left Front before the 1977 assembly election, panchayats received nothing more than a cursory reference. What made them change their policy in such a significant manner after assuming power?

To answer this question, one has to take into account the politico-administrative realities facing the party in 1977. First, there was the fear of arbitrary imposition of President's rule under Article 356, as the memories of 1960s, when democratically elected governments were overthrown twice by the centre, were still fresh in the minds of the CPI(M) leaders. Second, being practically new to the seat of administration, the party was sceptical of cooperation from the bureaucracy, particularly from those belonging to the all-India services. The CPI(M) was in need of legitimate power-centres from where it could exercise power without the mediation of bureaucracy. Third and most important, the Left did not have a strong political base in the rural areas. It was during the tenures of UF governments in the late 1960s that they could penetrate the villages significantly. But due to very short tenures of these governments, they did not find time to consolidate their position. During President's rule and Congress (I) rule in the 1970s, the Left found it difficult to pursue its agenda. Hence, the immediate political task of CPI(M), after gaining a rather surprising victory in the Assembly election, was to consolidate its organizational base quickly in rural areas.

The CPI(M) found the solution to all these three seemingly unrelated problems in the institutionalization of panchayats. In 1978, conditions were favourable for the Left to win the panchayat elections. The front lost no time and went for panchayat polls within a year of coming to power. Having occupied these bodies after a landslide victory, the CPI(M) and its partners realized that decentralization of development functions would make it difficult for the central government to impose President's rule effectively. Besides, the panchayats would provide an effective organizational base to resist central repression in future. It was also found that these bodies provide an excellent medium for the distribution of state largesse without involving the bureaucracy. The most important political benefit derived from the panchayats by the CPI(M), however, has been the expansion of the organizations of the party in every nook and corner of the state. Successive electoral victories of CPI(M) and the Left have been largely facilitated by the institutionalization of panchayati raj bodies in the state.

It is necessary to note that the Left regime has allowed the panchayats to develop up to a certain stage, but has shown reluctance to grant them autonomy. The institutions, therefore, have remained 'agencies' of the state government for the implementation of its plans and programmes. They have not graduated into institutions of self-government capable of expressing the 'will' of the local people. In fact, decentralization of governance and creation of an antonomous space for the panchayats had not been on the agenda of the Left. Hence, having created these institutions it was found necessary for the party to control them. It is necessary to point out that in the CPI(M)-controlled panchayats, the elected representatives are not free to exercise their statutory powers. The party exercises strict political control over them. A mechanism has been developed which ensures that all major decisions of panchayats have the prior approval of the local units of the party.

Bihar

Among the four states we study, Bihar is the only one that enacted a legislation on panchayats as early as 1947. Under this Act, two institutions, the gram panchayat and the gram kutcheri started functioning in 1948. Both were elected bodies. While the former was the executive body, the latter was the local judiciary hearing local disputes and administering justice in petty cases. The gram panchayat had meagre power and little resources. In terms of local development, its role was negligible. When the community development programme was introduced in 1952, the real power of rural development passed on to the community development blocks. There was no institutional integration between the development blocks and the panchayats. Even though a gram panchayat had little to do in respect of local development, its chairperson or mukhia, commanded prestige and acted as the link between the government and the people. Given a feudal rural economy and a hierarchically based social structure, it was natural that the mukhia and other members of panchayats would come from the upper castes. Hence, this institution posed no problem in perpetuating existing power relations within rural society. It also fitted well with the patronage system that the Congress had built up with the alliance of the dominant castes in order to expand its influence. Bihar's gram panchayats survived up to the mid-1960s, but organizationally they remained weak and inconsequential, even though the mukhia was allowed to retain the power to distribute state patronage.

After 1960 the Congress government began to face a crisis. The death of Srikrishna Sinha, a veteran freedom fighter and the Chief Minister of the state since 1947, disturbed the political equilibrium. There were factions within the leadership of the party. This was also the time when the upper-caste supremacy in the politics of the state was challenged and the elite among the backward caste people began to make their presence felt. This was not the time for the ruling party to play with the concept of decentralization. In fact, even during the 1950s, the strategy of the Congress to ensure political stability by enlisting principally the support of the upper caste stood on fragile ground. It restricted seriously the capacity of the government to introduce any progressive reform. The dismal failure of the government to implement land reform is a case in point, though Bihar was the first state to enact legislation for the abolition of zamindari. Secondly, by denying the aspirants among the backward castes access to power structures of the state, the regime was sowing the seeds of discontent. As later events showed, the party had to pay a heavy price for this in the 1960s, ultimately leading to its defeat in the assembly election of 1967.

This explains why the Congress regime of the 1950s and early 1960s was not enthusiastic about panchayati raj. It allowed the gram panchayat and gram kutcheri to function, but was reluctant to make these institutions powerful. When the Balwantrai Mehta Report gave a new momentum for democratic decentralization, and Nehru himself gave full support to the process of institutionalization of panchayati raj, Bihar failed to fall in line. In order to implement the policy of the central government and leadership of the Indian National Congress, the state had to enact legislation in 1961 to create a three-tier panchayat system. But both the block and district panchayats had deliberately been made weak political organizations, as their members were either nominated or indirectly elected and lacked a popular mandate. The government of the day, and also successive governments, were afraid of setting in place even these innocuous institutions of local government. Till 1978, panchayat samitis and zilla parishads were set-up in not more than 8 out of 32 districts of Bihar. Even elections to the gram panchayats ceased to be held after 1964.

Panchayat elections were held in 1978 when Karpoori Thakur became Chief Minister. He took care to ensure that the three-tier panchayat system envisaged by the state's panchayat Acts of 1947 (gram panchayats) and 1961 (panchayat samiti and zilla parishad), were duly set-up. After 1978, no panchayat elections were held in Bihar until 2001, when the state government had to clear the ground for elections, as mandated by the Constitution, under direction from the Supreme Court.

In Bihar no regime, other than that of Karpoori Thakur, has cared to fulfil even the statutory obligation to hold elections to the panchayats. Even after the coming into force of the 73rd Constitution Amendment in 1993, the parties in power (Janata Dal or its successor RJD) led by Laloo Prasad Yadav chose to flout the constitutional mandate of holding panchayat elections under one pretext or another. Thus Bihar remained the only state where the three-tier panchayati raj system was practically a non-starter till 2001 (except for the brief period when Karpoori Thakur was Chief Minister). The reason for this has to be located in the character of different regimes as well as in their capacity to govern.

An explanation of the Congress party's lukewarm interest in democratic decentralization during 1947–67, beyond creating inconsequential gram panchayats, has been given earlier. In 1967, Congress went out of power, but returned in 1972 to rule the state for fifteen years until 1977, and again from 1980 to 1990. These terms of Congress rule are characterized by what has been termed 'plebiscitary politics'. As experienced in other states, panchayats received most shabby treatment under such rule. In the case of Bihar, the effect of pursuing such politics has been disastrous. No Chief Minister of Bihar could remain in office for the full term of five years. The heads of both the party and the government continued to be 'chosen' by the high command of the party. They would not emerge through sustained work within the party. Soon, the Bihar Congress became the hunting ground of the corrupt, opportunists and even criminals. The entire institutional order, party organization, legislature and bureaucracy included, broke down. The governments were deeply in crisis.

No wonder, then, that developmental work had very low priority.

It is tragic for Bihar that when a change of guard took place, bringing Janata Dal to power in 1990, the situation went from bad to worse. Laloo Prasad Yadav who has been at the helm of affairs of the state since 1990, first as Chief Minister and later as proxy Chief Minister (his wife Rabri Devi occupying the official chair), has been pursuing the same plebiscitary politics perfected by Indira Gandhi. Under Yadav, the ruling party of Bihar—initially Janata Dal and later Rashtriya Janata Dal—has continued to be a one-man show. To remain in power, Yadav depends on his own image as protector of the religious minorities and as the Messiah of the poor or the backward people, and not on the political organization he leads. Thus power remains centralized in him and his coterie. The new rich among the backward castes, such as Yadavs, support him as they have been co-opted to play the middleman role between the government and the masses. Such politics stands on a weak foundation. Yadav knew very well that creating alternative power centres in the form of panchayats was fraught with dangers, as the sections of people hitherto excluded from the power structure might challenge his claim to being the lone voice of the downtrodden. That his fear was justified is proved by the panchayat election of 2001, which has seen 'the decisive emergence of the lower backward castes'(Gupta 2001). This explains why Laloo Yadav tried his best to avoid panchayat elections.

It is during the 22-month rule of Karpoori Thakur during 1978–9 that institutionalization of panchayati raj system was given high priority. As mentioned, he held the panchayat elections and took steps to set-up a three-tier panchayat system for the first time in the state. Why did he give so much importance to panchayats? Thakur was a socialist. The social base of his party was the backward caste people, divided in Bihar among innumerable castes. Thakur wanted to build a rainbow coalition among them. In order to do this, opportunities had to be created to enable them to participate in democratic institutions. Panchayats, according to him, offered such opportunities, as they can create a political space for the excluded categories in far-flung villages. So he wanted to revitalize these grass roots organizations. Second, Thakur was a man of organization. He had the desire to expand the influence of his party. The panchayat seemed to be a convenient instrument for this. It may be recalled that around the same time, the CPI(M) in West Bengal also promoted panchayati raj in order to enhance the organizational strength of the party. All this explains why Karpoori Thakur accorded such high priority to panchayats during his short tenure as Chief Minister.

What follows in the next four chapters are detailed case studies of the four states. Based on secondary sources, they seek to unfold the history of panchayati raj in the background of the kind of politics pursued in the states. From this history, it is possible to identify the political variables that have so far determined the fate of panchayati raj in this country.

They confirm our hypotheses about the close links between the character of a regime and its capacity to govern and sustainability of panchayats. The case studies also enable us to make certain general statements about the conditions under which a regime takes a positive or negative stance towards these grass roots institutions. These have been indicated in the concluding chapter.

NOTES

1. During the freedom struggle, Gandhiji developed the concept of *gram swaraj*. The concept encapsulated three basic principles:
   - Economically, the village should be self-sufficient for its own vital needs, 'yet interdependent for any others where dependence is necessary'.
   - Politically, the state should have least power, as it represents 'violence in concentrated and organised form' and the rural communities should govern themselves through their elected panchayats. This is what he calls panchayat raj or a system of governance under which panchayats will discharge all such functions as can be discharged from that level leaving the residual functions to the authority of the state.

- Morally, everyone should try to attain *swaraj* by acquiring the ability to rule himself. He will rule himself 'in such a manner that he is not a hindrance to his neighbours'.

In Gandhiji's scheme, the structure of Indian polity should be based on *village republics*, 'self-sustained and capable of managing their own affairs and interacting with others outside their respective villages'. For an acquaintance with Gandhiji's social and moral-political thought, see Bose 1957. Also see Ghosh 2000 for a brief review of the evolution of the concept of panchayati raj in India.

2. Among some other members of the Constituent Assembly, Dr. B.R. Ambedkar mounted a strong critique against the concept of village republics. 'I hold that', he said, 'these village republics have been the ruination of India. . . . What is the village but a sink of localism, a den of ignorance, narrow-mindedness and communalism?' To understand the mindset of the constitution-makers on the question of village democracy, see the proceedings of the Constituent Assembly in AVARD, 1962.
3. Quoted in Bandyopadhyay 2001.

One

Maharashtara's Panchayats: Opportunity Structures for the Elite?

Maharashtra as a unilingual Marathi speaking state came into existence on 1 May 1960. Till then along with Gujarati speaking areas it was a part of the bigger bilingual Bombay State. Prior to that it was a part of Bombay Province. The state is basically known as the land of Marathas. Yet, in order to explain the dominance of the rich Maratha caste in the state and in the Congress party which, unlike several other states in India, had almost uninterrupted rule until the 1990s (except for a short interregnum), a brief description of the political geography and history of Maharashtra is required here. This will give us a clue as to how, panchayati raj institutions (PRIs), again unlike several states, have received continued support from the state leadership, which in turn has enabled them to survive in the state and how PRIs along with other organizations (like cooperatives) have helped the Congress party to remain in power over the last three decades.

Present-day Maharashtra is divided into four agro-climatic regions. The regions and districts falling into each of these are given in Table 1.1. This excludes the metropolis of Bombay which in itself is a district, but is better known as the industrial and financial capital of India, than merely the capital city of Maharashtra.

The areas belonging to the Marathawada and Vidarbha region were not part of the Bombay Province; they were incorporated together as Marathi-speaking areas only after the state was re-organized in 1960. Prior to that, Marathwada was under the Nizam (later Hyderabad State) and Vidarbha formed part of the Central Provinces and Berar.

TABLE 1.1: REGION-WISE PLACEMENT OF DISTRICTS IN MAHARASHTRA

Marathwada	West Maharashtra	Vidarbha	Konkan
1. Aurangabad	1. Jalgaon	1. Nagpur	1. Thane
2. Beed	2. Dhulia	2. Bhandara	2. Raigad
3. Osmanabad	3. Nasik	3. Chandrapur	3. Ratnagiri
4. Parbhani	4. Ahmednagar	4. Wardha	4. Sindhudurg
5. Nanded	5. Pune	5. Yeotmal	
6. Latur	6. Satara	6. Buldana	
7. Jalna	7. Sangali	7. Akola	
	8. Kolhapur	8. Amaravati	
	9. Solapur	9. Chandannagar	
	10. Nandurbar	10. Gadchiroli	
		11. Gondiya	
		12. Washim	
		13. Hingoli	

Source: Siriskar 1976: 220 and Map I, *Census of India*, 2001 (Series).

It needs mention here that for two centuries—from the rise of Shivaji in the seventeenth century to the surrender of the Peshwa to the British in 1818—the Marathas had ruled over this part of the country. Under British rule there was nothing called Maharashtra as such, but a part of the Bombay Presidency.

The demand for a separate state of Marathi-speaking areas came to the fore as early as 1920, when Congress had expressed its commitment to the reorganization of states on linguistic lines, but it gained momentum following the separation of Sindh from the Bombay Presidency in 1936. Although the Samyukta Maharashtra Samiti (dominated by the socialists in Bombay State) had been at the vanguard of the movement for the creation of an unilingual Marathi-speaking state, all credit for it was given to the then Chief Minister of Bombay State, Y.B. Chavan, perhaps most for his role in retaining Bombay with Maharashtra.[1]

Thus after centuries the Marathi-speaking people, then dispersed in several states, were united under a state of their own with Bombay, the biggest industrial centre of the country, as its capital. For this historic achievement the Congress party earned kudos from all sections of society and Y.B. Chavan emerged as the supreme leader of the state. The Congress had become immensely popular in the state, and as an immediate consequence of this, came the exodus of large numbers of party workers and legislators from the Opposition to the Congress party (Siriskar 1976: 223).

Social Structure

Unlike other states, Maharashtra's social characteristics are attributed to the presence of a single middle-caste group, the Maratha-Kunbis.[2] This peasant-proprietor cultivator caste group comprises about 40 per cent of the total population of the state (Siriskar 1976: 221). There was hardly any noticeable presence of big zamindars in the state except in the Vidarbha region, and the ryotwari system of land revenue was common. Therefore, the rural areas had a fairly large population of peasant-proprietors and self-cultivators of the land.

The Brahmins, the only upper caste in the state, comprised just about 4 per cent of the total population. The Brahmins were the first to receive English education, and they held positions of power under the British and by virtue of their official position by which they had exploited the poor Maratha peasants. They were therefore resented by the Marathas.[3] However, as a result of reform movements of the late nineteenth century, the Marathas too had access to education. They could not remain aloof from the politics of that period for long. The 1930s witnessed large-scale entry of Marathas into politics and they gradually outnumbered and outmanoeuvered the Brahmins. In 1957, for instance, the State Congress Committee had 22 members in its Executive Committee, of them 5 were Brahmins and 11 Marathas. By 1966, there was not a single Brahmin in the Committee.[4]

In fact, by the time Maharashtrians got a state of their own, most Brahmins had already started withdrawing from Congress politics and settling in urban areas. And like the educated middle classes elsewhere in the country, they too had entered the bureaucracy and other white collar professions.

Yet another seam of social conflict was between Mahars, and Marathas. Mahars, comprising nearly 9 per cent of the total Scheduled Caste population (about 13 per cent in the state), were relatively literate, socially conscious and known for their militancy. Due to the efforts of Ambedkar a large number of them had converted to neo-Buddhism, but what had angered the Marathas more in rural areas was their refusal to perform certain traditional activities like scavenging and carrying of carcasses (Zelliot 1970: 29–32). The point to be noted here is that knowing the strength, status and privilege of the Marathas in the countryside, the Mahars had preferred to migrate to urban areas.

In urban areas, particularly in Bombay, there was another form of tension, between the local populace and the migrants. The Shiv Sena was born out of this conflict by championing the cause of Maharashtrians against the immigrants, mainly south Indian workers settled in Bombay.

Economic Condition

When Maharashtra became a state its natural resource base was thin. It was not endowed with enough mineral wealth and had generally low quality soils, with very little irrigation potential. Besides, there was no indigenous, commercial trading or entrepreneurial caste. The Bombay-based entrepreneurs were mostly non-Maharashtrians—Gujaratis, Marwaris and Parsis. Apart from this Bombay-based trading class, the economic stratification, primarily based on the agrarian structure, was relatively less pronounced in dispersal as compared to other states, particularly in the Hindi heartland (Lele 1990: 177). The pattern of operational holdings of land as given in Table 1.2, would testify to this fact. It may also be mentioned here that the land reform measures initiated in the 1950s were largely successful in abolishing absentee landlordism.[5]

Medium and large size holdings belonged to absentee Brahmin landlords and Marathas (see Table 1.3). Among them, as another study reveals, 'the number of marginal farmers and landless agriculturists are roughly double among Kunbi households com-

TABLE 1.2: MAHARASHTRA: PERCENTAGE DISTRIBUTION OF NUMBER OF OPERATIONAL HOLDINGS AND AREA OPERATED BY SIZE GROUPS, 1980–1

	Number (%)	Area Operated (%)
Marginal (below 2.5 acres)	29.4	4.8
Small (between 2.5–5 acres)	22.6	11.0
Semi-Medium (5–10 acres)	24.0	22.8
Medium (10–15 acres)	19.6	39.8
Large (over 25 acres)	4.4	21.6

Source: All-India Estimates of Provisional Number of Operational Holding and Area Operated in 1980–1, Agricultural Census Bulletin No. 21 (New Delhi: Ministry of Agriculture and Rural Development, Agricultural Census Division): 8, 10, cited in Jayant Lele (1990).

TABLE 1.3: LAND OWNED BY CITIZENS BELONGING TO THE MARATHA-KUNBI CASTE CLUSTER (1985)

Size	Maratha Kshatriya	Maratha	Kunbi	Total
10 acres or more	14 (20.3)	8 (13.3)	15 (15.3)	37 (16.4)
6–10 acres	21 (30.4)	22 37.9)	10 (10.2)	53 (23.6)
3–5 acres	15 (21.7)	18 (31.0)	20 (20.4)	53 (26.6)
1–2 acres	6 (8.7)	4 (6.0)	25 (25.5)	35 (15.6)
None	13 (18.8)	6 (10.3)	28 (28.6)	47 (20.9)
Total	69 (30.7)	58 (25.8)	98 (43.6)	225 (100)

Source: As for Table 1.2.

pared to Maratha-Kshatriya and Maratha households'. The bottom layer of Maratha-Kunbi caste cluster merges with holders of small fragments of land and landless agricultural labourers. The caste-class overlap was 'clearest' in case of the scheduled caste population, 'over 55 per cent of whom were reported to be agricultural labourers in 1971' (Lele 1990: 178).

Expansion of the Congress Base in Rural Areas

Although it was the non-Maharashtrian business sector that helped Y.B. Chavan to wrest power in 1956, he soon started cultivating Maharashtrian elements in order to secure a dominant position for himself in the party and the government. It was quite logical that he would adopt policies favouring the development of the rural areas in order to widen his political base. The reorganization and upgradation of the cooperative sector was one of these (Rosenthal 1972: 1725–46). But to win support for his policies, which in turn would help perpetuate his domination in the state, mobilization of the people was a must. The basis for mobilization could have been either caste or class, but open support to either of the two would have amounted to playing with fire. At the same time, Chavan knew that given the limitations of distribution of patronage in terms of dispensing state resources, he could not fulfil everybody's political ambitions. He therefore focused his attention on the middle and big landlords. At the core of his rural development policies was the economic interest of big farmers.

Therefore, when Chavan became Chief Minister of the newly created state, he had three important tasks on his agenda. First, the integration of the various regions, giving special attention to the Vidarbha and Marathawada. Second, the creation of an opportunity structure at all levels, to accommodate the ambitions of the Maratha elites without antagonizing Scheduled Castes and other weaker sections. And last but not least, the construction of a cohesive party organizational structure in such a way that his position at the top, as supreme leader[6] remained unchallenged.

In short, the question before Chavan was how to ensure the fruition of political gains out of the development plans initiated by him strictly under his leadership and institutionalize the support base of the Congress party throughout the state.

We have mentioned earlier that the Congress in general and Chavan in particular had earned kudos for the creation of a separate state of Marathi-speaking people. The defeat of the Congress party in the 1957 assembly election had also come as a personal gain for Chavan in the sense that his adversaries in the party were demoralized since they were primarily responsible for selection of the candidates who were defeated in several constituencies. Therefore, the atmosphere as a whole was congenial, and favoured the implementation of his plans. Another point in favour of Chavan was the solid support of the Maratha elites, their dispersal almost in all parts of the state as well as an equally favourable caste configuration. An 'ideologically guided and economically differentiated caste cluster of this size' was somewhat unique in Maharashtra, not seen anywhere else in the country (Lele 1990: 180).

The Marathas, numerically the biggest peasant-cultivator caste, has traditionally been a flexible and open community (ibid.: 179–82; Rosenthal 1977: 24–9; Baviskar and Attwood, 1996: 16–18), adept at forging bonds of kinship and caste loyalty, irrespective of inherent economic and cultural disparities. It is this flexible and open attitude of the community which helped Chavan to carve out a modest democratic polity (read establishing a systematic linkage between the local and state elites) in the state with his persuasive, paternalistic styles.

At the core of this carefully controlled (linkage) system was the Maratha gentry (rich and middle peasants). Marginal farmers among Marathas and Kunbis formed the periphery. The success of Chavan's control mechanism, however, was the impression of openness the system gave to outsiders. As an observer points out, 'The illusion of openness is the primary ideology that sustains formal democracies where mere induction of new groups, inspite of their demonstrated inability to affect the structure of privilege, is treated as validation of the openness claim' (Lele 1990: 180).

Even if the openness of the system was an illusion, it worked to a large extent successfully through exclusion, or 'carefully guarded kinship alliances in which flexibility is often determined by considerations of relative privilege. The reality of exclusion shows its more malignant face when serious and direct challenges arise to the very structure of class dominance' (ibid.: 181).

Dalits, more particularly Mahars who in the past had ever dared to challenge the class dominance, had to face violence unleashed by Marathas, even though the recurrence of such incidents was not as pronounced as in other states. Since Chavan himself was apprehensive of this, he always urged his caste brethren to accommodate legitimate demands of the Scheduled Castes.

In order to accommodate the aspirations of Maratha elites from within his own party and also to absorb the leaders of the Opposition by offering them positions of power, Chavan set out to reorganize and expand the cooperatives, panchayats, educational institutions and the party organization.

The cooperatives were already in existence since the late nineteenth century but a reorganization, introducing a federal structure,[7] occurred during Chavan's rule, first as the Chief Minister of Bombay state, and later, when Maharashtra gained statehood. The expansion of cooperatives began at an accelerated pace. This included 'deurbanization' of the Boards of the District Central Cooperative Bank (DCCB) and the District Land Development Bank (DLDB), and also their apex bodies. Earlier, urban based Brahmin 'social workers' were members of these boards; they were replaced by committed political activists from the rural areas. In a way, Chavan succeeded in shifting the centre of politics from urban to rural areas by facilitating the entry of political activists from the countryside in positions of power. Similarly, he encouraged the setting up of private educational institutions. Above all, what helped Chavan to nurture the political ambitions of Marathas was the creation of three-tier panchayati institutions.

It was in due appreciation of the 'dynamics of this competitive, accommodative style of dominance that Y.B. Chavan fashioned and managed democratic politics in Maharashtra through a hierarchy of formal structures' (ibid.: 179). In fact, here we find a convergence of his wish to expand the social base of his party by allocating resources to the rural areas and his compulsion to allow the rural elites to have a say in the distribution of patronage that ultimately resulted in the setting up of a hierarchy of formal structures. For what ultimately mattered was not only to provide elites with access to public resources which were in any case limited, but also to induce a certain mode of competition among elites for wielding discretionary power to allocate resources. What was the mode of such competition? Election, obviously. But there was an apprehension that if everything was left to the electoral process, its outcome may not be always desirable. In order to avoid such an eventuality there was the need for regulating competition by setting boundaries for competitors, so that compromises could be worked out among the competitors. But such a system cannot function without an arbiter at every level. The one (arbiter) who would emerge at the top, 'must display an acute sense for the strength of various political forces, to pick and support the winners, while at the same time ensuring that contending competitors are also assured of a place and a share' (ibid.: 180).

Before going into the details of the functioning of such a system created and nurtured by Chavan, it would be appropriate to see how the panchayats were created and how this system ensured the continuation of panchayats in the state.

With the creation of PRIs and with the establishment of an elaborate structure of credit, input and marketing cooperatives, the district became the crucial unit of elite competition. In fact, by expanding the party organization and more importantly, by setting up PRIs, Chavan created a number of public offices to incorporate the leadership emerging within the ambit of his own party as well as from opposition parties. The all-powerful position of the Congress on the one hand and the dwindling base of the opposition parties on the other, forced several Opposition leaders, particularly Marathas, to join the Congress party at that stage. Chavan had gladly welcomed all of them. It would not be an exaggeration to say that the Congress became synonymous with democratic politics (and its institutionalization process) in the state.

Setting up Three-Tier Panchayat Bodies

It is worth recalling that following the Balwantrai Mehta Committee recommendations, PRIs had already been set-up in several states by the late 1950s. But Chavan preferred to wait until Maharashtra was created. In fact, Maharashtra became the eleventh state to introduce the panchayati raj system. V.P. Naik, the then Minister of Revenue, after examining the Mehta Report, had settled for a three-tier structure, but deviated from the original recommendations by way of making zilla parishads all powerful in the hierarchical panchayati raj structure.

> Democracy in its true sense, cannot be expected to have a stable and permanent existence if it is based only on democratic institutions at levels so remote from each other. [The] History of other democratic countries has shown that like stable and unstable equilibrium there can be also stable and unstable democracies. The latter easily succumb to undemocratic forces as is seen by events around us. In order, therefore, to ensure an integrated and stable democratic structure capable of survival under stresses and strains which are implicitly in this form of government, it is imperative that there should be democratic institutions at intermediate levels between the state government and village Panchayat. (*Report of the Committee on Democratic Decentralization*, Cooperation and Rural Development Department, Government of Maharashtra, 1960)

The advocates of decentralization maintain that

> the local administration can function more efficiently and objectively if it consists of a hierarchy of officials under direct control of the state with local advisory committees, if necessary. They concede that if local bodies are considered necessary, their functions should be limited purely to civic amenities. In first place, it will be extremely difficult in rural areas to demarcate civic and developmental functions when the development work in rural areas primarily consists of provision of civic amenities like education, communications, medical relief, water supply, drainage, public health measures, veterinary aid. (Govt. of Maharashtra 1960: 46)

It must be noted here that as per the recommendations of Balwantrai Mehta Committee, the highest body at the district level-zilla parishad (ZP) was to be composed of indirectly elected members from among the members of taluka/block level panchayat samitis (PS). Contrary to this design, the V.P. Naik Committee provided for 'direct election' of members of ZPs 'from small single-member constituencies. At the same time, each panchayat samiti was to consist of all the members of ZPs from the particular taluka, and twice that number of representatives selected in electoral colleges' comprising elected village panchayat members 'formed into electoral clusters' in each taluka. A provision for the further organic linkage from GP to ZP was established by 'making presidents of PSs ex-officio members of the ZP in those cases where they were not already directly elected to those bodies' (Rosenthal 1977: 48). More noticeable in the case of Maharashtra, unlike in many other states, was the exclusion of members of the Legislative Assembly and Parliament from both the taluka panchayat and zilla parishad. This provision was perhaps made to ward off any competition that the state and central legislators could pose to the members of this apex panchayat body.

While making the ZP the most powerful body, the Naik Committee had concluded that the district body is the 'best operative unit of local administration as it alone will be capable of providing the requisite resources, necessary administrative and technical personnel and equipment required for a properly coordinated development of the district' (Maddick 1970: 84).

Since all the subjects hitherto handled by the line departments of the state governments were to be transferred to the ZP, it was clear from the provisions laid down in the State Panchayati Raj Act, 1961, that the office of its chairperson would assume high status. For the ZP chairperson would take a wide range of decisions regarding the appointment of personnel, their transfer and promotion, the channeling of funds to different panchayat samitis and gram panchayats in the area and also enjoy

> the power to influence the setting up of schools, hospitals, dispensaries, clinics and other local government institutions. None can deny that the office is one which potentially has the possibility of considerable influence . . . whatever the circumstances of state and national politics, there is bound to be competition between the parties for the post. . . . In general, direct elections in the panchayati raj system, may be expected to

be utilised by the political parties for graining a foothold in the system. (Maddick 1970: 211)

The fact remains, however, that had the state leadership been basically interested in effective mobilization of poor people, they would have gone for the devolution of real power to the village (gram) panchayats. Instead, they opted for a powerful zilla parishad, which they could have easily monitored by diffusing the tensions arising out of competing elites at the district level. That apart, with the creation of zilla parishads Chavan had taken a major step in the direction of introducing greater political homogeneity across regions and ensuring the effective functioning of the Congress system.

The point that needs mentioning here is that merger of the Vidarbha region was the result of the Nagpur Agreement, which, *inter alia*, provided for the creation of a separate regional planning body to overcome the backwardness as compared to western Maharashtra of the region. But with the creation of the zilla parishad, the demand for such a body was also diffused since elites of Vidarbha had by the time realized that it would be easier to compete effectively for the allocation of developmental resources under a decentralized planning process with the district as unit. Indeed, studies of elites of the time had revealed that there was a marked preference for becoming a member of the ZP over the Legislative Assembly (Lele 1990: 182–3).

It needs mention here that the Congress party had successfully cashed in on the popularity it had gained after the formation of united Maharashtra, both in the 1962 assembly election and the general elections. Of 264 seats in the state assembly, 215 seats were bagged in 1962 by Congress candidates. Of them, 100 Congress candidates (MLAs) had won with a clear majority of more than 50 per cent. The Congress had bagged 51 per cent of total valid votes polled (Siriskar 1976: 223). In the same vein, the Congress party had captured all zilla parishads when the election for this most powerful tier of panchayati raj was held in 1962.

Some case studies of Satara, Poona, Akola and Aurangabad

districts testify to this fact. Also, a large number of the district level politicians, basically the office-bearers of the District Congress Committee (DCC), went on to occupy prominent positions in the PRIs. In Satara district, for instance, the Congress won 45 out of a total of 54 seats of the zilla parishad for which elections were held. Most of these successful candidates were long-time members of the Congress party and nearly all (95 per cent) of them were active in politics for more than a decade. 13 of a total 18 DCC members contested and of them 11 won the ZP election; one member was co-opted.

The person who became the president of the ZP was not less than the DCC chief; his deputy in the ZP had been a DCC secretary and yet another secretary became president of a panchayat samiti. In fact, 1962 witnessed a large number of DCC office-bearers being elevated to the offices of PRIs in the state. Thus the creation of panchayat bodies helped the ruling party in more ways than one. For instance, if there was some tension within the organizational wing of the party, when some of them moved to positions of power at the state level, it was eased with the establishment of PRIs; this offered an opportunity to the party functionaries to occupy positions of power at the district and taluka levels. It also gave an opportunity to the party to recruit new workers in its organizational wing.

Besides, a study pointed out, the vast majority of the successful candidates in the ZP election were men of substance, belonging to the rich and middle peasant category. Similarly, 40 per cent of the presidents of the village panchayat were members of the managing committees of the local cooperative society (Shrader and Joshi 1963: 143–56). This was equally true at the taluka and district level. For instance, the chairman of a sugar (cooperative) factory in Ahmednagar district was also the president of the Ahmednagar zilla parishad (Baviskar 1968: 492).[8]

It may be noted here that in 1962 itself Chavan moved to New Delhi as the Union Defence Minister. Despite his physical absence from the state, Chavan remained an unchallenged leader of the state. By virtue of the political clout he wielded in the state, Chavan deftly managed to contain intra-party factional conflicts without arousing hostility. This is also apparent from the fact that, unlike several other states in India, Maharashtra was one of the few states where Congress had managed to avoid defeat in the 1967 elections. This victory needs further explanation. For it is here that we find a clue to the phenomenon of continuity of PRIs in the state.

Expanding the Base of Elite Pluralism

It is well known that all those states where PRIs were dislodged in the mid-1960s, had one thing in common: the ruling Congress party had lost in the fourth assembly election of 1967. Following this, there was uncertainty, plagued by political instability, for the PRIs. In fact, the PRIs survived only in those states where the same party, that had initially introduced the three-tier panchayat system, had been able to continue in power. Its corollary was equally true: that in those states where PRIs were treated as a part and parcel of overall governance, the very continuation of the panchayati system ensured the survival of the party that had in first place had created and supported the panchayats in the state.

Along with Gujarat and Maharashtra, the Congress retained power in two more important states, Andhra Pradesh and Karnataka. Yet, in these two southern states the PRIs suffered serious reverses and were discontinued. Political developments in these two states *vis-à-vis* PRIs do not fit into our framework. But at the same time, we do not intend to overlook these two cases as exceptions. Suffice it to say that there were some specific factors concerning each state through which the relative dominance or loss of authority of the Congress party can be explained. For instance, though the Congress managed to win the 1967 elections in Andhra Pradesh and Karnataka, its organizational base had already shrunk to a large extent. This was due to the lack of adequate representation of the middle castes in the party structure; the absence of a numerically large single caste cluster; and the absence of a strong leadership that could contain the intra-party factionalism. These factors, on the other hand, were favourable in the case of Maharashtra. Under such favourable circumstances, Chavan laid the foundations of democratic polity and governance in Maharashtra.

Atul Kohli (1991) has defined governability as the capacity of rulers to do three things: (a) maintain coalition support, (b) initiate solutions to problems perceived to be important and (c) resolve political conflicts without force and violence. We have mentioned above that the Chavan-led Congress party was naturally capable of maintaining coalition support because of the preponderance of a single caste cluster. Development of rural areas was the immediate task, and for that it was necessary to reorganize rural institutions; the cooperatives were already in place but Chavan got them reorganized, and with the setting up of PRIs, he created opportunity structures to fulfil the ambitions of Maratha elites. And finally, by inter-locking power at the district level and below, he managed to create a (Congress) system which helped the Congress resolve amicably the conflicts that occur in any democratic set-up.

We have mentioned earlier that Chavan's style of functioning was persuasive but paternalistic. He had an astute sense of assessing the strengths and weaknesses of the emerging local leadership both loyal to him as well as his adversaries, practically in all the districts of the state. Accordingly, from the very beginning, not only had he extended support to all those who had demonstrated capabilities to manage the affairs of the party and later cooperatives and zilla parishads, but also played a major role in establishing them as party 'bosses' at the district level. At the same time, he displayed exemplary political sagacity in keeping such district bosses at arm's length. Chavan himself perhaps never encouraged internal divisions in the party, but among the players at the district level he would keep matters simmering and thus maintain his supremacy in all matters. There were rival groups at each level of the party structure, but his deft management of factions was such that each faction/group was dependent on him and his trusted lieutenants for its survival. Therefore, the district level bosses were most of the time, if not always, engaged in ensuring their own dominance within the district rather than posing any threat to Chavan's leadership (Rosenthal 1977: 130–2).

In his case studies of the elites based in three districts of Maharashtra including Poona (Pune), Rosenthal (1977: 59) observed that 'a large portion of the politics of Poona during the period from 1960 to 1973 could be understood by focusing on the interlocking network of institutional affiliations and personal relationships which existed among perhaps no more than a dozen individuals or families in the district'. Rosenthal did not mean, however, that these dozen persons had monopolized all institutional positions in the district, nor did he intend to show that no other politicians had any say in the happenings across the district.

> In a broader sense, each of the dozen men represented a larger group in his home territory and in some instances responded to those others in the way he played the game of district politics. Furthermore, there was some porosity to the power structure because rivalries among the leaders of the district and among the followers of each leader, created some opening through which individuals with sufficient ambition and adequate political resources (including both economic and skill resources) could move into positions from which they were able to exercise influence over the fates of great number of people. (ibid.)

All these 'dozen persons' mentioned by Rosenthal, were prosperous Marathas. The district level 'boss' (1962–72) was a person called N.S. Mohol, an MLA in 1952–7. After assuming the unofficial position of the district 'boss', he himself did not 'pursue additional opportunities', except on a few occasions when he tookover the chairmanship of the District Central Cooperative Bank for a while and also that of the Dairy Federation at a later stage. Otherwise, Rosenthal comments;

> He [Mohol] attempted to moderate the ambition of others. At various times, for example, he intervened to prevent rivals from taking that extra step which might have disabled the Congress-directed system as a whole. No doubt, his very mediation of such rivalries helped in a certain sense to keep matters simmering and, therefore, preserved Mohol's own superiority, but this is not to argue that Mohol either consciously created such rivalries or enhanced them. (Rosenthal 1977: 77)

Leaders like Mohol had acquired a significant place virtually in each district, and the system was working well with a number of offices available for new leaders or the followers of the established leadership.

> In the ensuring competition among the various ruling class elites some succeeded more than the others, but there were very few real losers among them. The losers were mostly on the periphery of the political arena. By means of symbolic incorporation of some outsiders through seat reservation in legislatures, local councils, in schools in colleges and jobs, the illusion of openness was maintained. (Lele 1990: 181)

Besides, Chavan was more careful about his own region, western Maharashtra, the citadel of prosperous Maratha elites. Therefore, in the beginning he had selected V.P. Naik, a Banjara (settled nomads in Vidarbha region) landlord, as his closest ally and second in command in the state. Chavan never allowed any Maratha leader from western Maharashtra to grow in stature—they remained dependent on him. Even when Indira Gandhi secured her position in the aftermath of her decisive victory in the 1971 general elections, she chose S.B. Chavan, from the Marathwada region; there was no one from western Maharashtra whom she could have used to counter the growing influence of Y.B. Chavan.

The base of elite configuration created and nurtured by Chavan was western Maharashtra and Vidarbha—two relatively prosperous regions of the state. In both these regions he had forged links with local elites and worked through the system of consensus. That local leaders from Marathwada had to operate and satisfy themselves with the terms and conditions set forth by state elites, was yet another example of Chavan's class bias favouring rich and powerful Marathas. The Marathwada-based Marathas were confined mostly to the district headquarters and below.

Significantly, when Chavan was Chief Minster, he had inducted eight ministers, five of cabinet rank and three deputy ministers, from Vidarbha—a much higher proportion than what was due to the Vidarbha region. With this move, he diluted Vidarbha's demand for a separate state.

Chavan's cautious appreciation of the interest groups of Vidarbha once again became clear when a search for his successor was on in the wake of his move to the Centre. Chavan's obvious choice was V.P. Naik, but there were two other claimants, S.D. Desai, Chavan's colleague from his home district, Satara, and M.S. Kannamwar from Vidarbha. Since Kannamwar was opposed to V.P. Naik's group and was also in a better bargaining position, Chavan had to settle for him. However, with Kannamwar's death in 1963, within barely a year of his becoming Chief Minister, Naik was able to occupy the coveted post in the state. To assuage the feelings of two other regions and to maintain equilibrium, V.P. Naik had to accommodate two Deputy Chief Ministers, one each from Marathwada and western Maharashtra.

The effectiveness of Chavan's (or Chavan-Naik's) well oiled party machinery was put to a test in the 1967 assembly election. For, despite his uncanny ability to deal with interest groups and individuals, he could not accommodate everybody. Some of those who were denied party tickets for the 1967 assembly elections defected from the party and formed the Jana Congress (Siriskar 1976: 228).[9] But they failed in their objective of derailing Chavan's influence and support base. How did the hegemony of the alliance system, created and managed by the Congress, remain intact in Maharashtra, when it was dismantled in as many as ten states in India?

The roots of Congress power (and success in the 1967 elections) have to be found in the panchayati raj structure and the district power-pool (in the zilla parishad, District Congress Committee, District Cooperative Bank, District Sale and Purchase Society, etc.).

Taking the offices of chairman/president and their deputies of the zilla parishad, District Central Cooperative Bank (DCCB), Dairy Federation, District Sales and Purchase Union, District Land Development Bank and Sugar Cooperatives (including the post of directors in case of these two institutions) and District Congress Committee (DCC), there were about two dozen positions available at the district level to satisfy the ambitions of the resourceful aspirants. Further, there were a large number of positions available in the village itself, and also at the taluka level.

Branches of credit cooperatives, dairy societies, and panchayat bodies were also available at the level below the district headquarters down to the village.

Although as a matter of policy, a network of credit and service societies was set-up in each taluka and district during the 1960s, these institutions were more successful in western Maharashtra. Moreover, there was a dearth of cooperatives, particularly sugar factories in the Marathwada and Vidarbha regions. Therefore, district level players were few in number and less resourceful in these regions as compared to western Maharashtra. (This also explains why, until the late 1970s, very few prominent states level politicians had emerged from these regions.)

Notwithstanding the differences between the socio-economic characteristics of these three regions, a sense of new opportunities was spreading across the state. It gave the Congress system an opportunity to enrich itself politically in all the three regions. 'The institutional nexus within which competition occurred penetrated deeply into the rural areas during this period. It had all the essential elements of a formal mass democracy' (Lele 1990: 181).

All the organizations were under the control of the dominant Congress party in all the 25 districts (then, now 34) and this fact alone helped the party to retain its hold in the Assembly in more ways than one. First, the party could take credit for all development programmes carried out by these institutions with public funds. The panchayat leaders, even in GPs, were mostly prosperous farmers and were said to have distributed patronage selectively among the masses. Nevertheless, it had helped the party to mobilize rural voters, despite charges of corruption. Second, the party recruited young people but those experienced in running PRIs; nearly 50 panchayat leaders had contested the 1967 elections. Moreover, this move left a good impression on budding aspirants—that through panchayati raj they could move to the upper echelons of power. That apart, cooperative leaders played an equally significant role in providing funds for electioneering in the state as also in mobilizing their shareholders and workers in favour of Congress candidates.

Cooperatives, particularly sugar cooperative factories with their own funds, had invested a lot in development of villages by way of constructing link roads in villages, community buildings and school buildings, and even providing scholarships to poor students. Therefore, it was natural for the party or leader(s) who had control over these factories to exercise their influence over other organizations including PRIs. Barring a few exceptions it was the Marathas who had held sway over the chairmanship of such factories, by allowing one of the minority caste leaders, either a Mali or a Karekar, to assume the vice-chairmanship (Baviskar 1968: 490–5; 1971: 54–77; 1997: 94–5).

Thus the Congress party, with its overwhelming command over the state-wide network of institutions controlling manpower and resources, could easily maintain single-party rule in the state right from the Assembly and zilla parishad down to the levels of taluka and village panchayats. It is hardly surprising that when elections to the panchayat bodies were held shortly after the 1967 assembly election, Congress candidates emerged victorious at all levels of power. And in some of the zilla parishads, in Poona for instance, Congress candidates won all 43 seats, the same number they had captured in the 1962 panchayat election (Rosenthal 1977: 71).

The defeat of S.K. Patil, the Bombay Pradesh Congress Committee leader, in the 1967 general elections strengthened Chavan's position in Bombay also. Convinced of all out support from the Congress rank and file throughout the state, Chavan later took a stand against Indira Gandhi in the wake of the presidential election in 1969. Despite being aware of her preference and support for V.V. Giri, an independent candidate, all the MLAs and MPs of Maharashtra, barring a few staunch Indira Gandhi loyalists, voted for N. Sanjiva Reddy, the Congress party candidate, at the behest of Chavan. However, following the formal split in the party, Chavan supported Indira Gandhi, and the MPCC followed suit. Again this was in conformity with the wishes of Chavan rather than any ideological pressure. This particular episode was more than enough to demonstrate Chavan's absolute hold over the state party unit until the late 1960s. This was made all the more clear by the fact that members of the powerful 'Syndicate' were either despised by the Congress leaders in Maharashtra or were relatively unknown to them.[10] Yet they did not hesitate to vote for Reddy, once Chavan expressed his desire to support him.

Interestingly, once the formal split took place, Chavan's allegiance to Indira Gandhi did have its problems, with certain stresses and strains surfacing in their relationship. Equally notable is the fact that despite his expressed allegiance to Indira Gandhi, Chavan later denied party tickets to two sitting MPs in the 1971 parliamentary election. Along with few others, they had openly defied Chavan's instructions during the presidential election of 1969 (Rosenthal 1977: 144–5). Prior to that, during the Rajya Sabha elections some MLAs were alleged to have voted for the Opposition candidate, yet no action was taken against them. These two instances once again confirmed Chavan's cautious approach in handling the delicate affairs of the party. He did not hesitate to deny tickets to sitting MPs: this decision could have been based on his firm realization that those MPs did not carry much weight in the state party apparatus, therefore cutting them to size would be easy and would not be seen as an open case of prosecution. In the latter case, any disciplinary action against MLAs would have resulted in open antagonization, which may have had other implications. Therefore, Chavan maintained a discreet silence. In the ultimate analysis, what we wish to underline is that Chavan's style of functioning was not dictatorial but highly persuasive, and he avoided taking decisions that seemed to be openly antagonistic.

This was the reason why, despite her efforts, Indira Gandhi could not weaken Chavan's hold over the state Congress unit. Her attempts to use Naik to upstage Chavan proved futile; on the contrary it gave a new lease of life to Naik as Chief Minister. During 1971–2 in many states she had replaced Chief Ministers considered to be political heavyweights who could have posed a threat to her leadership.

STATE PARTY UNIT *VS* THE HIGH COMMAND

Since her overwhelming victory in 1971 parliamentary elections, Indira Gandhi had resorted to plebiscitary politics[11] in which the supreme leader was no longer dependent on the organizational network of the party. On the contrary, the party was dependent upon the charisma of the leader for electoral victory. Under this system there was no scope for any other leader to emerge from within the party. The supreme leader would nominate somebody as Chief Minister who would remain in the office at her pleasure. In Maharashra, initially Ms. Gandhi failed to apply this strategy because of two reasons. First, she was indebted to Chavan for his loyalty.[12] And second, non-availability of a non-Maratha leader with a leftist (pro-poor) leaning who could be projected as an alternative to the Chavan-Naik combine. Yet, in order to forestall any move on the part of Indira Gandhi, the Chavan-Naik combine resorted to further expansion of the base of the party by accommodating other caste leaders into the folds of the Congress owing allegiance to Indira Gandhi's leadership.

A fifteen-point programme adopted by the state leadership proves this point. This programme was meant to securing minimum wages for agricultural landless labourers with guarantees to employment in the villages; waiving of debts of small farmers and assurance to provide them with credit facilities; economic uplift of the Scheduled Castes and Tribes and the other backward castes; concessions in education to all backward communities and also to the economically backward including those belonging to higher castes, such as Brahmins and Marathas. Although there were proposals regarding slum improvement, a ceiling on urban property, etc., this was basically an exercise to woo all castes in the rural areas and neutralize the sense of resentment against the rise of Maratha castes in politics and the cooperative movement (*EPW* 1971: 1743–4).

These stated programmes were no doubt aimed at broadening the support base of the Congress, but at the same time they were in continuation of Chavan's earlier strategy (of forging an alliance with the Republican Party) to include nearly 2.9 million STs and millions of OBCs into the folds of the Congress by rewarding leaders of various caste groups with positions of power.

One can ask, if Chavan had always emphasized the need to accommodate leaders of other caste groups, then what was the need for reiterating the fact on the eve of the 1972 Assembly elections? The reason was that despite his pro-poor rhetoric, the policies adopted by the Congress had entrenched the power and influence of relatively big landowners and the cooperative lords in rural areas. And the way in which the rich farmers were displaying their wealth and power on account of holding positions in the party and the cooperatives, they had alienated themselves from the poor and masses. Added to this was the apprehension that the experienced cooperative leaders might prose a serious challenge to important state leaders. Yet, despite prolonged debates on the issue, the reform proposals were finally put into cold storage (Rosenthal 1977: 231–68). That apart, during 1971–3 Maharashtra was hit by a severe drought which gave rise to large-scale unemployment in the countryside.

Despite this sorry state of affairs, if the Congress party could manage to retain its hold in the state, it was largely because of a disorganized Opposition that had hardly any solid base in the rural areas.

The 1972 Assembly election was held with this backdrop, and the Congress (R) again came out successful with Indira Gandhi being forced to allow Naik to continue in power. Prior to this, the state government had launched a drought relief programme which ultimately took the shape of the Employment Guarantee Scheme (EGS) in May 1972. Under EGS, crores of rupees were spent on providing employment to landless labourers and financial assistance to the poor in the form of assets with multiplier effect. But the PRIs were hardly involved in this programme. On the contrary, the EGS helped the rural elites who, by virtue of their hold on PRIs, managed to gain favour for their supporters under this programme. It was mainly a bureaucratic exercise, manned and supervised by staffs of the revenue department and the main beneficiaries were the medium and big farmers (MHJ, *EPW* 1980: 2043–5. Also *EPW* 1982: 1226–7).

Panchayats losing steam and not caring for the poor was further established in 1972 when the Bongiwar Committee Report was made public. The Bongiwar Committee, no doubt, had appreciated the contribution of PRIs in the field of agricultural development, but, the report also noted that the poor were not getting representation in the PRIs, and there was a lack of dynamism in panchayati raj leadership (though in the same vein the Committee had appreciated the panchayati raj system for encouraging young leadership with agricultural background); the apathetic attitude of the bureaucracy and, above all, the fact that panchayati raj had failed to project itself as an institution working for the welfare of common man. Apart from suggesting changes in the recruitment of the administrative officers for panchayat bodies, the Bongiwar Committee also recommended, 'alterations in the kinds of persons co-opted to serve alongside elected members on specialized committees'. It also needs mentioning that the committee 'commented unfavourably on the practice of coopting persons who didn't have technical qualifications to committees where expertise was needed'. On the question of political control, however, the Bongiwar Committee Report recommended that taluka panchayats be composed of directly elected members besides persons from the taluka elected to ZP, and co-opted members. Yet, 'on the whole, the Report took for granted the existing separation of political and administrative roles and made it clear that the Chief Executive Officer (CEO) would be supreme in day-to-day administrative matters' (Rosenthal 1977: 297–305).

There were discussions on separating education from the domain of PRIs, but hardly anything was said about the participation of the people in the affairs of panchayat. Perhaps it was not on their agenda either. To them panchayati raj was an extended arm of the government, a welfare institution to deliver goods to the people.

Enhanced representation of OBCs, SCs, STs and minorities in the party organization and in the government, helped the ruling party immensely in Maharashtra whereas governments in other states, even in neighbouring Gujarat, collapsed under such external pressure. Naik earned kudos from Jayaprakash Narayan for his progressive policies. No doubt, elites from SCs, STs and Muslims had been 'more generously accommodated within the Congress system in Maharashtra than elsewhere', and as a result they had developed a vested interest in the maintenance of the system. It must be noted, however, that OBCs and Muslims probably had no choice than to fall in line, since they had neither control over land or trade nor a 'caste-cluster ideology equivalent to that of the Marathas or Mahars'; 'without spatial concentrations, mobilization against Maratha hegemony or the Congress system [could not] yield a lasting alternate system of rewards' (Lele 1990: 188–9). Besides, the Social Welfare Committee, constituted almost on the lines of the Social Justice Committee in Gujarat in 1970s, had commissioned several welfare programmes for SCs and STs. Notwithstanding these facts, the Congress's hold over poor masses was not as strong as it was a decade ago. But the Chavan-Naik combine had dared to explicitly blame the Centre for the shortcomings in the state development programmes.

The advent of the Emergency saw Naik being replaced by S.B. Chavan as Chief Minister. The latter was a strong contender from the Marathwada region but again a Maratha. With this change, though the elite pluralists suffered a setback at the hands of the copopulists, the Maratha hegemony remained intact. What coincided with the change in the state leadership was the setting up of a District Planning and Development Council (DPDC), a powerful body in each district which was to supervise all matters pertaining to district planning and resource allocation from the ZP. Although this body was created more at the behest of the Central Planning Commission (similar councils were also set-up simultaneously in many states including Gujarat and UP), whatever powers the ZP had on such vital matters, prior to the formation of DPDC, were taken away in one stroke. The chairman of the ZP, along with other elected representatives in the district, was made an ordinary member of the DPDC. The very composition of this body was enough to indicate that the elected representatives, of particularly the ZP had lost their power to the bureaucracy and the higher level political leaders. For, the DPDC was to be headed by a minister-designate and the Divisional Commissioner was to occupy the post of vice-chairman with the District Collector being its member-secretary.

It is equally important to note that the Emergency era witnessed the growth of an all-pervasive centralized authority. The first casualty was the democratic politics ushered in and consolidated during the 1950s and 1960s, and by implication, state autonomy. 'The organization of the Congress itself, in some regions where it provided a base for potential rivals to Mrs. Gandhi, was systematically dismantled—the most vivid example being the Maharashtra machine that had been created by Y.B. Chavan' (Manor 1991: 71). In a sense, it was the culmination of over-centralization which Indira Gandhi had initiated since 1971. Most importantly, the 'twenty-point programme'—the mother of all centralized rural development programmes (which have gradually grown out of proportion in later years)—also started during the Emergency, the responsibility for implementation of these programmes and their monitoring being given to the bureaucracy and higher-level political authorities. Maharashtra, obviously, could not remain an exception to this trend. For instance, special poverty alleviation programmes for small and marginal farmers (SFDA), the programme for farmers in the drought-prone areas and the Intensive Tribal Development Programme (ITDP) were kept outside the purview of the PRIs. As in other states, all these agenices were headed by bureaucrats and panchayats had practically no say in their day-to-day activities. Taking stock of the changes which came to occupy centre-stage, it appears that had it not been for the unique interlocking system of power-sharing at the local (district and below) level institutions, reinforced by the preponderance of a single caste cluster, the PRIs in Maharashtra would have probably met the same fate as their counterparts in northern India.

Consequences of Plebiscitary Politics

S.B. Chavan was not a leader with a mass following; instead, his ascendancy to the Chief Ministership was largely due to the support of Indira Gandhi. This became clear when his nominees from the Marathwada region were defeated in the 1977 parliamentary election.

The result of the 1978 assembly election was hardly any different, though the election was held under the influence of political change that had already occurred at the centre. For the first time the Congress was removed from power; this was by the Janata Party, a loose amalgamation of socialists, the Old Congress and the Jana Sangh. Some of the constituents of the Janata Party were quite active in Maharashtra. Besides, there had emerged two Congress parties, Congress and Congress (I) [the suffix (R) had later given way to (I) for Indira Gandhi]. The elite pluralists like Y.B. Chavan, V.P. Naik, Sharad Pawar and Vasantdada Patil were with the former. Populist leaders basically loyal to Indira Gandhi, like Ramarao Adik, A.R. Antulay, B.S. Bhosle, S.B. Chavan and Tripude, led the other Congress faction. For the first time the contest between the well-oiled political machine of the elite pluralists and the populists relying primarily on the charisma of Indira Gandhi, was clearly articulated. Not surprisingly, the results of the 1978 assembly election were in conformity with the earlier regional variations.[13]

A Congress-Congress (I) coalition government was formed, with Vasantdada Patil as Chief Minister and Tripude as his Deputy. But the coalition alliance could not last long as Sharad Pawar, the youngest among the pluralist leaders, resigned from the coalition government, floated a parallel Congress, and in alliance with the Janata Party, formed a Progressive Democratic Front government. Y.B. Chavan then leader of Congress (Urs, a faction formed after another split in the Congerss in 1979), opposed Pawar's move which led to the two main Congress groups opposing the Pawar-led Progressive Democratic Front. The question therefore arises: why did Pawar choose to lead an uneasy coalition? The unfolding of subsequent events perhaps provides the answer. In fact, the timing of Pawar's action was crucial, since elections were due for both the cooperatives and panchayat institutions.

It is a well known fact that the Patil faction yielded considerable influence over cooperatives and if he was allowed to continue as Chief Minister, he would have made maximum use of his position to destabilize Pawar's support base in the PRIs. Pawar also knew that in his state 'political power is not consummated unless one tightly holds the cooperative strings in one's hand' (*EPW* 1979: 1039–40; Baviskar 1997: 93–6).

No doubt Pawar fought aggressively at all levels of cooperatives, right from primary cooperative societies to district cooperative banks, sale-purchase societies, marketing committees, cooperative sugar factories and their apex bodies. He did succeed in capturing some of these bodies, including cooperative sugar factories. Some of the camp followers of Patil switched loyalties towards Pawar. Yet, Patil demonstrated that his support among the cooperatives had hardly diminished, notwithstanding the losses he suffered at the hands of Pawar.

On the other hand, Pawar's party reaped maximum benefit out of the panchayat election held in May 1982. His experienced followers were already controlling two ZPs where elections were not due, but after having won the election in thirteen more ZPs (*EPW* 1979: 930) Pawar managed to prove to his adversaries that he was in command in the rural areas. With such impressive gains in the panchayat election, Pawar indeed managed to kill two birds with one stone. First, Pawar dealt a severe blow to the official Congress led by N.M. Tidke, by his claim that the majority of the party's rank and file supported him and not the faction led by Tidke. Second, the Congress High Command could not afford to ignore him in the next Assembly election. Finally, with his demonstrated superiority over his alliance partner (Janata Party) in Maharashtra, Pawar managed to silence those dissidents in the Janata Party who would otherwise have revolted against his leadership. Yet, the fact remains that the Congress as a whole was hopelessly divided into several factions and parallel Congress parties, including that of Pawar, which was indeed doing more harm than good to each faction. No wonder, during the brief interregnum, a majority of the pluralists closed ranks with the populists to rejoin the Congress (I). However, despite the expansion of populism since the mid-1970s, and the increasing level of politicization in the backward regions and among the poor, the domination of the Marathas in Maharashtra state politics remained unchallenged. For, as the logic of populism goes, it has had the 'consequences of blunting the potential for systematic and effective mobilization of these classes at the mass level' (Lele 1990: 191). Not surprisingly, of the four Chief Ministers after Y.B. Chavan, three (Naik, Patil and Pawar) were leaders of the elite pluralists and one was populist (S.B. Chavan), and except Naik all were Marathas.[14]

The instability later in the 1970s, it must be noted, was bound to affect the party structure at the local level. Indeed, that is precisely what happened.

State Politics in the 1980s

The pluralists suffered a major setback in the 1980 parliamentary election when out of twenty-four candidates fielded by them only Y.B. Chavan could win. That was probably the last well-articulated contest between the pluralists and populists. Subsequently, Pawar's government was dissolved and the pluralists by then had realized that, 'attempts to gain or retain power from outside the Congress system were bound to fail and also that Indira Gandhi could not simply dismiss or ignore them; at best, they could be held in check by means of a coalition' (ibid.: 193).

This calculation of the elite pluralists proved to be correct when two loyal proteges (A.R. Antulay and B.S. Bhosle) of Indira Gandhi failed to tilt the balance against the pluralists during their short-lived tenures as Chief Minister. Although these non-Maratha aspirants who had entered the political arena for the first time were more educated and articulate than the masses in their communities, unlike newcomers from among the Maratha elites, they had no experience of controlling political institutions.

Moreover, the old system of dispensing patronage and garnering popular support through cooperatives and PRIs, particularly ZPs and educational institutions run by trusts, were still in the hands of the Maratha elite pluralists. Therefore, in order to help his MLAs develop support structures in their constituencies, Antulay set-up new informal committees for the allotment of loans, pensions, etc. The Sanjay Gandhi Niradhar Anudan Yojana and the Sanjay Gandhi Swavalamban Yojana (created to allocate pensions to destitutes and loans for artisans) were the result of these compulsions (ibid.: 194). Realizing the potential threat to their support base by these parallel institutions manned by the populists, the Maratha elites launched an attack on Antulay. The Bombay High Court was to find that Antulay had misused his discretionary powers in promoting these organizations, and he was forced to resign. Bhonsle, another protege of Ms. Gandhi who succeeded Antulay, also had to step down under similar pressure.

After two or three abortive attempts to marginalize the elite pluralists, Indira Gandhi was almost forced to give state leadership to one of them. Vasantdada Patil became Chief Minister in 1983 though he had to accept Ramarao Adik, a populist loyal to Ms. Gandhi, as his deputy. Prior to that, in 1981 Chavan had returned to the Congress (I) after having suffered humiliation in his efforts at 'home coming'.

Acceptance of Vasantdada Patil as the leader was a forced choice and populists had reluctantly accepted him. It was not surprising, therefore, that the populists began to play the destabilization game by raising the bogey of regional imbalance. Under the given circumstances such rivalry and intra-party tensions were inevitable, but what is relevant for our purpose are the findings of the Committee on Regional Imbalance (CORI 1984) which, *inter alia*, pointed out that interest in regional imbalance had been revived in the beginning of the Sixth Five-Year Plan (1980–5) and that, 'until then, most elites from the backward regions had silently accepted the change in the focus from the region to district' (ibid.: 199).

According to the CORI Report, what had resurrected the regional sentiment was the announcement of separate programmes for backward regions by the then Chief Minister, A.R. Antulay, without specifying any schedule or means to implement them. Thus the CORI Report had concluded, 'the policy of cavalierly announcing . . . programmes for Vidarbha, Marathwarda and Konkan, instead of planning properly to ensure availability of adequate funds necessary to do away with regional imbalance, has strengthened the distrust of the people in the state administration'[15] (CORI 1984: 13).

As usual, no action was taken on the report, but it had indirectly confirmed that the relative prosperity of western Maharashtra was largely due to the organizational structure of the party, assiduously nurtured by the Maratha pluralists. What was implied was that if populists wanted to gain benefits from the Congress system, they had to reorganize the party and other opportunity structures in their region (also giving due representation to Dalits, as the pluralists had done in western Maharashtra). Only then could they regulate or control competition amongst their camp followers, in the absence of which smooth access to public resources could not ensured.

At the same time, the report also confirmed that the Maratha pluralists were more interested in retaining power (in reality, their access to public resources) through opportunity structures including PRIs created by them, than in providing relief to the poor or in the larger objective of developing the rural areas, as was expected from the panchayati system. That PRIs had failed to meet the expectations of the rural poor was explicitly clear in both the CORI (1984) and Bongiwar Committee (1971) reports.

There was a gap of more than a decade between the two committee reports. Therefore from their common observations one can easily gauge that during the intervening period no attempt was made to change the functional approach of the panchayat bodies. If any change had occurred—such as giving more powers to the bureaucracy and higher-level political leaders—that too, under the given scenario, had failed to deliver the goods to the rural poor.

The Patil Committee Report

This point was reiterated once again in 1986 when the Panchayati Raj Evaluation Committee Report, popularly known by the name of its Chairman, P.B. Patil, was published. The Patil Committee Report is still considered to be very comprehensive, as this committee went into an in-depth analysis of the rise and delcine of the panchayat system, including the issues related to the autonomy of panchayat bodies. Its recommendations were radical in their approach. For instance, the report emphasized that if the panchayat system were to function as an autonomous self-governing system it had to be accorded the status of a third tier of the government at the district level. Accordingly, the committee recommended an appropriate devolution of power and functions between all three tiers of panchayats, through a Constitution Amendment. Likewise, it also called for a comprehensive legislative enactment for all the three tiers of PRIs. The appointment of a District Development Commissioner, an IAS officer, senior to the District Collector in each district; enhanced representation of elected representatives in the DPDC; reorganization of blocks and district; timely holding of periodic elections; additional financial resources for panchayat bodies; involvement of NGOs in implementing development schemes and imparting training to both elected representatives and officials; and 25 per cent reservation of seats for women in all the tiers of PRIs, were other notable recommendations of the Patil Committee Report (Govt. of Maharashtra 1986: 131).

Meanwhile, elections to PRIs, scheduled for 1987, were deferred on account of stay orders issued by the High Court. The Patil Committee Report was made public in 1986. For the next four years, to the end of the 1980s, no significant developments occurred on both these counts. It was only in the early 1990s that the state government decided to accept some of its recommendations. The timing was crucial. The union government was contemplating the introduction of the 73rd Constitution Amendment Bill, which, *inter alia*, had provided for a statutory recognition of PRIs. Its smooth passage in parliament was ensured in view of the overt concern expressed by all political parties for the 64th Amendment which had led to suitable modifications in the Bill. Meanwhile, the elections to PRIs were due in 1992. Among the suggestions accepted and duly implemented, were an increase in representation of PRIs in the DPDC. Accordingly, all chairpersons of subject committees and two to three heads of taluka panchayats were given membership of DPDC, besides the president of the ZP who was already a member of DPDC. The ZP president was also given the status of a deputy minister. As far as finances of the ZP and TP were concerned, their share in revenues and cess on land revenue were raised. Similarly, 30 per cent of the seats for women were also reserved in all the tiers of PRIs. That apart, a separate committee exclusively for the welfare of women and child was constituted.

The state government also agreed to create the post of an Additional Chief Executive Officer and to upgrade the post of the Social Welfare Officer in the zilla parishad.

Barring these last two proposals, the rest of the provisions were implemented before 1992—when the panchayat elections were held after the gap of thirteen years. The most noticeable feature of that election was that for the first time there were large number of women in the fray, both SC and ST too who contested and won, though most of them contested from the constituencies reserved for them, thanks to the recommendations of the Patil Committee. This did not, however, remain a novel feature of the Maharashtra panchayat system. By that time, the 73rd Constitution Amendment had already been passed by parliament, calling for not less than one-third of the total seats in PRIs throughout India to be reserved for women and for SCs and STs, according to their proportion in the total population in a given state.

What was the impact of a large number of women[16] and SC and ST persons on the functioning of panchayats? It is too early to evaluate but it appears that after three or four subsequent panchayat elections, panchayat bodies would become responsive to the need of the weaker sections of the society.

The political developments of the 1980s, particularly since the mid-1980s, have shown that the degree of intra-elite adjustments, competition and cooperation that existed in 1960s and 1970s was no longer permissible in view of the lack of space for all aspirants staking their claims. With so many contenders vying to utilize local institutions as vehicles for personal gain without affecting change in the political system, conflicts are bound to be bitter. Under the given circumstances, it was quite logical that the dynamics of development would throw up many more aspirants who would eventually challenge the established order. Restrained political behaviour on the part of such budding but ever-increasing leadership is perhaps not expected. Lack of endurance and perseverance are the hallmarks of impatient populists who invariably rely on short-cut methods to gain instant success. The populists in Maharashtra were no exception. The result was not unexpected. Open rivalry between the established pluralists and the populists, and the latter's quest to grab all opportunities at any cost, heralded a new phase in the Congress system by early 1980s. The situation gradually went out of hand, so much so that the 1984 elections for PRIs had to be 'postponed' and actually were not held at all on the pretext of certain cases pending before the courts.

This is partly evident from the fact that the Congress system nurtured by elite pluralists during the 1960s had started showing signs of cracking up by the late 1970s. The rural elites, who for the last twenty-five years had monopolized the party organizations, cooperatives and PRIs, had, in later years if not all along, been busier pocketing the spoils of the system than delivering goods to the poor. Consequently, the SCs, STs and OBCs were increasingly alienated from the Congress system managed by elite Marathas. Simultaneously, the Marathas had been so involved in promoting members of their own clan over the years that it had become almost impossible for new aspirants to gain entry into the opportunity structures. This was almost true for the young, educated Marathas also who had no truck with elite Marathas except for their caste allegiance.

The shrinking of the rural base for the Congress had started by the mid-1980s but the slid accelerated since 1990 and reached its nadir in the 1995 Assembly election, when the BJP–Shiv Sena alliance secured a decisive victory against the Congress party.

Decline and Fall of the Congress-led System

In the 1990 assembly election the Congress party had won only 141 seats out of a total of 288, and 38.3 per cent of the total votes polled. But Sharad Pawar managed to form the government by winning over thirteen Congress rebels who had won as independent candidates. As his mentor Y.B. Chavan had done before him in 1962, Pawar in 1991 joined the central government as Defence Minister. Following the precedent set by Y.B. Chavan, he choose as his successor Sudhakar Rao Naik, a politician from Vidarbha, who happened to be a nephew of the late V.P. Naik who had for long faithfully played second-fiddle to Y.B. Chavan. Pawar had assumed that Sudhakar Rao Naik would continue the tradition, acting as his proxy in the state. But by then the circumstances as well as the players had changed. Naik lost no time in asserting his independence in day-to-day affairs of the state and within the party, and to the chagrin of Pawar, also exposed the latter's alleged links with underworld kingpins. The first casualty in their fight to the finish was the party organization, which lost whatever little dynamism and direction it had retained. Subsequently, in March 1993, Bombay witnessed the worst-ever communal riots in the wake of the Babri Masjid demolition, followed by serial bombings in various parts of the city.

If these two episodes drove Muslims away from the Congress, they also offered additional leverage to the Shiv Sena-BJP combine to mobilize the majority Hindu opinion against the Congress government. A few months later came the news of starvation deaths from the remote parts of the Vidarbha region inhabited by tribal people. By that time Pawar had returned to Bombay as Chief Minister and had reportedly confessed that there was no dearth of funds but lamented at the absence of a machinery to reach out to the suffering tribal masses. The majority of the victims of starvation deaths were children.

With this statement, which he perhaps gave unmindful of its implications, Pawar himself demolished the myth of a responsible Congress administration as well as the reach and impact of services delivered by the PRIs. Under the Tribal Development Plan not only were there special agencies responsible for tribal welfare, but a separate subject committee was also constituted under the ZP to take care of children—these facts were simply ignored by the Chief Minister. The fact remained that there were several institutions carrying out similar functions and much duplication or even triplication of manpower, which had been found wanting when required to demonstrate its presence and ability in the field.[17]

But this episode was soon forgotten in the wake of the massive earthquake in October 1993 which hit two districts of the Marathwada region. Here again, systematic distribution of relief was not properly supervised by the Congress party, the district administration or the PRIs.

The insensitivity and callousness of the Congress and the government machinery became all the more apparent following the death of over a hundred Gowari tribals in Nagpur in a stampede in November 1994, when the state assembly was in session. They were pressing for their long-standing demand for inclusion in the state schedule of tribes. Even then Pawar did not think it fit to come to Nagpur to express his sympathy for the victims or offer condolences to the people as a whole. And finally, the then Deputy Municipal Commissioner of Bombay openly levelled charges of corruption against Pawar and his alleged nexus with builders and underworld kingpins.

The exodus from the Congress was led by the OBCs and the rural poor as a whole, who were joined by certain sections among the Marathas, the Muslims, women (in the wake of the Jalgaon Sex Scandal in which local Congress leaders were found involved), and the tribal people—all these sections gradually withdrew their allegiance to the Congress due to the insensitivity of its leaders placed at different levels of the power structure, including the government, district administration and local level institutions. The Chief Minister himself was in the dock. The biggest beneficiary of all these events and circumstances was the Shiv Sen-BJP alliance that won in the 1995 Assembly election.

1995 Assembly Election: Congress *vs* Sena-BJP Alliance

As figures given in Table 1.4 reveal, the BJP improved its position in the 1995 assembly election by adding 44 seats, in addition to what it had gained in 1990. The Congress (I) lost as many as 61 seats compared to its total strength of 141 seats in 1990.

TABLE 1.4: PERFORMANCE OF CONGRESS AND SHIV SENA-BJP IN LAST TWO ASSEMBLY ELECTIONS

Year	No. of seats won and percentage of votes polled				Total Seats
	Cong-I	Sena-BJP Alliance	Cong-I	Sena-BJP Alliance	
1995	80	138	30.37	29.28	288
1990	141	94	38.17	26.64	288
Loss(-)/Gain(+)	(-) (61)	(+) 44	(-) 7.8	(+) 2.62	

Source: Vora 1996.

But the defeat of the Congress was much [*sic*] serious than these figures tell. Many of the stalwarts and faction leaders, and ministers of the Pawar ministry, could not get elected. . . . District-level leaders, with a stable support structure for years together, were defeated in these elections. Out of the 72 constituencies having sugar cooperative factories (within and outside the sugar belt), the Congress lost 26 seats. (Vora 1996: 171–3)

The Congress party in fact lost in all the regions of the state, as Table 1.5 indicates. But unlike in other regions the defeat of the Congress (I) candidates was relatively less demeaning in western Maharashtra where cooperatives and panchayati institutions have been fully integrated with the party. Nevertheless, it is interesting to note that apart from the factors mentioned above, what hastened the defeat of the Congress was the presence of a large number of Congress rebels as independent contestants.

TABLE 1.5: REGIONWISE BREAK-UP OF 1990 AND 1995 ASSEMBLY ELECTION RESULTS

	Western Maharashtra		Marathwada		Vidarbha		Bombay+ Konkan	
	1990	1995	1990	1995	1990	1995	1990	1995
Cong (I)	54	37	23	12	25	17	18	0
BJP-Sena	6	15	16	24	23	33	40	51
Cong Rebels	–	18	–	5	–	11	–	–
Total	175	75	46	46	66	66	65	65

Source: Vora 1996.

The fight against the party nominees by those denied party tickets is not something new in the Congress. But it acquired alarming proportions in the 1995 assembly election when as many as 200 rebel candidates entered the fray against the official candidates of the party. In fact, as many as 35 Congress rebels won as independent candidates. In another 43 constituencies, Congress nominees were defeated 'because of high percentage of votes secured by rebels who did not win. It means that the Congress could have secured approximately 78 seats over and above the 80, which it actually won. Thus the root cause of the Congress defeat was to be found within congress organization rather than outside' (ibid.: 172).

From the above analysis it is obvious that the well oiled machinery of the party which had earlier helped the Congress system to run effectively had not only bcome rusty but perhaps also obsolete. No doubt, there was a lack of a powerful yet flexible and dynamic leadership that could have otherwise ensured working unity among different faction as per the rules of the game. But that was not all. As the saying goes, change is the inevitable course of life, and politics, like other activities of life, is no exception; therefore, change was inevitable. As a matter of fact, the debacle of the Congress could also be attributed to its failure to keep pace with the changing economic scenario.

In the present era of liberalization and globalization the Congress was bound to lag behind since its entire mechanics was geared to serve its rural constituents, led by its rural elite. Comprising nearly 40 per cent of the urban population (compared to the all India average of 26 per cent), Maharashtra is one of the most industrialized states in the country. Rather, Maharashtra alone contributes about one-fourth of the total industrial output of the country. The contribution of the manufacturing sector to the state income has gradually increased over the years, amounting to 25.6 per cent in 1993–4. On the other hand, the contribution of agriculture to the total state income has declined from 33 per cent in the 1950s to 21 per cent in 1993–4. Similarly, the service sector's contribution has also gone up to 20 per cent. The manufacturing and service sectors are bound to increase their levels of growth under the new economic policy, since approximately 1,535 industrial projects with an investment worth Rs. 1,96,708 crores (Vora 1996) including investments from NRIs are in the pipeline.

The increasing marginalization of the Congress party in the state, particularly in the cities and towns, has to be explained through this fast changing economic scenario. As a matter of fact, in all 91 urban or semi-urban constituencies, the Congress has won only in 11, whereas the Sena-BJP alliance won in as many as 63 constituencies. Ironically, Pawar, the Congress leader who took the lead in implementing new economic policy initiatives in the state, simply failed to communicate this message to his partymen. Hence the marginalization of his party's position.

The predicament of Congress leaders like Sharad Pawar could also be seen in the apparently contradictory interests they had been unsuccessfully trying to balance. For instance, Pawar knew that his party was rooted in rural areas and its backbone was the centralized public sector economy. Yet, he espoused the cause of liberalization and privatization whereas influential Congress leaders, having a base in the cooperative sector, voiced their opposition to privatization initiated by the government led by their own party.

Current Perspectives

What was the impact of this change on PRIs in the state? Did it alter the dominant caste composition in the state? Did it affect the course of democratic decentralization? To look for answers to these questions, we will have to take stock of the background and caste compositions of the state-level regional ruling elites. For the first time (1995) in the history of Maharashtra, Manohar Joshi a Brahmin came to occupy the position of Chief Minister who owed his prosperity to the growth of the metropolis where he had started his career in the 1960s. Eleven of his twenty-two cabinet ministers belonged to urban constituencies including seven from Bombay alone. Similarly, more than one-third (six out of sixteen) state ministers came from cities and towns. Two of the three Regional Development Corporations and the State Planning Board were also headed by leaders born and brought up in the urban milieu.

Yet the Maratha and Kunbi caste cluster, taken together, still had 138 of the total 288 seats in the new assembly. Therefore, Marathas as a dominant caste, managed to retain their position. Like the Patels in neighbouring Gujarat, they have shifted their loyalties to the Sena-BJP alliance. Nearly half of them belonged to non-Congress parties, excluding rebel Maratha Congressmen who won as independents. The Shiv Sena, which till the late 1970s, had remained an urban middle-class party, initially made inroads into the rural areas by voicing the concerns for OBCs who had been left out of the Congress system. Gradually, it attracted newcomers among Marathas also. It was these newcomers who had found the Sena-BJP alliance to be an alternative platform of power for them. This did not necessarily mean that the Marathas had completely switched over from the Congress to the new alliance. In fact, they were in both in Congress and the Shiv Sena-BJP alliance; the essential difference between the two was that the Shiv Sena-sponsored Maratha MLAs were those who were 'young and have little or no support structure in the form of co-operatives, etc. They are those disgruntled elements who are not absorbed in the local power structure by clanish Marathas of the Congress' (Vora 1996: 173). Also included were those Marathas opposed to the renaming of the Marathwada University after Ambedkar. In fact, the Shiv Sena had mobilized the Marathas of the Marathwada region particularly by opposing the Congress government's decision to rename the University.

The representation of OBCs in the Assembly remained the same (around 50–3) but the strength of Mali and Dhangar, two important peasant castes was reduced: from eleven to four in case of the former, and from five to three in the case of the latter. Further, the Sena-BJP alliance captured eleven constituencies reserved for Scheduled Castes (out of a total of eighteen) and eight out of a total of twenty-two seats reserved for the Scheduled Tribes (Vora 1996).

Clearly, there was not only a split in the votes of Marathas but also of the OBCs, SCs and STs taken together. Thus it can be safely argued that the Sena-BJP alliance wrested power in the 1995 assembly election by splitting the traditional vote bank of the Congress party.

What was the overall impact of the assembly elections on the future of panchayat bodies in the state? It was obvious that the PRIs would remain there, but they would survive largely because of the 73rd Constitution Amendment of 1992. For a highly centralized party like the Shiv Sena, run on dictatorial lines, to support the idea of decentralized governance was beyond comprehension and logic of any sort. Therefore, the form of the panchayats bodies would be maintained owing to constitutional obligations, but in all probability they would be devoid of any real powers to affect decentralization.

The cooperatives and panchayats were still under the control of the Congress. Initially, the Sena-BJP government hardly said anything publicly pertaining to the local level institutions, though the press reports indicated that the state government was likely to change the old management structure of the cooperative sector.[18] In any case, there were reports of mismanagement of the cooperative assets and accounts; and also that sugar cooperatives were running into heavy losses.[19] To cap it all, these sugar factories had not paid dues worth crores of rupees to farmers who had sold their sugar cane to them.

Paradoxically, an authority vacuum that earlier led to the defeat of the Congress party in 1995, became all the more visible during the Sena-BJP rule. And the reasons were two fold. First are the compulsions of a coalition government, compounded by the fact that the government was under the remote control of the leader of the major partner, the Shiv Sena. Second, the inability of the partners in power to strike a balance between their immediate interests and the long-term interests of the state.

Moreover, under the new dispensation, the focus shifted from rural to urban areas, with 'populism' occupying the central place in major policy pronouncements. It was hardly surprising therefore that the new rulers failed to provide an alternative to counter the old Congress system. As a matter of fact, what all the BJP-

Sena government could manage to do was to further weaken the local level opportunity structures which the Congress had created over the years in the state. To be fair to the new rulers, however, it must be mentioned that both cooperatives and panchayats had lost their dynamism of 1960s and 1970s.

There was a marked decline in the performance of both the cooperatives and panchayats. Yet, instead of revitalizing these institutions, the new regime tried to further destabilize them. For instance, the tenure of ZP and PS chiefs as well as vice-presidents of various subject committees were reduced to one year;[20] earlier a two-thirds majority was required to move a no-confidence motion against a chairperson, now a simple majority is enough. Above all, the (ZP) presidential powers of recruitment, transfer and purchase were withdrawn and vested with the state government. Clearly, all these steps were taken to demonstrate the new regime's mistrust in the institutions below the state capital and also to cut at the roots of their rival (the Congress), still in control of the majority of local level institutions. In the process, however, it caused more harm to these institutions of decentralized governance. Incidentally, the above-mentioned changes were brought about through an ordinance, particularly the reduced tenure of panchayat chiefs promulgated in late February, just a month prior to the zilla parishad and taluka panchayat elections held in March 1997. Of the total 29 ZPs in the state, Shiv Sena could bag only 5.[21]

Although the Shiv Sena has lately had made inroads into the rural areas and had also lured OBCs into its fold, this party and the BJP are nevertheless products of the Indian urban milieu. No wonder the Shiv Sena did not care for the rural cooperatives or panchayati bodies. In fact, neither of these parties, whether in power or in opposition, believes in decetralization. The neglect of urban local bodies in the states ruled by the BJP in the last decade testify to this fact. At the same time, it is equally true that the institutions of decentralized governance cannot be revitalized with the old tools and techniques of the Congress party. The grand old party of 1950s and 1960s, was already moribund. It saw another split[22] before the 1999 assembly election. The newly born

Nationalist Congress Party (NCP) fought the assembly elections on its own, heralding the beginning of a triangular contest in the state. Although in the ensuing political battle the Sena-BJP alliance lost majority, neither of the Congress parties could win enough seats to form government on its own strength. Therefore, both the Congress parties joined hands and with the help of many smaller parties[23] formed a Democratic Front government.

The Front is in power since then but it has never been a smooth sailing for its partners. Firstly, most of the smaller parties have earlier fought against the policies of the Congress and the BJP-Shiv Sena. And they also resent the big brotherly attitude of both the Congress parties. Secondly, the relationship between the two Congress parties are not cordial either. Both the Congress and NCP claim to have wider support base among Marathas and in order to buttress their claim they have been engaged in a fierce battle. It was this lingering tussle between these two parties that they chose to fight separately the panchayat elections[24] held in the state in February 2002. The BJP-Shiv Sena alliance, on the other hand, fought unitedly. The results of the consequent triangular contest were almost in tune of the previous Assembly election results. The votes of the pre-split Congress were almost equally divided between the Congress and NCP as they emerged as single largest parties in 11 ZPs each. To quote a perceptive observer:

> The Sena-BJP alliance succeeded in emerging as a major force agaisnt the Congress and the NCP in rural areas. Successive Assembly elections have indicated that Shiv Sena has been penetrating Congress rural bastions in north Maharashtra, Marathwada and to some extent in western Maharashtra. This penetration is visible in the recently held ZP (zilla parishad) elections . . . (the) results of ZP elections indicate the disastrous effect of split of Congress vote as far as both Congress and NCP are concerned. (Palshikar 2002: 1278)

From the above observations it is apparent that the split has adversely affected both the Congress and NCP. Thus the battle between them remains inconclusive. But what are its implications for the state politics and panchayats as well. To begin with, it should be noted that following the return of the Congress—

both the Congress and the NCP as coalition partner—in power there has been no major shift in the polity and economics of the state. In fact, on these accounts there is hardly any difference between both the political formations, BJP-Shiv Sena alliance and Democratic Front. In the arena of panchayats, except for some minor changes like the extension of the tenure of panchayat chairpersons from one year to two and half years, the new regime is as directionless as its predecessor was. This explains the negligence, even callousness that abounds in the governance of Maharashtra.

Recently, all political parties contested panchayat elections with all seriousness and deployed all possible means to win as many seats as possible but all these efforts were directed to capture panchayats which, they believe, will help them to strengthen their position in the state politics. In a way they recognize the importance of panchayats, not as an institution to facilitate decentralized goverance but as a tool to further their political interests. The political crisis to which the state government has recently undergone (which is far from over, no matter whether the government has survived no-confidence motion) too has stemmed from their fight over the control of panchayats.[25]

Beyond that, the present regime is hardly making any attempt to invigorate the third tier of governance. The provisions of reservations of seats for women, OBCs, SCs and STs could have been used to widen the social base of the local leadership. Instead, practically all the political parties used this provision to co-opt candidates from these reserved categories. One wonders, whether these co-opted leades would ever be able to assert themselves and work for the cause of democratic decentralization in the state. As a matter of fact, all the four major political actors in the state—Congress, NCP, Shiv Sena and BJP—are insensitive to the needs of the weaker sections of the society. They are more interested in promoting their kith and kin. It is apparent from the fact that a large number of candidates in the recent panchayat elections were family members (wives, daughters, sisters, brothers, nephews, etc.) of the political leaders operating at the district level and below.

Under the given circumstances, panchayats would continue to stay and their elections would be held regularly too, since they are now constitutionally mandated. But their mere existence would not be a guarantee of their emergence, even in distant future, as autonomous institutions of third tier of governance. Shorn of the honour they are entitled for, panchayats would remain as an extended arm of the government, merely as an agency to implement the schemes conceived and designed at the higher level of governments.

CONCLUSION

Maharashtra, as an independent state, came into being under a set of unique circumstances. When the Maharashtrians got a state of their own, their clamour for linguistic identity was assuaged. Bombay, the finance capital of the country, became the state capital. The Congress party, instrumental in the creation of Maharashtra as an unilingual state, earned kudos from all sections of society. Y.B. Chavan emerged as the most popular leader of the state, aided by the fact that he belonged to the dominant peasant caste of Marathas, who, along with Kunbis, are referred to as a single caste cluster and account for about one-third of the total state population. The preponderance of a single caste cluster helped Chavan-led Congress to maintain the required coalition support.

The avowed objective of Chavan's politics was to accelerate the pace of development in rural Maharashtra, so that maximum benefit could accrue to the party. For this it was necessary to expand and consolidate the social base of the party. Thus Chavan first gave a pro-rural tilt to existing structures such as the Land Development Bank and Cooperatives. Then he expanded these organizations by opening branches at the taluka and village levels. But these alone were not sufficient to accommodate the ambitions of the Maratha elites. Therefore, Chavan introduced institutions such as PRIs and several marketing, sales and purchase unions.

If cooperatives and marketing, sales and purchase unions helped party loyalists to raise resources, PRI offered them an opportunity to exercise political authority. This, for all practical purposes, meant providing them access to state resources and the power to dispense patronage. On the other hand, it also helped the state leadership provide party office-bearers positions of president of ZP, or TP; thus ordinary members of the party found an opportunity to move up the party hierarchy. All the development work done during this period naturally established PRIs as an important government institution in the eyes of the people.

It is hardly surprising that in the 1967 assembly election nearly fifty panchayat leaders became MLAs. Their places were taken by office-bearers of the party or from among cooperatives, etc. With this, Chavan managed upward mobility for partymen, and created an image of the system as an open one. The OBCs and SCs were also accommodated in the Congress system, but they were offered relatively insignificant positions such as vice-presidentship of TPs or membership of subject committees.

Unlike the provision for direct election of members of both GP and ZP, their chairpersons were elected indirectly from among the members of both these bodies. This provision also helped the state leadership to regulate the selection of key positions in PRIs. And resourceful party loyalists occupied these coveted positions.

Over and above, Chavan's style of functioning was unique. An astute politician, he anticipated the strengths and weaknesses of both his loyalists as well as his adversaries, and perfected the art of conflict management.

It was through the networking of the (Congress) party organization, having linkages with other opportunity structure, that helped sustain the system centred around elite pluralists, and worked well and paid rich dividends at all levels of power till the early 1970s. Subsequently, tensions or conflicts emanating both from within the state system and outside, surfaced. Moreover, Indira Gandhi was keen to replace the old guard of the state unit with hand-picked leaders from the marginalized sections.

Through the 1970s and 1980s the state party leadership applied both the techniques of compromise and resistance to withstand pressures. The Emergency not only witnessed the installation of a nominee (S.B. Chavan) of the central leadership as Chief Minister, but also the introduction of a plethora of welfare and development schemes (twenty-point programme) to be implemented by the state bureaucracy. This led to a struggle for supremacy between the camp followers of the party high command and the old elite; ultimately it was the institutional base of the Congress system that declined.

Populists had gained an upper hand in the state politics in the early 1980s with the support of the Congress (I) high command, but they could not retain power for long. First, all the important centres of power below the state level were still under the dominant influence of the elite pluralists. Second, by the very nature of their recruitment and style of functioning, the populists lacked perseverance and patience and created parallel organizations to dispense patronage. The success of this strategy was short-lived and the populists lost power, forcing the Central leadership to close ranks with pluralists in Maharashtra. By then, however, the damage had already been done to the old system.

This could not remain a secret for long as the infighting amongst the various factions and groups within forced the state leadership to postpone elections for the ZPs due in 1984–5. It may be recalled that earlier also ZP elections due in 1977 could be held in 1979 only and the elite pluralists had retained their control over a majority of these local level institutions.

Meanwhile the Patil Committee had submitted its report in 1986. Some of its recommendations, were accepted by the state government but only on the eve of the 1992 panchayat elections for all the three tiers. This was a forced choice since those recommendations were by and large identical to some of the mandatory provision of the 73rd Constitution Amendment, 1992. In April 1994, the Maharashtra government also brought out a new Panchayat Act in conformity with the Constitutional requirement.[26] Accordingly, certain changes were brought out in the form of panchayats and supporting structures were also created. These changes, however could not stop the slide into which PRIs, along with the entire state machinery, had already slipped.

The death of dozens of tribesmen in a stampede at Nagpur

and starvation deaths of hundreds of children across several tribal districts revealed the insensitiveness of the Congress regime towards the sufferings of the poor and marginalized sections of the society. The collapse of the administrative machinery was all the more glaring when Muslims were selectively targeted in the Bombay riots of 1992–3. Above all, Pawar had a hard time doing the balancing act between harping on the imperatives of economic reforms and defending the interests of a Congress party firmly rooted in the rural areas. The Congress machinery was, however, worst hit by the mismanagement of both the PRIs and cooperative, corruption and increasing criminalization of politics.

It is against this backdrop that the 1995 assembly elections were held and the Congress party was voted out. This defeat was far more striking than that of 1978, when for the first time in the history of Maharashtra state a non-Congress party came to occupy the seat of power. Although the numerical strength of Marathas in the state assembly, as earlier, was maintained, their social composition was changed. In fact, the Maratha legislators who won the assembly elections on the BJP-Shiv Sena ticket were relatively young and had little or no linkages with cooperatives, panchayats or any other local level rural institutions. The majority of them came from urban or semi-urban constituencies.

The fall of the old Congress system, in the final analysis, was the result of the increasing 'authority vacuum' in the party, primarily caused by the incapacity of the elite pluralists among the dominant Maratha caste, in the face of populists' upsurge, to regulate or influence the political actions of the new generation leadership, including those below them in the social hierarchy. This inability of the elite pluralists, in a way, was the consequence of their failure to create a rational basis for generating new leadership through formal institutions. This was the major reason why an increasing authority vacuum was visible in Maharashtra. Unfortunately, this syndrome has been perpetuated further in the state for two reasons. First, there were compulsions of a coalition government in power, that too when the steering was frequently controlled by the supreme leader of the major partners. Second, there was an inability to strike a balance between the immediate interests of the holders of power and the long-term interest of the state.

Besides, even though the political order remained under the dominant spell of populism, under the new dispensation, the focus was shifted from rural to urban areas. No wonder, it failed to provide an alternative to effectively counter the old Congress system during its five years term. On the contrary, all the BJP-Sena government could manage to do was to weaken the opportunity structures through which the Congress system had earlier operated. This is not to deny, however, that both panchayats and cooperatives had lost dynamism and had become complacent.

One can also argue that both the BJP and Shiv Sena are essentially a product of the Indian urban milieu, therefore they did not care for the rural cooperatives or panchayati bodies. This may be true, but the fact remains that the leaders of these parties do not believe in decentralization *per se*. The neglect of urban local bodies in those states where the BJP has had been in power would testify to this point. At the same time, it is equally true that local level institutions are unlikely to be recharged with the tools of the old Congress machinery, itself dead for all practical purposes. This also explains why, after the return of the Congress, the party and the government are in a state of disarray. Lethargy, negligence and callousness abound in Maharashtra.

Given the pro-urban tilt of the political forces in power and those who are again waiting in the wings as well as the aptitude of leading political bigwigs of the present dispensation, it appears that the epicentre of state politics has come full circle to occupy the same place wherefrom Y.B. Chavan had begun four decades ago. The paradox, however, is that the present Maharashtra is one of the highly urbanized and industrialized states in the country, and state politics cannot be put back on the same old track. To redesign a state politics embedded in the spirit of decentralization would require a different kind of visionary leadership, capable of accommodating the hitherto underrepresented voices in a multilayered democratic institutions. Alas, it is not visible even in the distant horizon.

NOTES

1. Although the decision to bifurcate Bombay State into (Gujarati speaking) Gujarat and Maharashtra had already been taken in 1956, its implementation was stalled as long as Bombay was a bone of contention between Maharashtrians and Gujaratis. Thanks to the skilful negotiation of Y.B. Chavan with the centre, the Gujaratis withdrew their claim. Thus Maharashtra emerged as a new state with Bombay as its capital.
2. For a comprehensive reading on the Maratha community and the Kunbi identification with Marathas see Iravati Karve, 'Maharashtra: Land and Its People', in *Maharashtra State Gazetter*, Directorate of publications, Government of Maharashtra, Bombay, 1968, cited in Lele (1990).
3. Although the Maratha kingdom established by Shivaji lasted till 1818, the Marathas were relegated to a secondary position during the defacto rule of the Peshwa, the Brahmin minister of Shahuji, the grandson of Shivaji. The resentment against the domination of Brahmins was so strong that it led to the formation of Satya-Shodhak Samaj under the legendary social reformer, Jyotiba Phule (Sirsker 1976, p. 222).
4. For a review of the increasing numerical strength of the Marathas, in the composition of Maharashtra Pradesh Congress Committee from 1923 to 1966, see, Ataram Ganesh Kulkarni, 'A Study of Political Parties in Maharashtra' (Ph.D. theses University of Pune, 1968) cited in Rosenthal (1977, p. 32).
5. Most of the large landowners were Brahmins, who had already started migrating to cities following selective discrimination against them by elite Marathas in the wake of Mahatma Gandhi's assassination in 1948.
6. Following the defeat of the Congress in the 1957 undivided Bombay provincial elections, Chavan's position in the state *vis-a-vis* the national leadership was strengthened since his opponents in the state Congress unit had been vanquished. During the next three years he skilfully reorgnized the Congress party in the state by shifting its base in rural areas. He also managed to rope in the leaders of PWP by opening up opportunities in cooperative societies.
7. Reorganization included two aspects. Firstly, opening of branches of cooperatives in villages and at taluka level, thus making cooperatives a federal institution. Secondly, in order to forge links with expanding activities of cooperatives, Chavan either co-opted cooperators of demonstrated capabilities and having independent base in terms and

conditions put forth by his party, or encouraged (Congress) party members or sympathizers of proven organizational skill to set-up new cooperatives by providing them wherewithal including resources. For details see Rosenthal (1972), especially pp. 1731–2; also Baviskar (1968 and 1980).

8. For the details of linkages between cooperatives, panchayats and the state policies. See Baviskar (1968) and also for the interlocking of these institutions below the State level as well as their role in elections, see Baviskar (1971), Baviskar (1997, especially pp. 93–6).
9. In the 1962 election also Chavan had to face dissidents but then the popularity of the Chavan-led Congress party was its zenith, therefore the rebels were defeated.
10. Among five members of the Syndicate, only S.K. Patil, was from Maharashtra, Patil was basically known as spokesman of the Bombay-based finance capital and did not have followers among the overwhelming majority of legislators from rural areas. The other two—Morarji Desai and S. Nijlingappa—were despised by Marathas. During his Chief Ministership of Bombay State, Morarji Desai had let loose a reign of terror against the movement for the formation of unilingual Maharashtra state. And, owing to Nijlingappa, Maharashtra was deprived of border areas belonging to Mysore which had a sizeable presence of Marathi-speaking population. The other two of the five, Atulya Ghosh and K. Kamaraj, were hardly known to ordinary legislators in Maharashtra.
11. For a detailed discussion on plebiscitary politics, see Rudolf and Rudolf 1990.
12. Chavan went to the extent of suggesting that Naik consult Indira Gandhi (instead of him) about her choice for two party candidates to be elected as members of the State Parliamentary Board in January 1972. For details of Chavan's compromising move in order not to displease the party high command, see *EPW* (1972a).
13. The pluralists' strongest base was western Maharashtra where they won a maximum of sixty-nine seats. On the other hand, the populists won a total of sixty-two seats, mostly from Marathwada. The Janata Party won the maximum, ninety-nine seats. Its victory was confined to mainly urban areas particularly Bombay and several district towns and parts of the Konkan region which had traditionally been the base of the socialists. See, Lele (1990).
14. Naik was not a born Maratha but he was from the very beginning a strong pillar of Maratha politics, in Maharashtra.

15. The programme announced by Antulay had listed thirty-five items for Marathwada, fourteen for Vidarbha and thirteen for Konkan in order of relative backwardness of the regions concerned cited in Lele (1990).
16. For the genesis of reservation of seats for women in panchayats, the immediate impact of this policy as well as its distant prospects both for women and PRIs, see Kumar (1995).
17. Nothing has changed since than as different departments/arms of the state government have not learnt any lesson from such a tragic incident. It is apparent from the fact that during the last one year (May 2000 to April 2001) over 8,000 children up to the age of six have died of malnutrition. All these deaths have been reported from tribal belts spread across the districts of Nandurbar, Jalgaon, Dhulle, Nasik and Ahmednagar.

    The growing apathy and negligence on the part of the government machinery has once again come to the fore as all the concerned authorities/departments have blamed one another. Although the tribal welfare minister, Madhukar Rao Pichod, has confessed to 'negligence' on the part of his government by saying that 'the lack of employment has brought about this disaster'. Consider the following statements:

    - 'Blame the local administration. They are the ones who implement. We only plan release of funds'—Social Welfare Minister
    - 'Zilla parishad is to blame, we only monitor and maintain data. Besides, they did not die from malnutrition but of disease'— Deputy Development Commissioner.
    - 'The diseases were induced by malnutrition. It is revenue departments' job to provide food or employment. We come in when disease strikes'—Divisional Deputy Health Director.
    - 'Can't say anything now, Assembles in session'—Integrated Child Development Scheme official.
    - 'There is simply not enough food for the tribal kids'—Field level workers.

    See *Hindustan Times*, New Delhi, 16 April 2001.
18. For details, see *The Pioneer*, New Delhi, 29 April 1996.
19. For a detailed discussion on the reasons for the sickness of co-operative sugar factories and suggested remedial measures by an High Powered Expert Committee (set-up by the Government of India), see, Godbole 2000.
20. *Panchayati Raj Update*, November 1997, Institute of Social Sciences, New Delhi.
21. *Panchayati Raj Update*, April 2001.

22. The split occurred on the issue of Sonia Gandhi's leadership. Sharad Pawar wanted to don this mantle which, as every body knew, would eventually propel him to prime ministerial chair once the Congress was back to power in Delhi. He, therefore, raised the issue of the foreign origin of Sonia Gandhi and walked out of the party. The impact of the split was most visible in Maharashtra as sizeable section of the party workers joined the NCP, formed by Sharad Pawar after the split.
23. The Democratic Front government comprises ten political parties. This includes eight smaller parties: The Peasants and Workers's Party (PWP), Republican Party of India (RPI), Bahujan Mahasangh (BMS), Samajwadi Party (SP), Janata Dal (S) and CPI and CPI(M).
24. On 7 February 2002 elections for both the zilla parishads and panchayat samitis, the two upper tiers of three-tiered panchayati bodies were held simultaneously in the state in February 2002. Almost all the constituents of the Democratic Front fought the panchayat elections separately since they could not reach an understanding among themselves. The Congress had to establish that the rank and file of the old party is still behind Sonia Gandhi. The NCP had to disporve this point. Besides, the social base of both these parties are almost similar. Hence a pre-poll alliance between them was impossible. It was all the more paradoxical with the smaller parties like PWP, CPI(M), SP, BMS, etc. First, 'these parties believed that both Congress parties were overbearing and hence no understanding could be reached'. Second, 'all these smaller parties have so small pockets of individual influence that it would have been meaningless for them to forge an alliance among themselves. . . . The net result was that every small party wanted to cling to its small fortress, uninterested in what will happen statewide.' For an excellent account of these elections to both rural and urban local bodies and their implications for the state politics, see, Palshikar (2002).
25. Raigad district is considered to be the strong hold of the Peasants and Workers Party (PWP). Naturally, PWP was hopeful of establishing its strength in (Raigad) zilla parishad elections. But its candidates were defeated by the NCP with the help of the Congress and Shiv Sena. Subsequently, the PWP stalked its claim for the presidential post of the ZP (elected indirectly from among the members of the ZP) but there also the PWP candidate was defeated. Enraged by the deceit of the alliance partners, the PWP demanded the resignation of the NCP minister from the area who it considered responsible for its

defeat. The demand was honoured. But when the same minister was reinstated in May-end, the PWP ministers resigned from the government. The crisis reached a flash point in a couple of days when following a spate of defections and withdrawal of support by alliance partners, the coalition government was reduced to a minority. Ultimately the Democratic Front government was asked to prove its majority in the assembly. The point to be noted here is that earlier this party had voiced its differences agaisnt the government on several issues, such as Enron, distribution of irrigation water, commercialization of upper primary education in the state, etc., but unlike the CPI(M), it had not resigned from the government. That the Congress or NCP are hobnobbing with each other, and both the Congress take smaller coalition partner for granted, the PWP had been digesting all these indignities. It was only when its claim for ZP presidentship was denied the PWP raised the banner of revolt. Others also jumped into the ring, precipitating the crisis that had almost upstaged the government. For details see, *The Asian Age*, 5 June 2002; *Times of India*, 7, 10 and 13 June 2002.

26. It should be noted that the 73rd Constitution Amendment was ratified by the Maharashtra state assembly without any discussion on the subject. Again when the state government brought a comprehensive bill to amend the old Panchayat Act, the due process of legislative business was not observed. Even legislators from opposition parties were not given enough time to discuss various provisions of the Bill placed before the house. What these two instances reveal? That the then ruling party (now practically all the major political parties in the state) was more interested in safe passage of the Bill (and winning elections somehow) than providing adequate time to state legislators to voice their concern about the local level democratic institutions. Paradoxically, this happened in Maharashtra, the state which earlier had earned appreciations for extending uninterrupted support to its panchayati institutions.

    For details of the debate in Maharasthra assembly, see Kumar (2002, especially, pp. 14–34).

Two

Reconciling Ideology, Elites' Aspirations and Political Centralization: Panchayats in Gujarat

Like its south-western neighbour Maharashtra, Gujarat came into being as an independent state in May 1960 following the bifurcation of the erstwhile Bombay State. Historically and culturally speaking, Gujarat may be divided into two major regions, mainland Gujarat and peninsular Gujarat. Mainland Gujarat can be further divided, on the basis of its geographical and agro-climatic attributes, into three parts the north, centre and south.

There are altogether 25 districts in the state, of which 17 are placed in the mainland (Table 2.1) and 8 fall in its peninsular part. A major portion of mainland Gujarat was under British rule, excluding north Gujarat, the princely state of Baroda (now Vadodara) ruled by the Gaekwads and covering parts of central, south and the hilly regions in the east. After Independence this region formed part of the Bombay State.

Peninsular Gujarat comprises Saurashtra, traditionally known as Kathiawad and the Kachchh. Prior to its integration with Independent India in 1948, Kachchh was a princely state and Saurashtra was a conglomerate of nearly 500 small, medium and large politico-administrative units, including estates and jagirs.

Of the total 25 districts, Dangs and Gandhinagar (which happens to be the state capital) are small districts without talukas. In contrast, Bhavnagar district in Saurashtra is spread over as many as 12 talukas. The total number of talukas (at the level of block, an administrative unit below the district) in the state is 184.

Gujarat is spread in 195,986 square km (6 per cent of total area of the country) and its total population is 50.59 million (2001

TABLE 2.1: DIFFERENT REGIONS AND SUB-REGIONS OF GUJARAT

Mainland			Peninsular	
North	Central	South	Saurashtra-Kachchh	
1. Mehsana	1. Gandhinagar	1. Bhrauch	1. Jamnagar	1. Kachchh
2. Sabarkantha	2. Ahmedabad	2. Vadodara	2. Rajkot	
3. Banaskantha	3. Kheda	3. Surat	3. Porbander	
4. Patan	4. Panchmahals	4. Valsad	4. Surendranagar	
	5. Anand	5. Dangs	5. Bhavnagar	
	6. Dohad	6. Navṣari	6. Amreli	
		7. Narmada	7. Junagarh	

Source: Map 1, *Census of India*, 2001 (Series 1).

Census) as compared with 20.64 million in 1961. Of the total population 66 per cent still lives in the rural areas.

SOCIAL STRUCTURE

The upper castes, comprising Brahmins, Banias and Rajputs form about 12 per cent of the total population. Brahmins and Banias are found in almost all parts of the state. There is, however, something exceptional about the Banias of Gujarat in that, unlike other states, they have overshadowed Brahmins for centuries in the political and economic spheres.

The middle castes account for about half the total population. They are divided into several castes, sub-castes and into branches, leading to clans and families. Among them, however, two castes, Kolis and Patidars, are numerically large (Shah 1990: 63). Again, Kolis alone represent half (24.22 per cent) of the total middle castes, followed by Patidars (12.16 per cent). The Kolis, like upper-caste Brahmins and Banias, live all over the state, and some of them identify themselves as Kshatriyas[1] in central and north Gujarat, but as Patels in south Gujarat. Kolis are basically a cultivator caste comprising tenants, small land owners, and agricultural labourers, fishermen and sailors.

Unlike the Kolis, Patidars are unevenly distributed in the state, with the lowest concentration in south Gujarat. In central Guajarat, where their concentration is the highest, the Patidars are prosperous and have acquired a high status. In contrast, their status is considered to be low in north Gujarat and Saurashtra, particularly in areas belonging to the erstwhile princely states (Kothari and Maru 1970: 98, n. 14). Traditionally, they have been farmers[2] but many of them have entered into business, industry and white-collar professions. What is more, the Patidars represent the largest section among the Gujarati migrants to Africa, Europe and the USA.[3]

The SCs and STs constitute 7 and 14 per cent of the population respectively. SCs are settled almost throughout in the state whereas STs are found in a few districts of eastern and south Gujarat. Apart from being small and marginal farmers and landless agricultural labourers, some of them are still engaged in their traditional occupations: scavenging, carrying carcasses, etc. Similarly, a majority of STs also happen to be small and marginal farmers and agricultural labourers. Among SCs and STs who have settled in urban areas, there are casual workers, some of them are also employed in factories and white-collar professions.

Muslims, who account for 8 per cent of the population, are spread throughout the state, many of them being cultivators, artisans, petty traders and industrial workers.

Occupational Patterns

Among the three upper castes, the Rajputs, comprising nearly 5 per cent of the population, are heterogeneous in terms of agricultural holdings and occupation. As Rajas, Thakurs, and Jagirdars they enjoyed positions of power in the past, but after Independence, not only lost political power but also the ownership of their land which they controlled as absentee zamindars.

The main beneficiaries of the zamindari abolition, introduced after Independence, were Patidar tenants, and as a result Rajput landlords and Patidars still nurture an antagonistic relationship. It is also significant to note that unlike Brahmins and Banias, a large number of Rajputs earn their livelihood as landless agricultural labourers. Besides, those Rajputs who own land get yields per acre far lower than do the Patidars. For, being ex-zamindars they are not used to physical labour, which they consider being below their dignity. Besides, their women folk do not share in the farm work with their husbands. 'Hence the Rajputs and patidars of the same or nearby village with equal size of land have different fortune. The latter have better economic condition than the former' (Shah 1996: 9–20).

Along with Rajputs, Banias had also enjoyed a dominant position in the rural areas until the late eighteenth century, but in present-day Gujarat a large number of Banias are still engaged in their traditional occupation—money lending and petty trading, besides dabling in business; some of them are in white-collar professions, but very few are cultivators. Similarly, the Brahmins for long have been in secular professions (doctors, lawyers, government servants, traders, etc.) other than performing traditional functions. The percentage of such Brahmin professionals was as high as 61 per cent even in late nineteenth century (ibid.: 13).

In contemporary Gujarat, however, the rich farmers come mainly from three castes, Patidars, Rajputs and Brahmins, and all these three big landowning castes compete with each other. The relationship between the Patidars and Rajputs is antagonistic whereas between Banias and Patidars it is competitive. On the other hand, the Kolis, being nearly one-fourth of the population in Gujarat, represent the biggest caste cluster in the state. They are basically small landholders or work as agricultural labourers. Some of them who could avail the facilities of higher education in the early part of this century, were absorbed in government jobs and some, as shipworkers and labourers, migrated to England, Africa and New Zealand.

Social base of the Congress party

Owing to their higher status in terms of educational background and landed assets or business, it was basically the Brahmins and the Banias who dominated the Congress party in the pre-Independence period. They were followed by the Patidars, whom

Sardar Vallabhbhai Patel had initiated into politics and the freedom struggle but the representation of the latter in state politics was far below that of the two upper resourceful castes. This is apparent from the fact that of the total seventeen elected members of the State Executive Committee of the Congress party in 1948, thirteen were Brahmins and Banias taken together. The number of Patidars was just four. But the Patidars, owing to their improved status were catching up with the upper castes.

Since three castes were competing in the political arena there was little scope for monopolization by a distinct caste group. Along with the traditionally dominant commercial culture, the politics in the state was largely moderate, gentle and cohesive,[4] which was further strengthened by the dominance of a supreme leadership—beginning with Mahatma Gandhi and Sardar Patel. Gujarat to a large extent remained free of rabbid casteism, at least until the late 1960s, when it was ruled by the undivided Congress party. Morarji Desai, the most important leader of undivided Bombay State, held sway over Gujarat after its bifurcation from Bombay. In fact, the first four Chief Ministers were either Brahmins (Morarji Desai, Hitendra Desai) or Banias (Jivraj Mehta, Balwantrai Mehta). While the state power rested in the hands of Banias or Brahmins, the Patidars, were a dominant and resourceful caste that controlled district level politics. Thus, one can safely argue that the Brahmins and Banias in alliance with Patidars to a large extent controlled the Congress party and state politics until early 1970s. But this smooth and gentle era of politics had a 'narrow political base. It was dominated by a few wealthy upper-caste men in Gujarat' (Kohli 1991: 243).

It was not that the Congress leadership was unaware of this fact but given the ground realities it was helpless to change things. The Congress leadership in Kheda district, for instance, was of the view that assembly and parliamentary tickets should be given to effective party workers. An effective party worker was one capable of 'dealing with government on behalf of agriculturist and businessmen; as also establishing and managing cooperatives, conducting social service, settling disputes' and finally 'organizing to win elections'. Since Rajputs and Bariyas (the social groups who had formed Kshatriya Sabha) were lacking in these skills, the Congressmen were not inclined to give these numerically strong social groups positions in the party (Weiner, 1967: 105–6).

Besides, the Congress was under the spell of Patidars with whom the Bariyas (a majority sub-caste of Kolis) had developed an antagonistic relationship following the implementation of land reform legislation. It needs mentioning that owing to this legislation the Bariyas' position had been reduced from tenancy to agricultural labour. Besides, 'Bariyas were aware that many Patidars viewed them as an indolent people unworthy of higher status within the community until they achieved a higher educational level, became better agriculturists and harder workers, and were ready to share in the work of the development bodies in the district—in short, until they were, in attitudes and behaviour, more like the Patidars' (ibid.: 109).

With such a narrow base, how did the party manage to mobilize people? To find an answer to the question, we have to look into the roles the various caste and professional associations played at that time. It is important to remember here that practically all castes have their own associations, registered or unregistered, in the state. This phenomenon, started with upper castes, was quickly followed by the middle castes such as Patidars. Lower castes also formed their associations at later stage (Shah 1990: 101–5).

The Role of Caste Associations

Not all caste associations entered party politics. Yet, they invariably inculcated a sense of fraternity among their members. Patidars, particularly the rich and middle peasants among them, for instance, had started mobilizing their caste group[5] through a Khedut Samaj or association of farmers. But the name of the association was deceptive, for over 80 per cent of its office-bearers come from the Patidar caste alone. It is interesting to note that the leaders of the Khedut Samaj would not invoke their caste name (i.e. Patidars) from the forum of the Samaj. At the same time, several caste associations of Patidars and their journals had been using the term 'Khedut' synonymously with 'Patidar'. Unlike the Patidars, the Kshatriyas (Rajputs and some sub-castes of Kolis who had proclaimed themselves to be Kshatriyas) had formed their association, the Gujarat Kshatriya Samaj (GKS), as early as 1948, to participate actively and directly in electoral politics of the state. The GKS was instrumental in fostering Kshatriya consciousness and unity by invoking a feeling of a common culture and a glorious past; this fed the ego of the poor Kolis, particularly those of central and north Gujarat. These Kolis felt closer to the Rajput leaders of the Sabha because the latter was hostile to the Patidars who were also their exploiters. In order to lure poor Kolis, the GKS also went on to demand the inclusion of Kshatriyas in the list of Backward Classes. Besides, the GKS adopted a resolution on 'the problems of poor cultivators, tenants and labourers and raised its voice against the Patidar landowners who ill-treated Bariyas'; but it ignored similar treatment meted out to the Bariyas by the Rajput landowners. The Sabha did not organize the Bariya labourers against the landowners as a class, but its leaders became actively involved when the Rajput landlord interests were in danger. For instance, the Sabha opposed the Zamindari Abolition Acts and pressurized the government in favour of the Rajput Girasdars' (Rajput landlords in Saurashtra), who enjoyed property rights and collected their shares of the agricultural produce from cultivators in 1948 (Shah 1990: 104).

Rich Patidar peasants were obviously not in favour of land reforms. Accordingly, their caste journals opposed land reforms, saying that small holdings were uneconomical. It was felt that the majority of Patidar cultivators who were small and marginal farmers, and whose interests clashed with those of big farmers, would not join them in their opposition to land reforms. But that was not the case. Small farmers felt that if the government would concede the demands of rich peasants by lowering the prices of agricultural inputs (such as seeds, fertilizers or electricity charges), they too would be beneficiaries.

No doubt, emphasis on caste unity amounted to preserving the status quo. Yet there was hardly any attempt to organize the poor agricultural labourers or marginal and small cultivators on class lines that cut across caste barriers. There were many reasons, but most important was the absence of a respected leader or party to espouse the cause of small farmers and farm labourers. In fact, no leader attempted to do so, out of the fear that 'any attempt to divide the community in terms of classes, they argue, would lead to conflict and give opportunities to communism which would turn "individuals to animals" without any freedom'. Also, 'the small and marginal farmers of the Patidar caste, like the members of any other caste, imbibe prejudices against other communities and thus create cultural barriers to their unity across caste' (ibid.: 92–3). Apart from invoking caste sentiments these caste associations had been helping their members to organize welfare programmes including the running of schools, hostels and co-operative societies and provide medical facilities and financial assistance. Yet, it must be noted that all castes did not have enough resources to run such programmes. In fact, apart from Banias, only Patidars and Kshatriyas had been able to do so.

These associations were naturally then used by their leaders to mobilize caste men during elections. The GKS was the first to openly bargain with the Congress party in the first two assembly and parliamentary elections (1952 and 1957). Continuing the legacy of its prominent role in the independence movement, the Congress party won the maximum seats in the first two assembly elections. With 56 to 67 per cent of votes polled in its favour, the Congress party bagged 141 out of total 157 seats in 1952, and 101 of 133 in 1957. Mention may also be made of the fact that though the Congress victory was spread all along the state, it lost almost 15 per cent of votes in northern and central Gujarat on account of the linguist movement. It is in these two regions that the party suffered major reverses in the 1962 and 1967 Assembly elections at the hands of the Swatantra Party (Seth 1976: 70). Let us recall here that when the first two elections were held, Gujarat was part of Bombay State. Gujarat as an independent state came into existence in May 1960.

Following bifurcation, the Congress secured a landslide

victory in Maharashtra but suffered a major setback in Gujarat. No doubt there were historic reasons for the immense popularity of the Congress in Maharashtra, but if a single factor could be attributed for that it was the support of a single caste cluster (Maratha-Kunbi). In contrast, Gujarat's caste composition and class formation was entirely different.

Apart from the GKS, the Kshatriyas had also floated the Khedut Sangh in 1951, basically to mobilize the peasantry to oppose the tenancy legislation. This and a couple of similar organizations had contested elections (see Table 2.2) for a limited number of seats, but their gains were marginal.

Later the Khedut Sangh succeeded in mobilizing ex-rulers adversely affected by land reforms along with a large section of peasantry, by forging a caste alliance between Kshatriyas and Patidars. The political manifestation of this grand strategy was the Swatantra Party, founded in 1959. Along with the Khedut Sangh, some of the leaders of GKS became instrumental in this new political formation. Nevertheless, the Swatantra Party could win only 26 seats (24 per cent of the votes in the 1962 assembly election) but managed to increase its strength to 66 seats out of 168 in 1967. Thus the proportion of Kshatriya MLAs doubled from 10 to 20 per cent from 1962 to 1967. This is not to suggest, however, that the Kshatriyas had gone out of the Congress fold. In fact, when in 1962 the Congress was defeated in Kheda district (considered to be a stronghold of the GKS), it tried to win over the Kshatriyas by offering more political positions, including two parliamentary seats, to them. On the other hand, the Congress party also helped float a parallel Kshatriya organization, particularly of Koli Kshatriyas. Consequently, there was a split among Kshatriyas, finally leading to disunity of Kshatriya and Patidar leaders.

Interestingly, the Congress party unit in Kheda district was then considered to be one of the well organized parties of 'one of the more prosperous rural areas of the country'. Therefore, its defeat was surprising. But it proved that the Congress could not accommodate the rising expectations of upwardly mobile social group

TABLE 2.2: PERCENTAGE OF VOTES POLLED AND SEATS WON BY POLITICAL PARTIES IN GUJARAT ASSEMBLY ELECTIONS, 1952–80

	1952		1957		1962		1967		1972		1975		1980	
	Seat	% of votes	Seat	% of votes	Seat	% of votes	Seat	% of votes	Seat	% of votes	Seat	% of votes	Seat	% of votes
Congress	141	56	101	57	113	51	93	46	140	51	75	41	141	50
Congress (O) (came in existence after 1969						-	-	-	16	24	56*	24	21[f]	22
Swatantra (founded in 1959)					26	24	66	38	-	-	2	-	-	-
Lok Paksha[a]	2	12	-	-	-	-	-	-	-	-	-	-	-	-
KMLP (founded in 1974)				-	-	-	-	-	-	-	12	11	-	-
BLD (founded in 1974)				-	-	-	-	-	-	-	2*	1	-	-
Jan Sangh	-	+	-	1	-	1	1	2	3	9	18*	9	9[g]	13
Hindu Maha-sabha[b]	-	3	-	+	-	1	-	-	-	-	-	-	-	-
Socialist[c]	4	9	3	4	7	8	3	3	-	1	2*	1	-	-
MGJP (founded in 1956)			29	31	1	4	-	+	-	-	-	-	-	-
Communist[d]	-	+	-	+	-	+	-	+	1	1	-	-	-	-
Other Parties	-	1	-	+	-	+	-	+	-	1	1*	1	-	2
Independents	10	19	-	7	7	10	5	10	8	12	13[e]	12	10	10
Total	157	100	133	100	154	99	168	99	168	100	181	100	181	97

Notes: Percentages are rounded, and therefore the totals do not add up to 100.

[+]Less than 0.5 per cent votes

[a]This included the Khedut Sangh, Krishikar Lok Paksha and Praja Paksha in 1952.

[b]This included the Ram Rajya Parishad.

[c]This includes SP, SSP and PSP.

[d]This includes CPI and CPM.

[e]7 Independent candidates were supported by the Janata Morcha.

[f]Janata Party

[g]Bharatiya Janata Party

*Coalition Partners in the Janata Morcha.

Source: G. Shah (1990).

(Kshatriyas) which was numerically powerful than the dominant castes, the traditional supporters of the Congress party (Weiner, 1967).[6]

It may also be noted that on the choice of candidates seeking tickets for the 1962 election the Congress party had faced a major dilemma. For the GKS had demanded a larger share. That apart, 'they wanted their own selections for the legislative assembly'. In other words, the GKS wanted the Congress to give them a number of tickets *en bloc* and they in turn would give it to the candidates of their choice. For the Congress, acceding to the demands of the GKS meant giving up the party's prerogative to select its own candidates. To quote a Congress leader:

> They tried to recruit as many Kshatriyas as possible so that they could get control of the mandal committees. And then they would try to get control of the taluka and district committees and then the entire party organization. Because they do constitute such a large part of the population of Gujarat it might have become possible for them to get control of the Congress party organization. (Weiner 1967: 107)

Apart from the fear of destroying party discipline, the Congress was apprehensive that if the demands of the GKS were honoured, it would lead to large scale alienation of Patidars.

Setting up Pachayati Bodies

After the creation of Gujarat in 1960, one of the first few steps the state government took was the setting up of a committee under Rashiklal Parikh (the then Revenue Minister) to examine the recommendations of the Balwantrai Mehta Committee Report. The recommendations of the Parikh Committee on democratic decentralization (1961) were incorporated into the Gujarat Panchayats Act, 1961. The Parikh Committee had accepted the three-tier structure of panchayats envisaged in the Balwantrai Mehta Committee Report. However, in terms of distribution of powers and functions, it drew inspiration from both the Maharashtra and Rajashthan models. Like Maharashtra, the zilla panchayats (ZP) in Gujarat was vested with maximum powers and functions. At the same time, the autonomous status of the taluka panchayats, on the Rajasthan pattern, was given due recognition. Again, unlike Maharashtra, the MLAs and the mamlatdar (a revenue officer at the level of block/taluka) were made associate members of the taluka panchayat. Under the Gujarat Panchayat Act 1961, provisions were laid down for adequate transfer of powers, authority, functions and required resources at all levels of PRIs. Taxation powers were also given to all three tiers, so that they could have their own resources, along with provisions for matching grants. Gujarat became the first state in the coutnry to give 100 per cent of the land revenue to PRIs and also a share in forest revenue and stamp duties. Gujarat perhaps was also the pioneer in setting up a State Panchayat Service Selection Board (PSSB) and also a Service Selection Committee at the district level, to recruit Class III and IV employees for the PRIs. Similarly, services of Class I and II officers engaged in implementing schemes transferred to ZPs were also put under the effective control of the ZPs.

It also needs mentioning here that the chairpersons of all the three tiers were indirectly elected from amongst their members. Besides, the taluka panchayats and zilla panchayats were composed of both directly and indirectly elected members.

In terms of distribution of powers and functions, the ZP as an apex body had control over both the TP and GP. Again, of the three bodies, the one at the termediate level, the TP, was relatively weak (though stronger than its counterpart in Maharashtra).

Over and above this, with the creation of a more statutory body, the State Panchayat Council (SPC), the state government expressed its commitment to support the PRIs. But the SPC was basically an advisory body. Under the Gujarat Panchayat Raj Act 1961, the ZP particularly was vested with adequate administrative and executive powers. The setting up of a Gujarat PSSB and District Panchayat Service Selection Committee comprising a nominee of the chairman of PSSB and also an officer nominated by the state government and president of the ZP are just an illustration of this point. Not only the ZP was endowed with power to the recruitment of Class III and IV staff of different categories of post, the state government also trnasferred many schemes pertaining to as many as twelve departments to the ZP. Accordingly, all the district level state government officers (belonging to Class I and II cadre) were transferred to the district level panchayat which had effective control over them (Vakil 1973: 96).

The District Collector was not responsible for the implementation of schemes transferred to the panchayat bodies, though he was a member of the ZP. Therefore, the authority of executing development schemes and their supervision and monitoring was largely vested in the office of the president of the ZP.

Against this backdrop, the first two state-wide elections (1963 and 1968) were held for panchayat bodies. The Congress won a majority of seats both at the ZP and taluka levels (Seth 1996: 38). It was not surprising since the Congress party had an all-pervasive influence throughout the state and also that it had accommodated the dominant castes, particularly the rich and influential Patidars, in its organizational network. In fact, the interlocking of power structures (panchayats, cooperatives, Congress party units, etc.) was also visible in Gujarat. For instance, the founder chairman of the Kheda Milk Cooperatives (Amul dairy) Union, Tribhuvandas Patel, by caste a Patidar, held this position for decades and also headed both the Pradesh (State) Congress Committee and the (Kheda) District Congress Committee for years together. He was a MP on a Congress ticket. After nearly three decades, he was succeeded by one of the vice-presidents of the (Kheda) zilla panchayat who was also a well-known member of the Congress party. This was equally true of some of the directors of Amul dairy who held important positions in other power structures. 'But unlike in Maharashtra their power was not cumulative in the sense that their being in Amul did not directly help them to capture other power positions[7] nor did their positions elsewhere seem to help them in becoming directors of Amul' (Baviskar 1997: 105). Thus it was mainly Congressmen who occupied positions of power, in all ZPs and most TPs. In the second panchayat election (1968), however, the Swatantra Party managed to win some seats at both the ZP and TP level, but not enough to control these bodies anywhere in the state.

It is well known that the GP election was not held on party lines, but it is also common knowledge that village leaders, having links with taluka and district level political leaders in general, had won the election for the post of sarpanches. It is important to note here that elections for sarpanch were not direct. Sarpanches were elected from amongst the members. Naturally, a member who was resourceful and having links with higher level political leaders had a better chance to capture the top position at the GP level. A few case studies of the elected representatives at the level of GPs reveal that the dominant caste in the area, and not the majority caste, won a sizeable number of seats, the majority of sarpanches had invariably belonged to the rich dominant caste. Also the voting pattern was to a large extent influenced by the 'kinship' factor.

A study of panchayat leaders in ten villages selected randomly in Kheda district substantiates this fact. Of these, Kshatriyas were in a majority in 7 villages, Patidars in 2, and in one GP, Muslims were in the majority. However, in the district as a whole, the Patidars constituted about 20 per cent of the population, Kshatriyas (Bariyas, particularly those belonging to the lower strata among Kshatriyas) and Rajputs taken together accounted for 50 per cent of the total population. The Patidars of the district, as elsewhere in the state, were rich, educated and influential, having linkages abroad and stakes in trade, industry and services. On the other hand, among the Bariyas and Rajputs some were either small or medium landowners, but a majority were tenants or agricultural labourers on land owned by Patidar landowners. The survey revealed that of 10 sarpanches of GPs, 6 were Patidars, one each belonged to Bania and Muslim castes, and 2 were Kshatriyas. The study had concluded the majority caste is not always the dominant one in the villages (Patel 1986).

A majority of the leaders including ex-sarpanches, totalling 30 in number, were found to be actively associated with the village cooperatives as chairmen, secretaries, or executive board members. In fact, more than 80 per cent were active in milk cooperative banks. Also, half of them had more than 20 acres of land and another half had land in the range of 10 to 20 acres.

Moreover, of them, 8 panchayat leaders had cars, another 6 had scooters and 6 others had tractors at their disposal.

A study[8] of the panchayat of Mogri GP in Kheda district also reports similar findings. Of the 257 land owning families in the village, 67 per cent were Patidars and 13 per cent, Bariyas. Besides being economically powerful, the Patidars were numerically the largest group in the village. In addition, during the rule of the Gaekwads, it was from among the latter that mamalatdars used to be appointed. Thus, the traditional hold of the Patidars helped them perpetuate their dominance after Independence. In fact, the first election of Mogri village panchayat, in 1951, was

> merely a formal exercise in reinforcing the dominance of the traditional leadership. The second panchayat election (1956) was nothing but another exercise and perpetuating the hold of the traditional leadership. The head of a family which enjoyed tremendous economic status in the village was chosen as the Sarpanch. The rest of the members were the same as in the first panchayat. (Shah and Pandya 1989: 143–53)

The above study also highlighted the dynamics of caste factionalism among the Patidar elites.

> Factions have emerged on the basis of kin-groups. Each major family behaves as a faction and is primarily concerned with defeating its traditional rival. They are three major factions in the village. They are known as 'Ahmedabad', 'Local' and 'Gadiwala' all belong to the dominant Patidar caste. The second dimension appears when factional fighting turns into class conflict. The Patidars as a class of landowners and employers, are politically challenged by the Bariyas and the Harijans, who represent the labour class. The Patidars get united, forgetting their rivalry, to counter the challenges posed by the new rising class. (Shah and Pandya 1989: 153)

Till then the Bariyas and other communities, comprising more than half the total village population, had no place among the village elites. But their sheer numerical strength could not be ignored for long once the electoral process started gaining roots and in the 1961 panchayat election, two Patidar contenders were defeated by people from the Bariya and Valand communities. Subsequently, in the fourth panchayat election (1965), out of a total of 13 seats, 5 went in favour of the Bariyas and SC communities. With the change in leadership democratic consciousness spread further and grew among the weaker sections in Mogri village, but did not fully penetrate the rural society, still bound by hierarchical and paternalistic attributes. The study therefore concludes that

> the formal observance of democratic rule in the panchayat is not enough. The greater barrier seems to be the marked disparity in economic, social and cultural status of the various sections of the population. The less privileged social groups and minorities still find it difficult to participate meaningfully in the democratic functioning of the panchayat. (Shah and Pandya 1989: 153)

There is no denying the fact that the Patidars have dominated the public domain particularly at the district level and below, be it cooperatives (oilseed, cotton or milk) or panchayats or the Congress party unit. But this phenomenon has socio-cultural roots. The Patidars, to begin with, have been major political players in the Congress party since before Independence (Weiner 1967: 76); education spread rapidly among them during the first quarter of the last century owing largely to the reforms launched by enlightened Patidaras who had received early education and were exposed to the world outside. Usually they held a bigger share of land as compared to any other caste in the state. It is hardly surprising therefore that Patidars took initiative in setting up cooperatives. The incentive was two folds, first to promote and protect their interest and second to expand their area of influence that would help them play a larger role at all the levels of power—from the state capital to down the level of villages (Rajaram 1996).

As Rajaram, paraphrasing Weiner, put it, 'Cooperatives serve the two aspirations of a good Patidar—to make money and to get credit for doing welfare activity' (1999: 2103). By virtue of their official position, the cooperative leaders used to be influential during election; state level leaders would try their best to get their loyal supporters inducted in cooperatives at all levels. It was because of this two-way linkage that aspiring politicians (especially among the Patidars) find the cooperative route appropriate for fulfilling their political aspirations. A village-level leader can, by becoming a leader in a cooperative, extend his influence to a group of villages. The politicians who are members of board of directors of co-operatives are or have been members of district panchayats. (Rajaram 1999: 2099)

Notwithstanding the traditional bias against the Bariyas, the Patidars had also imbibed the spirit of cooperation and accommodation, as is evident from the fact that in many Patidar headed village panchayats, the post of deputy sarpanch was invariably held by Kshatriyas and groups considered inferior in the caste hierarchy (Patel 1996: 262).

The 1967 Assembly Election and After

We have seen that Brahmins, Banias and Patidars, particularly rich and powerful ones from among those castes, were managing state politics through their hold over the party organization, cooperatives and panchayat bodies. But the Kshatriyas started asserting themselves from the early 1960s and when their demands were not met, they became instrumental in raising a rightist formation whose political manifestation was the Swatantra Party. This political development was in contrast to the then prevailing scenario in the Hindi heartland, where the socially and economically backward stood united under the banner of socialist ideals. In Gujarat the associations of various castes, the dominant ones to begin with, had never attempted to organize the poor among the respective castes, or cutting across the caste barrier on class basis. That would have been a surrender to communism, they believed, whose tenants went against the ethos of the trading communities in Gujarat (Shah 1990: 93).

In any case, the Swatantra Party largely represented the Kshatriyas who were numerically large, and emerged as a major player in the Assembly after the 1967 Assembly election. Its strength had increased from 26 in 1962 to 64 in 1967. On the other hand, the numerical strength of the Congress was reduced to 93 members in a House of 168. However, the Swatantra Party could not retain its position for quite long, since the Congress had already started alluring some of the Kshatriya leaders. What helped the Congress further at this juncture was the pro-poor image of Indira Gandhi. Moreover, the Congress was not only holding power in the state capital; it had a well-knit party organization. It was, besides, controlling the PRIs and cooperatives in the state. Therefore, despite its reduced strength in the Assembly, the Congress could put up a brave face against the Opposition. Within two years, the Congress managed to increase its strength from 93 to 101, as the Swatantra Party's strength was reduced from 64 to 55 members (anti-defection laws were then not in operation).

By this time there was a split in the Congress and unlike Maharashtra, the Congress ministry in Gujarat defected to the Congress (O). The then Chief Minister, a staunch supporter of Morarji Desai, one of the prominent Congress (O) national leaders, had to face challenges from the Prime Minister on the one hand and the Swatantra Party on the other. To counter the defection moves of the Opposition, the Chief Minister not only held meetings with party workers, he also summoned panchayat leaders, particularly the chairmen of ZPs, to the state capital to exert pressure on the MLAs of their respective districts.

For some time this strategy worked, even leading to the disintegration of the Swatantra Party. But ultimately, the Congress (O) ministry could not ward off the increasing threats from the Congress (R). What went against that was increasing awareness among backward caste leaders, mainly from the southern part of the state. Although the Congress (O) had offered these backward caste leaders positions of power in the party organization, panchayat bodies and cooperatives, they were lured by Indira Gandhi's pro-poor rhetoric and allied with her Congress (R). Moreover, 'the growing popularity of the Congress (R) at the national and state levels 'forced some Congress (O) leaders of Gujarat to review their political plans. The Congress (O) alliance with the Jana Sangh and Swatantra Party to forge a Grand Alliance gave many of them an opportunity to give ideological cover to political considerations' (Seth 1976: 72–3).

Two ministers in the Hitendra Desai government, including

Chimanbhai Patel, who later emerged as a key player in state politics, resigned. The discontent grew more intense in the Congress (O) government and the party received a final blow in the 1971 parliamentary election in which the Congress (R) won as many as 11 seats, equal to that of the Congress (O); two went in favour of the Swatantra Party.

The Chief Minister, Hitendra Desai, resigned on 31 March 1971. He was replaced by the Congress (R) leader, Kantilal Ghia, but owing to large-scale defections his ministry could not last long. Hitendra Desai was reinstated but he too met the same fate as he failed to secure a majority, despite large-scale horse-trading. Finally, President's rule was imposed for the first time, on the state on 12 April 1972. This period of uncertainty came to an end only after the 1972 assembly election, but the era of stable politics was over.

The 1972 Election

Before Gujarat went to polls, the state party unit was badly riddled with factionalism that had attained unmanageable proportions. Chimanbhai Patel, along with other dissidents who had already defected to the Congress (R), had a good support base among the rich peasants, particularly Patidars, the caste to which he also belonged. The affluent peasant castes, with Patidars at the forefront, had a sizeable influence in the countryside, by virtue of their hold over cooperatives and panchayat bodies. This helped mobilize the electorate in favour of the Congress (R). Besides, the weaker sections particularly Scheduled Castes and Tribes, who had received benefits from the welfare programmes of the government, had also thrown in their lot with the Congress. Jinabhai Darji, a Scheduled Tribe leader, and former president of the Surat zilla panchayat, who had by then become the president of the Congress (R), also played a crucial role in mobilizing the poor in support of the Indira Gandhi-led Congress. Added to this was the pro-left image of Indira Gandhi, enriched with her slogan, *Garibi Hatao.* All, these factors led the Congress (R) to a comprehensive victory at the hustings.

Thus the Congress (R) alone bagged 140 of total 168 Assembly seats. The Congress (O) had to be satisfied with a poor second position having just 16 seats. The Jana Sangh bagged three seats, the Communists one and the rest went to Independent candidates (Table 2.2).

Despite such a massive majority, the Congress remained a divided house. The internal bickerings started with the imposition of a Chief Minister from New Delhi. Ghanshyam Oza, a Brahmin from Saurashtra and then a MP, was chosen as the Chief Minister by Indira Gandhi. All including Chimanbhai Patel had to comply with the wishes of the party High Command.

But the Chief Minister failed in his efforts to unite ambitious factional leaders. For the Congress party in the state was an unstable amalgam of ambitious men from contrasting political and ideological backgrounds. They included former Congress (O) dissidents, socialists and communists, who were anti-business, and ex-Swatantra Party members who strongly defended free enterprise. In any case 'ideology was hardly the principal factor in the factional division which cystallized between "loyalists" and "dissidents"; calculations about power were primary, even among those who already shared it' (Jones and Jones 1975: 1014–16).

The party was apparently divided into loyalists and dissidents with the former commanding a majority in the House. Although these factions were

> basically marriages of ambition and convenience, there was one interest-based element of cleavage: Jinabhai Darji and Chimanbhai Patel were rivals for control of both the party organization and ruling classes, with Darji appealing more to the disadvantaged agricultural labourers and Chimanbhai to the prosperous farm owners. (ibid.: 1015)

The dissidents led by Chimanbhai Patel and Kantilal Ghia (Finance Minister in the Oza ministry) ostensibly fought on the grounds of autonomy (against the imposition of the leadership by the party High Command) and ultimately brought down the Oza ministry with a no-confidence motion in June 1973. Soon the dissident leaders also fell out as both of them sought the Chief Ministership. Though Chimanbhai Patel was able to wrest the initiative, the way he and Ghia fought with each other, 'left an indelible public impression upon which Chimanbhai's opponents capitalized in the Nav Nirman agitation' (ibid. 1975: 1015).

The 'Nav Nirman movement' was a massive urban protest initiated by students in 1974. This upsurge had started against rising prices and scarcity of essential commodities, perceived by the urban masses as a sequel to large-scale political corruption. The students were soon joined by the urban middle class (Shah 1974).

As a result of the movement, Chimanbhai Patel was forced to resign in February 1974. But it would be erroneous to conclude that rural areas or at least rich peasants, supporters of Chimanbhai Patel, had nothing to do with the movement. On the contrary, prior to the agitation, the middle and rich peasants too had waged a non-cooperation movement, and called a general strike to protest against the government's policy on land-ceiling and paddy levy. But as soon as the students demanded the removal of Chimanbhai Patel, the rich peasants under the banner of the Khedut Samaj not only withdrew their agitation but also offered to pay a higher paddy levy, even more than what the government had demanded. Obviously, their purpose was to defend Chimanbhai Patel, who hailed from a family of peasants. Even when Patel was removed, and President's rule was imposed, these farmers became instrumental in getting the assembly dissolved in March 1975. For defying the party High Command and also for indulging in anti-party activities, Chimanbhai Patel was dismissed from the party. Not deterred, he soon floated his own party, the Kisan Mazdoor Lok Paksha (KMLP), that turned out to be major contender in the 1975 assembly election.

It may be mentioned here that before the 1975 election an anti-Congress (I) wave had started gaining momentum in northern India, particularly Bihar and Gujarat. Jayaprakash Narayan, a highly respected leader who had never aspired for political office, led the movement in Bihar and visited Gujarat to win support for the crusade against the populist and authoritarian politics of Indira Gandhi. The end result was the emergence of an anti-Congress front called the Janata Morcha, comprising the

Congress (O), the Swatantra Party, the Jana Sangh and the Socialist Party. Incidentally, the same alliance partners had contested unitedly both in the 1971 general elections and the 1972 Assembly election. Thus the Congress (I), the Janata Morcha and KMLP were the major contenders apart from some other minor parties. What was more interesting in the contest was that the two leading caste-clusters in the countryside, the Patidars and Kshatriyas, had the largest representation in all three parties, though Kshatriya candidates had found more berths in the Congress (I) and the Patidars in the Janata Morcha (Shah 1976: 273).

It may also be noted that a local election committee, comprising the State Congress (I) leaders, was constituted but the entire election process was supervised and controlled by the nominees of the party High Command.

The Congress (I) however, won only 75 seats in a House of 181 members. The position of the Janata Morcha was slightly better, with 86 seats. The KMLP came a poor third, but the Janata Morcha and the KMLP together formed the government.

The Congress (I) not only lost in urban constituencies but was also defeated in the reserved constituencies for SCs and STs. For instance, of a total of 26 reserved seats, the Congress lost as many as 11 to the Janata Morcha. For the first time, the Congress 'political base among the tribals was shaken and political division among them had become sharper' (Shah 1976: 281).

Similarly, the Congress also lost 7 of total of 12 seats reserved for Scheduled Castes. By and large a similar trend was noticed in the constituencies reserved for Scheduled Tribes [out of 26 ST constituencies, the Congress (I) had lost 11 to the Front (Table 2.3)] and Muslims. What the 1975 assembly election results revealed was that the traditional support base of the Congress (I) had developed deep fissures. Therefore, the question of bringing the old supporters back to the fold of the Congress (I) became a central issue for the survival of the party in the state.

By this time, Indira Gandhi had already emerged as a popular and powerful leader at the national level. This is not to deny that despite her well-projected concern for weaker communities of the society, including minorities, she adopted a populist

TABLE 2.3: PARTY-WISE PERFORMANCE IN THE ST CONSTITUENCIES

Party	Assembly Elections			
	1962	1967	1972	1975
Congress	17	16	20	15
Opposition	4	6	4	11
Total	21	22	24	26

Source: G. Shah 1976: 281.

strategy so that the realignment of weaker sections could work as a winning formula for elections.

Accordingly, the KHAM—Kshatriyas, Harijans, Adivasis and Muslims—strategy was chalked out in Gujarat. Hitherto politically suppressed communities comprised nearly 60 per cent of the total population of the state. The leaders chosen by Indira Gandhi to implement this formula were Jinabhai Darji (Adivasi), Ratubhai Adani (Muslim) and Madhavsinh Solanki (lower Kshatriya). What was beneficial for this KHAM strategy, was the 'twenty-point programme' launched during the Emergency. Although the state machinery was entrusted with the task of its implementation, it primarily being a central government plan, the state leaders of the Congress (I) claimed credit for it.

During the Emergency itself when democratic activities were put on hold, the Gujarat government went in for panchayat elections which had been due since 1973. This showed the level of commitment of the political parties towards panchayat bodies. Although they were seeking political legitimacy, they were sincere in their support to PRIs, political rivalries notwithstanding. But the implications went beyond mere reiteration of their faith in local self-governance. The dominant caste/class led by Patidars, who till then were controlling PRIs, particularly the GPs, found it a good opportunity to renew their control over PRIs for a while longer. No doubt, the proportion of underprivileged communities among the local elites had increased after every election, and the 1975 panchayat elections were no exception. But the fact remains that it was not the poor but the elite among these communities who came to occupy positions of power in local level institutions.

By the early 1970s, however, the dominant Congress party system had developed cracks in its structure and its influence showed signs of waning, though it had managed to withstand the immediate effect of the formal split in 1969. At another level, the Scheduled Castes particularly were getting restive with growing incidence of atrocities against them by the upper castes in the countryside. This was the time when a high level committee to review the working of PRIs was constituted under the leadership of Jinabhai Darji.

The Darji Committee submitted its report in 1972. It recommended direct elections for the post of sarpanch, as well as for members of TPs and ZPs. Another important recommendation was the creation of a Social Justice Committee (SJC) at each level of the PRIs, comprising representatives of Dalits, tribes and other weaker sections.

The point to be noted here is that the change in the mode of election of sarpanches from indirect to direct had, perhaps, something to do with the weakening of the party's organizational network. By that time it had become clear that the party was losing ground. This could have been so because the powerful socio-economic position of dominant castes in the villages, the disadvantaged groups were not getting a chance to become sarpanch. Be that as it may, elections to TPs and ZPs, due in 1973, could not be held in the state. When held in 1975, these bodies were formed for the first time with directly elected members. Some of the recommendations of the Darji Committee Report had been incorporated in the Gujarat Panchayat Act, 1973. These provisions helped the leaders of Backward Castes, SCs and STs to induct disadvantaged groups into the PRIs. By facilitating the participation of weaker communities, the political leaders managed to work out new equations among these traditional supporters of the party who, of late, had become more assertive.

Although direct elections to TPs and ZPs, in a way, had the effect of disrupting the organic inter-tier links between PRIs, the PRIs again became an instrument to mobilize the weaker sections in favour of the party. Given their assertive stance, the dominant castes had no option but to concede to this change.

The Congress, being in the Opposition, was in a better position to project itself as the saviour of the weaker sections of society. In fact, the process of political realignment that began in 1969 accelerated during 1975-80, leading up to a crystallization between the Congress (I) and the disadvantaged groups. Undoubtedly, political instability at the national level had direct bearing on political developments in the state, which during the same period witnessed the installation of as many as four governments—two led by the Janata Morcha and two by the Congress (I). In case of the former, Banias, Brahmins and Patidars had the upper land (14 and 16 ministers respectively) as compared with the disadvantaged groups (Kshatriyas, OBCs, Muslims, SCs and STs). The proportion of the privileged castes (7 ministers) as compared to the less-privileged castes (15 and 11) was just the reverse in the two Congress (I)-led governments. It may also be noted that with these developments the social base of the Congress (I) was radically altered. This is apparent from the fact that among the Congress legislators in 1967, 60 per cent hailed from upper castes whereas their representation was sharply reduced (in 1980) to just 30 per cent. On the other hand, the number of legislators belonging to the OBCs, Muslims, SCs and STs dramatically increased from 40 per cent in 1967 to as high as 70 per cent in 1980. It was this shift in the social base of the Congress that resulted in the allocations of powerful ministries to the disadvantage groups. Their rising strength was clearly apparent as for the first time Gujarat saw the elevation of a lower Kshatriya politician, Madhavsinh Solanki, to the Chief Ministerial chair.

The result of the 1980 assembly election clearly demonstrates that the less privileged groups had finally started pushing the powerful Patidars, Brahmins and Rajputs to the background. Shall we then say that the process of democratization, reinforced by electoral politics, had taken a swing to the extent that leadership had started emerging from hitherto under-privileged caste groups? This would amount to exaggerating the consequences of the democratization process, as the ground realities were different.

Plebiscitary Politics

It may be recalled that following the split in the Congress party in 1969, Indira Gandhi lost the party organization to her opponents, who formed their own party, the Congress (O). But her landslide victory in the 1971 parliamentary elections confirmed that she was the most popular national leader who had a profound influence over the masses. From then onwards, she introduced a different kind of game what has been described as plebiscitary politics (Rudolph and Rudolph 1990) in all the Congress ruled states to the extent that all state-level leaders with a solid political base of their own were gradually sidelined. She did not allow anyone to mediate between her and the masses and it was obvious that an organizational network within the party would be futile. To win elections somehow became her sole aim and she started cultivating leaders devoid of a political base, particularly from underprivileged groups, but strictly on her own terms and conditions. These newcomers had never gone through the rigours of the recruitment and training process. Their only claim to legitimacy was that they were either known to Indira Gandhi personally, or to her lieutenants. With bank nationalization and privy-purse abolition together with her rhetoric, she successfully conveyed the right impression of being pro-poor and a defender of the under-privileged. What further worked in her favour were the negative features of the old party system, built over the years on the norms of authority and the old social order. The party managers of the old order in Gujarat as elsewhere in India, had by then degenerated to such an extent that they favoured only those who had belonged to their own clan or class. There was no scope for newcomers or first-generation leaders from these underprivileged groups/classes. But they were also keen to join the privileged political classes which had access to enormous state resources that had enabled them to create a core group of their followers.

In Guajarat also those who joined or shifted their loyalties to Indira Gandhi in the early 1970s had not come from among the rank and file of established local politicians (generally represented by Patidars but were newcomers, mostly Kshatriyas). In fact the 'old Congress was all full, one needed ten to fifteen years of experience before getting promotion in that party. There were many new opportunities in Indiraji's Congress' (Jinabhai Darji quoted in Kohli 1991: 44).

In a micro-level study of a district-based leadership, an analyst commented,

> Those who were attracted to the new Congress in Kheda (district) were individuals who felt excluded from the established power structure and wanted power in a hurry. These people had not spent their formative political years participating in the nationalist movement. Rather, they had grown up observing that lucrative careers could be built in a society of scarcity if one had access to the abundant resources of the interventionist state. These were not people who were interested in joining an organization at the bottom and working their way up slowly, while learning the political ropes and contributing to the strength of the organization. Their underlying motivations were quite different. Their view, for which there was some justification, was that the dominant Patidar Congressmen were not individuals who were about to share power and privileges with the Kshatriyas. Rather, the Kshatriya upstarts saw the Patidar elites as highly partisan players, who were more likely to act for their own benefit and for the benefit of their caste community. Thus, shortcuts to power were sought as a means of simultaneously displacing the dominant groups and gaining access to state resources, and Indira Gandhi provided a quick opportunity. The slow laborious task of building a party organization was never carried out. (Kohli 1991: 44–5)

It must be noted, however, that these 'newcomers' did not belong to the economically poor strata of the underprivileged caste groups; rather they were the elites among oppressed castes. In sum, the class profile had not undergone any major change. The whole churning process of electoral politics had resulted in the displacement of established elites by neo-elites belonging to the OBCs, SCs, and STs. A class profile of these new elites as we shall see later, will testify to this fact.

What was the implication of this changed social base of the Congress party for the panchayat bodies in Gujarat? The changes had occurred at the district level and below. In Kheda district (a stronghold of Patidar caste) for instance, the representation of the Koli Kshatriya caste cluster had gone up to 54 per cent in 1983 from 26 per cent in 1949. But who were they? Did they belong to poor families? An emphatic no would be the answer. Unlike the overwhelming majority of their caste members who were poor, these elected representatives were men of substantial assets. Again in Kheda district itself, out of 33 zilla panchayat members, 19 (57 per cent) had at least 10 acres of land or more and another 7 member (21 per cent) had land between 2 to 9 acres; 3 others were lawyers, and 4 had not disclosed their landed assets. Thus it was concluded that despite the lack of similar data for other districts, 'there was no reason to believe that Kheda district was an exception' (Shah 1990: 107).

However, even such change (replacement of established caste elites by neo-elites from less privileged castes) had not percolated down to the village level. In Anand taluka for isntance, in Kheda district, Koli Kshatriyas comprise 55 per cent of the total population as compared to Patidars who constitute 34 per cent. Yet 37 per cent of the village panchayats in that taluka had sarpanches belonging to the Patidar community, as compared to 34 per cent of sarpanches in 1984.

> It is also noteworthy that while a few persons belonging to the low castes initially gained political positions in panchayats, they lost ground subsequently for two reasons. First, the upper castes and classes had succeeded in co-opting defectors among the low caste leaders. Second, although the members of the lower castes gained political positions, they remained economically dependent on higher castes, middle or rich cultivators. In a few cases, affluent lower caste leaders offered stiff resistance to high caste leaders; they had behind them the numerical strength of their caste groups and they were not economically dependent on the high castes. (Shah 1990: 108)

It was these deviations from the estbalished norms of the panchayat system that prompted Rikhavdas Shah (then president of Mehsana zilla panchayat who chaired another committee to review the functioning of panchayat bodies) to recommend, in 1978, the deploticization of local bodies and restoration of the earlier mode of indirect election to TP and ZP, so that inter-tier linkages could be re-established among PRIs. At the same time, it must be emphasized that the Rikhavdas Committee received the least number of suggestions for improving the functions of ZPs. This was by and large considered to be an indication of proper functioning of the apex body till the late 1970s.

The Second Phase of the Congress 1980–1990

By early 1980, the Congress (I) re-emerged as the dominant party in the state, but was in no way near the old Congress of the pre-1967 phase. First, its social base had changed from the rural elite (Brahmin, Bania, Patidar) to a party of elite from less (socially and economically) privileged castes. But this change was significant, for it had come a long way from a minority to a majority dominated party. Second, as mentioned earlier, notwithstanding this change, the Congress party in its new incarnation was devoid of any organizational network. The consequences were farreaching.

The dominant caste, particularly Patels (Patidars), remained in control of much of the state's socio-economic resources (such as agriculture, cooperatives of different varieties, educational institutions, to a lesser degree trade and commerce as well as the press) but they had lost political power to the less privileged majority group. In a real sense, the loss of power meant losing access to state resources and consequently, being deprived of government patronage. This was something which a powerful minority group was not prepared to accept and as soon as they found an opportunity they challenged the legitimacy of a constitutionally elected government.

The opportunity came in the form of the government's decision to provide reservation of seats to OBCs, SCs and STs in technical colleges and government jobs. As soon as this decision was made public, the students of the powerful Patidar community took to the streets and violently protested against the decision. They were joined by the urban middle classes and even several professional associations such as unions of university and school teachers, a union of police inspectors, etc. (Kohli 1991: 252–7). In fact, what initially started as student's protest against reservation, subsequently turned into a caste war, resulting in large-scale arson and atrocities against Harijans.

This violent fallout of the reservation policy lasted for several months and could be quelled only when the army was deployed. The violence not only exposed the weakness of the government, but also robbed it of its legitimacy. Most importantly, a powerful minority made it clear that if their interests were theratened they could hold the powers that be to ransom. This was apparent from the fact that the Patidars even went to the extent of making a statement almost in a threatening tone that even though Patels were out of power, all governments would be well advised to take their interests into account.

That the Madhavsinh Solanki government failed both politically and otherwise, was a clear indication of the fact that it had assumed power in the state formally, without having organizational strength and social support.

We have mentioned earlier the manner in which the Congress (I) had managed to win the elections without an adequate party organizational structure. The consequences of such a facile victory were intense factionalism among leaders; Madhavsinh Solanki's rise to Chief Ministership proved to be no exception as it was primarily because of Indira Gandhi's blessings.[9] Her nation-wide popularity combined with pro-poor rhetorics among the oppressed castes and promises of patronage to them had helped Congress to win the 1980 election. Therefore, the party leaders deserted Solanki's efforts to unitedly counter the opposition led by a minority powerful group. The lack of a committed cadre was another handicap which did not help Solanki's cause.

It is surprising therefore, that despite all odds, the Solanki government completed its five-year tenure. Perhaps that was the only achievement of a government of the majority caste group, which did nothing to cater to the needs of the underpriviledged sections of the society. The Solanki government neither implemented the Agricultural Land Ceiling Act nor took up the issues of land distribution and implementation of the 'twenty-point programme' which could otherwise have gone in favour of the

Dalits, tribals and minorities. In other words, Solanki completed his tenure by compromising the interests of the lower strata of the state. Yet his party won the 1985 parliamentary election largely because of the sympathy wave following the assassination of Indira Gandhi in 1984. Added to that was Solanki's strategy of whipping up lower caste sentiments by announcing fresh reservations for backward classes in government jobs and educational institutions. This reservation policy was announced in January. As usual, the upper caste students again launched an anti-reservation agitation, which, unlike the earlier riots, could not spread because of two important reasons. First, the government quickly responded by closing all educational institutions till the assembly election was held; second, no political party could take up an anti-reservation stance on the eve of election for fear of losing the backward class vote bank.

Not surprisingly, the assembly election held in March not only passed off peacefully but the ruling party also reaped full benefit from its reservation policy. The OBCs and other weaker sections largely comprising the KHAM equation of the Congress (I), won as many as 125 of the total 149 assembly seats captured by the party in the election, with the Kshatriyas bagging the lion's share. Even in the cabinet comprising 20 ministers, 14 were Kshatriyas, controlling all the key portfolios. However, immediately after the election and the assumption of office by the new government (on 18 March), rioting began afresh (on 19 March), and lasted for six months.

The question that needs to be asked, therefore, is: Aware of the consequences of the earlier (1981) experiment with reservation, why did Solanki resort to the same course again? Had he become oblivious of the fact that given the hold of the Patels on the society and economy of Gujarat, they would vociferously oppose the government if they were denied political power?

Answers to these question can be found in the strategy adopted by Solanki, close to the Party's central leadership, which effectively meant being in the good books of Indira Gandhi and later Rajiv Gandhi.

By then the top-down approach of nominating leaders in state capitals had already been established. Solanki therefore had known that as long as he could carve out an invincible coalition, his position at the top was secure. He was not at all concerned about the recruitment of party cadres and building up party organization from below. Thus the KHAM strategy (to Solanki), was a formula to win the election. To be fair, Solanki himself had never claimed to be a radical reformer. To appreciate the efforts of the leaders of the winning coalition, he 'offered leaders of those groups direct access to states patronage: control over ministries and seats in the Assembly, government controlled jobs, admission to colleges, and positions in local governments (read panchayat bodies) and cooperatives'(Kohli 1991: 259). At the same time, he tried to placate the traditionally dominant caste (Brahmins, Banias and Patidars) by pursuing policies favourable to them. In other words, Solanki tried to give symbolic satisfaction to underprivileged groups, at the same time continuing with policies that would appease the privileged ones.

> Thus, implementing economic policies favouring the highest groups, holding control over the state and politics in the name of the disadvantaged groups, and using goons to control the opposition's street violence must have been Solanki's ruling strategy. That strategy did not work. (Kohli 1991: 260)

In fact, violence and rioting came to an end only when Solanki was forced to resign and his successor openly agreed to fulfil all the demands of the anti-reservationists. Besides, the new Chief Minister, Amarsinh Choudhary (a tribal leader from south Gujarat) also inducted some Patels into his ministry.

Choudhary had the distinction of being the first tribal Chief Minister in Gujarat. He lacked organizational skill or administrative capabilities. Earlier, he had proved himself to be a lame duck Home Minister in Solanki's government. Corrupt and weak as he was, Choudhary spent his time buying peace from faction leaders at all costs. His elevation to Chief Ministership was more in pursuance of the KHAM strategy of the party. In the process, however, he preferred to sacrifice the interests of the underprivileged classes who were increasingly disillusioned with the party. In fact, towards the latter part of the 1980s, the Congress in Gujarat was witness to a strange spectacle. Darji, for instance, despite being an ardent supporter of reservation for backward classes, could not remain for long with Solanki in view of the latter's pro-rich economic policies and neglect of party organization. He was greatly disturbed with the compromises Choudhary was making for the sake of the dominant classes, but could not go against Choudhary for fear of being misunderstood.

In such a situation the state of affairs in the party as well as government had become like a house of cards. Choudhary was biding his time by appeasing all factional leaders in the party. Since he himself was not an elected leader of the legislature and was thrust upon the state legislature, he lacked moral strength to enforce any plan or policy. It was too much indeed to expect from the government in which the Chief Minister could not see eye to eye to with as many as half a dozen of his cabinet colleagues, to make any policy pronouncements. In the absence of any government policy on any issue, the party as well as the administration was reduced to a farce. The Prime Minister as party president was largely responsible for such a scenario, but publicly expressed his anxiety by saying that Gujarat had become a problem state; so for all practical purposes the state was being governed in an ad hoc manner. Choudhary had appeased the dominant class and castes by giving ministerial positions to their representatives, while, on the other hand, he had also kept the elites among the deprived at bay, giving them a free hand in their domain including the working of panchayat bodies. With the reservation issue still unresolved, Choudhary was apprehensive of the recurrence of riots at any time and despite his conciliatory moves, he displayed exemplary courage in using his administrative powers to detain large numbers of anti-social elements, including those with powerful connections. Yet commnual riots erupted in Ahmedabad in July 1986. His efforts to organize relief measures in the wake of three years of consecutive famine ravaging most parts of Gujarat were equally impressive, though he was accused of mismanaging the relief programme.

The last phase of Congress rule (1980–9) was marked by political instability in which, Chief Ministers were allowed to occupy their chair for a considerable periods to complete their terms, and both governments were plagued by dissidence. And since their hands were tied by the party High Command, they were not in a position to discipline the party leaders or their ministerial colleagues. Yet, both Solanki and Chowdhary attached due importance to panchayat bodies. This is apparent from the fact the elections to panchayat bodies were held twice in this period, 1981–2 and 1982–7 (when the state was badly hit by drought and famine) strictly on schedules.

The question that follows here is that if the state leadership was feeling handicapped because of an over-centralized party structure presided over by the High Command, and the state leaders themselves were not being elected to the top position, why did the axe not fall on panchayats?

The answer probably lies in the tradition of panchayat system which over the years had gained roots by becoming a part of the overall system of governance. The panchayat bodies had been the implementing agency of the Gujarat government's policies, and people had become accustomed to this system. Therefore, despite infighting in the party and government, no leader ever thought of postponing the panchayat elections or superseding those bodies. Besides, election was a mechanism through which all the successive leaders, even faction leaders have had managed to put their men in key positions of power at the district level and below. And this helped the state leadership to increase its bargaining position *vis-à-vis* other faction leaders. In fact, panchayat leaders helped in the mobilization of support, and state leaders in turn accommodated their supporters in positions of power in panchayats.

The setting up of several high powered committees to review the functioning of PRIs is yet another proof of the commitment shown by successive governments towards local level institutions. However, the mere survival of an institution is not an ipso facto guarantee of its better functioning. The PRIs in the state in 1980s were no match for their earlier incarnation in the 1960s. There were several internal and external factors that had led to the decline of these institutions.

Since the mid-1970s particularly, following the recommendations of the Darji Committee, some of the powers of elected representatives were transferred to the Chief Executive Officers at both the taluka and district level panchayat bodies. This was more than enough to indicate that state legislatures had lost confidence in the wisdom of the elected panchayat leaders in TP and ZP. Perhaps this step was a precursor to what was to unfold at a later stage. In mid-1980s two agencies in particular, the District Rural Development Agency (DRDA) and the District Planning Board (DPB), were created in Gujarat (as in other states). These agencies, manned and led by district level officials and technically working under the overall command of the District Collector, not only took over the district planning exercise but also the task of implementing centrally sponsored schemes. In theory both these agencies were supposed to work closely with the PRIs. It was not just an encroachment on the autonomy of the PRIs, but an indictment of elected panchayat leaders who were no longer considered impartial in the discharge of their duties and serving the rural poor.

Though the creation of DRDA and DPB was a country-wide phenomenon and practically all states including Gujarat had to silently accept the imposition of over-centralizing tendencies in governance, the PRIs in the state had already undergone significant changes. We have noted earlier that, owing to the KHAM strategy and direct elections, sarpanches from among the OBCs and other weaker section had come to occupy positions of power in PRIs; their presence was felt more at the village level gram panchayats. The Kshatriyas in particular had become the dominant caste group in a large number of PRIs. But they were not able to reorient the PRIs towards serving the rural poor. The reasons were many: first, the autonomy of PRIs had to a large extent been eroded; second, by then the party organization, which had earlier been influencing the decision-making process and recruitment of leaders, had become defunct. Therefore these first generation leaders indulged in self-aggrandizement rather than serving their constituents. It was not only the party structure that had become defunct but the state panchayat council and state panchayat parishad also met the same fate. These two state-level bodies had earlier been guiding, and running training programmes for, the elected panchayat representatives.

The combined effect of all these was the decline and fall of the PRIs whose outer shell had somehow remained intact even as they had lost their souls. In an official report, the Gujarat government (GOG 1990) had also observed that the PRIs had failed to impact the lives of poor. Besides, the system was not empowering them thus making them indifferent. In fact, there was hardly any attempt to motivate the people to participate in the political and economic process. The report had concluded: 'Local participation was at a low key and totally disappointing' (Cowlagi 1994: 212).

It may be recalled that when Ahmed Patel (a nominee of Rajiv Gandhi whom the party High Command later made the GPCC president) tried to brow beat the Surat zilla panchayat president, he could not succeed. Sahdev Chaudhary (president of Surat ZP), like Amarsinh Choudhary, was a tribal, and, both were on good terms. When Patel expelled Sahdev Chaudhary from the party, all party workers aligned with Choudhary, with the result that the party was defeated in the ensuing by-election in the area.

Another point that needs mentioning is that regular elections to panchayat institutions have resulted in weakening the hold of the dominant caste in villages in Gujarat. Naturally then, elites of disadvantaged groups have come to occupy positions of power in PRIs. At the same time, it has given birth to intense competition among OBCs also; the latter do not want to lose any opportunity to share the spoils of the system. Therefore pressure is always built up to hold panchayat elections. Moreover, as pointed out in a recent study (Shah 1996), after every election almost 80 per cent of new faces assume leadership in the PRIs at all levels. It is this combination of factors—unbroken tradition of periodic election, pressure from prospective leaders-in-waiting and the fear of losing legitimacy in the eyes of the people—which have forced state leaders to keep PRIs alive.

Although panchayat leaders had been used earlier in the late 1960s and early 1970s to pressurize MLAs, when the Congress split for the first time, their use by faction leaders in their tussle for supremacy led to the decline of the PRIs and, subsequently, the party itself lost its support base in the state by the late 1980s.

It may be mentioned here that towards the end of the 1980s, corruption in high places occupied a central place in the political discourse at the national level. With this issue on their agenda the leaders of the Jan Morcha had gone to the people during the 1989 parliamentary elections. And on this issue alone the Congress party lost to the Janata Dal, a loose coalition of Jan Morcha and several splinter groups of the erstwhile Janata Party.

Following its defeat in the 1989 parliamentary elections, the Congress affected a change in the leadership in Gujarat. Once again Madhavsinh Solanki was made Chief Minister in January 1990. But by then the party was badly ridden with intense factionalism; so much so that all important leaders of the party were preoccupied more in the fight for supremacy among themselves and cutting each other's support base by whatever means possible, than with evolving a strategy to counter the opposition. Criminalization of politics, maladministration in the police and civil services, caste and communal riots which had erupted several times in the 1980s, all these ultimately resulted in the rout of the Congress party in the May 1990 assembly election. With a coalition government of the Janata Dal–BJP combine, under the leadership of Chimanbhai Patel, the second phase of Congress rule came to an ignominious end in Gujarat.

Ironically, Chimanbhai Patel—whom the Jan Morcha and Janata Party leaders had bestowed the honour of leading a crusade against corruption—was the same former Congress leader during whose Chief Ministership corruption had reached its peak in the early 1970s and whose government was dismissed following the 1974 'Nav Nirman movement'.

State Politics in the 1990s: BJP's Rise to Power

In the 1990 election the Congress won 33 of the total 182 assembly seats, whereas the Janata Dal and BJP, with partial seat adjustments against the Congress, captured 70 and 67 seats respectively.

And a coalition government, formed by both these parties led by Chimanbhai Patel, took charge of the state.

Since being dismissed as Chief Minister by Indira Gandhi in 1974, Chimanbhai Patel had been waiting for an opportunity to regain power. He had wrested power, but his political base had considerably weakened. Yet he was not prepared to give in easily. Therefore, as soon as the BJP withdrew its support in the wake of the Ramjanambhoomi issue, Chimanbhai Patel looked to the Congress for support. Since Rajiv Gandhi was keen to see the downfall of V.P. Singh's government, he extended support to Chimanbhai Patel, who had already aligned with Chandra Shekhar's group in the Janata Dal. These alignments culminated in the formation of a regional party called the Janata Dal (G).

At this juncture the state leaders whom Rajiv Gandhi had not taken into confidence while deciding in favour of Chimanbhai Patel, were faced with a serious dilemma. The Congress party, particularly since the floating of its KHAM formula, had been championing the cause of the poor, the downtrodden and disadvantaged groups and in the process, had fought against the pro-rich, dominant caste peasant leader Chimanbhai Patel in the last election. With Rajiv Gandhi deciding to extend support to him, they had to suddenly embrace him. This uneasy coalition turned out to be disastrous for both the Congress and Chimanbhai Patel, as the results of the 1991 mid-term parliamentary elections showed. For, out of 26 parliamentary seats, 24 were captured by the BJP.

This humiliating defeat clearly established the fact that the Janata Dal (G) was a party without any support base in the state. It was also clear that an alliance with it would be suicidal for the Congress. But the central leadership, worried about national politics, did not care to pay heed to the warning signals emanating from Gujarat. On the contrary, Rajiv Gandhi forced his party to play second fiddle to the Janata Dal (G). In the meantime, slowly but surely Chimanbhai Patel lured Congress MLAs to his side by offering them ministerial positons and thus paved the way for the merger of Janata Dal (G) with the Congress.

No doubt, with the merger the Congress could claim to have Gujarat under its belt but by all means it turned out to be merely a personal triumph for Chimanbhai Patel. The Congress party could not draw political mileage out of it. With the death of Rajiv Gandhi in May 1991, the Congress also lost its charismatic leader. The state unit was already directionless as the new central leadership was busy with its own survival in New Delhi. The party lost all touch with its support base in the state. To quote an observer of the Gujarat political scene,

> No effort was made to rejuvenate the party. All the faction remained busy in circuit house annexe politics with the aim of defeating one another. There was evidence of cross-voting in the Rajya Sabha election in 1993–94. The party avoided facing the electorate as far as possible (it) postponed panchayat and municipal election under one pretext or the other. (Shah 1996b)

As apprehended, panchayat elections due in 1992 were not held. Meanwhile, the Constitution (73rd Amendment) Act came into force. Paradoxically in the state that had pioneered panchayat institutions in terms of holding regular elections since 1963, the leadership was trying to avoid election as far as possible.

The BJP, on the other hand, was drawing maximum mileage out of the prevailing political situation. Slowly but gradually, the BJP made inroads into the expanded support base of the Congress such as Kshatriyas, Scheduled Castes and Tribes. Its strategy of religion-driven mobilization had already paid rich dividends in the 1990 assembly election. Subsequently, the Congress party's vascillating stands on the mosque/mandir issue drove Muslims away. The pre-final test between the two major contestants took place in 1994 when a High Court order forced the government to hold municipal elections. The BJP won more than half of the seats in as many as 54 municipal bodies (Patel 1999: 2425). This turned out to be a prelude to the decisive 1995 assembly election. The long-term strategy of the BJP was to win over the SCs, STs and Kshtriyas, by fielding a large number of candidates from these sections. By then the Patidars had already turned to the BJP to protect their own interests. The BJP's strategy of religious mobilization, also paid rich dividends to the party in the 1995 assembly election. The BJP emerged as a most powerful victor with a mandate to rule. Overlooking all these facts, the outgoing Chief Minister, analysing the Congress defeat, went on record to say that 'pampering the minorities by the Congress party was the main reason for the defeat' (Joshi 1995: 20).

Subsequently, by capturing an overwhelming 82 per cent of the district and taluka panchayat seats (624 out of total 767) the BJP heralded the beginning of a two-party system in the state. With 18 out of 19 zilla panchayats and 154 out of total 183 taluka panchayats under its command, for the first time in the history of Gujarat panchayats, the BJP came to rule on a popular mandate.

1995 and After

The euphoria created over the victory of the BJP at taluka, district and the state level, soon turned sour when the BJP came to govern the state. Traditional rivalry between the Patidars and Rajputs and Kolis soon surfaced as a result of an extremely lopsided and politically unwise sharing of power. And as the conflicts over the dispensation of resources sharpened, Shankersinh Vaghela (a Rajput leader with mass support among Kolis) broke away from the BJP to form another party, the Rashtriya Janata Party (RJP). The split in the party, and that too within a few months after the BJP had assumed power in the state, shattered the tall claim that the BJP is a 'party with a difference'.

Vaghela formed the government with Congress support and tried to project himself as the leader of OBCs. He did not succeed.[10] To his dismay, polarization of votes on caste lines did not occur during the 1998 (mid-term) assembly election. Also the non-Patel votes, comprising that of Durbars, the Backward Castes, Muslims and SCs, were divided between the RJP and the Congress. On the other hand, Patels rallied behind the BJP to avenge the injustice done to their leader. The BJP returned to power with Keshubhai Patel at the helm of affairs.

During the first three years after the rout of the Congress in 1995, the state witnessed as many as five governments with

Keshubhai assuming charge second time. As the state entered the next century, it became clear that the BJP leader of the Saurashtra region had not learnt any lesson from his past experiences. Not only did the Chief Minister refuse to accommodate leaders of different social groups, once again he allowed the concentration of power in the hands of a coterie, including extra-constitutional authorities. Besides, as he went on raking up controversial issues, his government was seen as being a flop in the realm of policy making and overall governance.[11]

That people are getting disillusioned with the BJP government, became clear in the polls for the local bodies, both for the municipalities and panchayats. The point to be noted here is that the election to the gram panchayat, due in May-June 2000, was deferred to December 2000 on account of drought. Subsequently, yet another ordinance was promulgated in November 2000 to postpone GP elections for another three months (*Panchayti Raj Update* Dec. 2000). In September 2000 elections to taluka and district level panchayats were held, and at both levels the BJP failed miserably. The Congress captured 22 of the 23 zilla panchayats[12] for which elections were held.

In a way this was a reversal of the 1995 election result in which the BJP had won all but one zilla panchayat. This time the BJP won only the Porbandar zilla panchayat in Saurashtra region, the native place of the BJP Chief Minister. Similarly, at the taluka level, of the total 210 taluka panchayats, the Congress won 150.

Commenting on the BJP's performance in the panchayat elections, an observer said, 'the BJP lost also because of the "Congressization" of its culture. The leaders lost touch with grass roots level workers. The BJP was also bogged down by Keshubhai Patel's kitchen Cabinet' (Bavadam 2000: 113). The BJP's defeat in local bodies had been interpreted in different ways, but the observation noted above to a large extent summed up BJP rule in the state. In fact, there were many parallels between the Congress of the early 1990s and the BJP under Keshubhai. That there was intense rivalry among the leaders, all powers were centralized in the hands of a kitchen cabinet that took all decisions in the name of the Chief Minister, and a very ham-handed performance of the government in handling the drought as well as earthquake relief. Above all, the Chief Minister himself was widely perceived as a regionalist-casteist (according special status to Saurashtrian Patels over Patidars of mainland Gujarat) and a patron of the corrupt and wrongdoers of all sorts, a static old man under the spell of his son and son-in-law who made decisions on his behalf (*Frontline* 18 June 1999).

Notwithstanding these apparent failure and his style of functioning, Keshubhai was ensconced in his chair since he knew that he had the suppot of the influential central leaders of the party. After all, they had bailed him out over and again. The moment of reckoning ultimately came when the BJP lost in the by-elections held in August 2001. This included the Sabarmati assembly seat that forms a part of the prestigious Gandhinagar Lok Sabha constituency held by Advani, the present Home Minister and the second most important leader of the BJP.

It was at this juncture that the state witnessed change of its guard. An almost failure ridden Keshubhai Patel was replaced by Narendra Modi in October 2001. It was again akin to adopting the Congress style. Modi is known as a party whole timer who does not have mass support. He has never been an elected leader either. He is also seen as a man who lacks experience in the matters of governance. Yet he was hoisted as the head of the government. Commenting on what prompted this change, a journal wrote:

> Gujarat is the only state where the BJP is in power on its own, and it was also widely dubbed as the 'laboratory for the party's Hindutva experiment'. However, while with the NDA alliance at the centre, incidence of communal violence have actually dropped across the country, the party's ascendence in Gujarat has been marked by frequent incidence of communal violence against minorities. . . . That he is the first BJP CM (Chief Minsiter), who has risen from the RSS[13] ranks, also indicates that the party may well be planning to use its Hindutva card. (*EPW* 2001: 3797–8)

The subsequent communal riots that engulfed Gujarat for months together confirmed this worst apprehension. The communal riot is not something new to Gujarat. Yet the way the houses, shops and property of the minortiy community were selectively targeted,[14] it was obvious that the attacks were premeditated. The law enforcing machinery either looked the other way or it connived with the marauders. Altogether, this worst carnage took the heavy tall of hundreds of lives, destroyed properties worth crores of rupees and also drove over a lakh of people into camps as refugees in their own state. A couple of months after, an indifferent and insensitive state administration showed its most malignant face when it took upon the task of forcibly closing the refuge camps. In first place, the state failed to protect the lives and property of the people, then forced the hapless victims of violence to live in cramped refugee camps, devoid of any basic facilities. And to cap it all, the demonic state is now forcing them out of the camps to a world of despair, without any home, asset and future. That the impact of these steps will not only alienate a minortiy community but will also drive the wedge deeper in the society as a whole, the present dispensation is oblivious of this fact. On the contrary, this is what it had intended to achieve for its short-cut narrow political gains.

It is apparent from the fact that while the earlier BJP government was mortally afraid of facing electorates, the Modi government is now gearing up for an early Assembly election,[15] otherwise due in 2003. Having taken a dip in the blood of innocent minority community people, the party has rejuvenated itself, striking a chord with the majority community which has been thoroughly polarized on communal lines. It was this resurrection of the party—from the ebb of despair to the throes of ecstasy—that amidst the chaos it conducted gram panchayat elections[16] in the middle of April 2002. It was beyond comprehension of any rationale mind that in a state which was bleeding amidst unchecked communal conflagration for so long, election of any sort would be conducted. Yet that is precisely what the present regime did and paradoxically, in pursuance of decentralized governance in the state. What flows from it?

That interests of the ruling party taking precedence over those of governance. What is the immediate interest of the party? What is it aiming at? And what it wants to achieve? The answer to all these questions are sequential. First and foremost, to boost the sagging morale of the party not only in Gujarat but most importantly in Uttar Pradesh where it lost power in recently held assembly electoins. In order to do so the party has once again aimed at consolidation of Hindutva forces which, the party believes, will garner sufficient votes on communal lines. If this strategy succeeds in Gujarat then happily, the BJP will apply it in other states where elections are due next year, and eventually, prepare the runway for the next general elections. The ultimate aim of the party, as is well known, is to form its own government in Delhi so that it could translate its cherished dream—remaking India a Hindu *Rashtra*—into reality. Modi was chosen by the party to give shape to its well thought out strategy. Therefore, to believe that the Modi government failed to check the communal violence would amount to misinterpretation of the fact. For Modi and his companion knew that by prolonging communal violence they were serving the interests of the party. And in all likelihood, they seem to have reaped benefits for the BJP.

For until recently, it was believed that the BJP might suffer heavily in the next assembly elections. It is to a large extent going the same way the Shiv Sena-BJP government had gone in neighbouring Maharashtra. The state of Gujarat, like Maharashtra, happens to be a stronghold of the Congress. It may be mentioned that prior to 1995, Gujarat had experienced only two spells of the non-Congress regimes—first in 1975 and then in 1990. And on both occasions, the non-Congress government could not complete its stipulated five-year tenures. That this might happen once again, was a feeling that was gaining ground. However, it was obvious that the Congress had not mended its ways as it was commonly known that the victory of the Congress in the last elections to municipalities and panchayats was more by default than design. There has been negative voting in India for long. People punish non-performing government irrespective of the party to which they belong. There was every possibility of the BJP government meeting the same fate in the ensuing elections. The incumbency factor was almost certain to play its role. But after these gruesome incidents the political landscape seems to have been completely changed. And so is the mood of the militant Hindutva forces. They form the core of the BJP and after winning them, the Modi regime seems to be fervently trying to whip the mass Hindu sentiments in its favour. The *rath yatra*, which was temporarily shelved,[17] was resumed as *gaurav yatra* to achieve this objective.

By all indications it is now clear that the governance as such has no place on their agenda. Therefore to expect them to work for strengthening panchayats is simply ruled out. By postponing elections to the gram panchayats initially and later, by conducting them under abnoraml circumstances, the BJP government has revealed where panchayats stand in its scheme of things.

Unlike in many states in India, elections to panchayat bodies in Gujarat have been regular for nearly four decades. Notwithstanding the fact that panchayats have failed to evoke people's participation, people attach value to them. As we have noted earlier, that almost 80 per cent of sitting panchayat members are changed by new faces in almost all panchayat elections held so far in the state. In any case, the findings of a major survey[18] conducted in 1996 show that about 40 per cent of people (sampled respondents) had the highest extent of trust (a great deal) in the institutions of local government. The corresponding numbers of the people having a similar level of trust in other democratic institutions like political parties, political representatives, and the state government were 12, 18 and 22 per cent respectively (Patel 1999: 2430).

So people have faith in panchayats (and municipalities), more than in any other representative institution, and logically they appreciate regular elections to these bodies. It is also a constitutional requirement. And yet the BJP regime does not pay any heed to either of these obligations.

Most importantly, the way panchayats have been treated under two successive BJP governments in the state, it has established the fact that the Constitution (73rd Amendment) Act in itself is not sufficient to ensure the continuity of panchayat institutions. This also validates our hypothesis that the continuity of panchayats is intrinsically linked to (good) governance and both in turn are dependent on the regime in question.

Conclusion

In this study we have tried to analyse the significance of PRIs within the realm of overall governance in Gujarat. Therefore, to look at the broad elements of operational linkages between state politics and PRIs has been our endeavour. Such operational linkages have been examined in terms of the role of PRIs in facilitating consensual ways of resolving conflict that emanate when dominant social forces compete with each other for access to state resources and to dispense state patronage among their followers. By providing access to positions of power to the traditional elites, and subsequently to newcomers in the arena of politics from village to district level, PRIs have not only played a prominent role in resolving conflict, but also in bridging the gap between the people and the government that is located in the state capital.

Moreover, if not for the de-facto devolution of power, the very creation of PRIs provided an opportunity to the state leadership to at least ensure adequate representation of the peasant-proprietor cultivating caste (Patidars and later Kshatriyas including Kolis) in the *de jure* power structure at the district level and below. This chasm between the local level governmental institutions including cooperatives and the party organization helped widen and consolidate the support base of the ruling party. That in turn, helped mobilize people in support of the party, and thus ensured its victory in successive assembly elections. On the other hand, the continuation of the same political party in power helped the PRIs survive in the state.

As mentioned earlier, Banias and Brahmins, the two traditional dominant castes, were occupying the top positions in the state politics when Gujarat came into existence in 1960. But these castes were numerically not large enough to control all the levels of power within the state. Therefore, to strengthen the hold of the Congress in the state, it was necessary to create more opportunity structures and share power with the other dominant caste, the Patidars, at the district level and below. The latter comprised 12 per cent of the total population in the state. The Patidars, though belonging to the middle castes and inferior to Brahmins and Banias in the social hierarchy of Gujarat, were resourceful by virtue of their landed assets and business interests enriched with the wealth that migrant Patidars had ploughed back in their native villages. Besides, they had already entered the political scene in the 1930s, following the rise of Sardar Patel in the Congress. They became the natural allies of Banias and Brahmins.

The Congress in Gujarat had been influenced by the charisma of a supreme leader: beginning with Gandhiji, this tradition continued up to Morarji Desai, whose followers controlled the state so long as the state was ruled by the undivided Congress party.

In Gujarat, as elsewhere in the country, the traditional dominant castes, the Brahmins and Banias in association with Patidars, formed the social base of the Congress. Being numerically large and given their hold in the counryside, the Patidars were more easy to co-opt. And panchayats became the instruments to achieve this goal. In fact, in certain parts of Gujarat, Patidars were already controlling the village panchayats when the state was a part of the Bombay Province and later Bombay State. It is not surprising, therefore, that in the first two panchayat elections held in 1963–4 and 1968–9, the Congress party won most of the seats in the PRIs. It is equally significant that both TPs and ZPs consisted of both directly and indirectly elected members. Also, as per the State Panchayat Act, the chairperson of PRIs at all levels were to be elected from among the members of respective panchayat bodies. This rule was perhaps introduced to regulate the election of chairpersons, who for all practical purposes, mattered more than all the elected (whether directly or indirectly) members at any level of PRIs. In this way the ruling party ensured the dominance of elites at all levels of panchayats.

Interestingly, some of the elites among the Patidars who had also been vying for state level leadership, had even aligned with the upcoming Kshatriyas under the auspices of the Swatantra Party in the 1967 assembly election. This hampered the fortunes of the Congress as it lost several seats to the Swatantra Party in the 1967 election.

The role of PRI leaders, particularly the chairpersons of ZPs, became crucial following the 1969 split in the Congress party. Unlike neighbouring Maharashtra, in Gujarat the party and the government had remained in the hands of the Congress (O). The then Chief Minister, therefore, had to face both a hostile Prime Minister and the opposition simultaneously, and he was apprehensive that some of his party legislators might cross the floor. At this juncture he had mobilized panchayat leaders to exert pressure on MLAs in their respective districts not to defect from the party.

The game plan succeeded until March 1971, but later internal bickering in party led to instability with the change of guard and also after reinstating the same Chief Minister; finally the state was put under President's rule. Stability could be partly restored with the massive victory of the Congress (I) in the 1972 assembly election which also witnessed a change in the caste profile of the legislature as well as intense dissidence and factionalism within the party. The point to be noted here is that again unlike Maharashtra, where Marathas and Kunbis had formed a caste-cluster, here in Gujarat the Patidars and Kolis had been rivals for quite long and their dislike for each other had hampered the Congress party.

It is also to be recalled that Indira Gandhi, who by then had emerged as the undisputed leader of the country, had introduced a different kind of politics; she was not bothered about the party organization nor with a concern for the devolution of power and by extension for the PRIs. Notwithstanding the central leaders' reluctance towards devolution of power, once a majority Congress government assumed power after the 1972 assembly election, the then leadership again showed its concern for PRIs by constituting a powerful committee under the leadership of Jinabhai Darji. By then the leadership profile of the party was changing, as the party was trying to expand its base among the hitherto disadvantaged groups. In consonance with the Congress (I)'s professed pro-poor commitment, the Darji Committee changed the mode of election of GP chairpersons from indirect to direct, so that a less privileged and politically resourceful person could also aspire to become a sarpanch.

It also needs mentioning that owing to the ongoing work of the expert committee coupled with the changing social base, the then state leadership postponed the third panchyat election due in 1973. Credit must be given, however, to the Gujarat legislators that even during the Emergency they pressed for panchayat elections. Later, elections were held once again when the state was reeling under a severe drought in 1986.

To sum up, the chronology of developments in Gujarat politics clearly illustrates the extent to which the panchayats have been wedded with state politics. The linkages between the two have been strong enough to influence each other's course of happenings. But then, Gujarat has some exceptional attributes that have helped PRIs to emerge as local centres of power and also made it a part of the overall system of governance in the state.

Gujarat was one of the few states where the state panchayat parishad and state panchayat council, the former an advisory body and the later a statutory body, played an active role in advising and coordinating activities of the PRIs as also in running training programmes for panchayat leaders. It may be a coincidence, but the fact remains, that all the notable architects of panchayats (Gandhiji, Balwantrai Mehta, and Asoka Mehta) hailed from Gujarat. The setting up of several expert committees to review the functioning of PRIs, the introduction of the Social Justice Committees at all levels of PRIs, and the total devolution of land revenue to PRIs, are some of the examples that testify to the tradition and commitment of the state leadership to their panchayat bodies.

By the 1980s, traditional elites had finally given way to a young populist leadership to whom politics was a means for self-aggrandizement. In this period, we notice a perceptible decline in the panchayat autonomy. By constituting the District Planning and Development Board and the District Rural Development Agency, the wings of the panchayats were sought to be clipped and, on the other hand, more powers were given to the bureaucracy and the legislature.

In fact, it was the presence of a large number of lower caste leaders in the PRIs who helped mobilize poor people under the KHAM umbrella in favour of the Congress (I), which won both the 1980 and 1985 assembly elections. By then however, ideology and any kind of commitment had taken a back seat as the new Congress leaders were those who had never gone through the political rigours and lacked the patience and perseverance to move gradually the political ladder. Their motivation was different; to them politics was only the pursuit of power. It is under them that the panchayats lost their dynamism, and state politics became directionless, divorced from any social or community cause. Later, by delaying panchayat elections for no apparent reason, along with uncontrolled factionalism, the Congress party provided the basis for its crushing defeat in the 1995 assembly election. In fact these reasons turned out to be decisively against the Congress when it subsequently lost the PRIs to the BJP, the party which had formed its government in the state and had organized the 1995 panchayat election in the state.

Once in power, the BJP turned out to be no different from the Congress. Soon, there was split in the party due to reluctance of the Chief Minister to share power with the leaders of other social groups which in first place helped the BJP to wrest power from the Congress in 1995. This led to factionalism and increasing dissidence in the party and resultant political instability. It is hardly surprising, therefore, that during the first three years (1995–8), following the departure of the Congress, the state witnessed as many as five governments. Although Patel returned back to power again in 1998, increasingly he behaved like a sectarian caste leader. Devoid of any vision and agenda for governance, the Patel regime epitomized misgovernance. The government delinked itself from the grass roots workers and did not even want to face the people. So much so that the State High Court had to force the government to hold elections to municipal and panchayat bodies.

Consequently, when elections to taluka and district level panchayats were held in September 2000, the BJP was defeated miserably. The party met the same fate again in bye-election for assembly seats. Ultimately, the central leadership of the BJP was forced to sack this lethargic state leader.

His successor Narendra Modi took over in October 2001. Within six months of his rule, the communal violence broke out which went on unchecked for months together, making the wedge deeper between the Hindu and Muslim communities. Ironically, when the state was passing through this prolonged phase of turmoil, gram panchayat election was conducted. Obviously, the intention of the government was to make use of the polarization of votes on communal lines. Narendra Modi, in any case, acts more like a militant Vishwa Hindu Parishad ativist than the head of a state government. He lacks administrative experience and prior to his elevation to the Chief Ministerial position, he has never held any elected office. No wonder, he works more like a devout foot soldier of the party. Serving the interests of the party is his top priority. Therefore, governance does not figure in his scheme of things. The outcome of the Gujarat assembly elections 2002 has shown that Modi has succeeded in his game plan. Naturally then, under the Modi regime, panchayats will be able to some how survive in the state, they will nevertheless loose their vitality.

NOTES

1. The Kshatriyas of modern Gujarat comprise a new social group, different from centuries old traditional Kshatriyas. The constituents of this new social group are Rajputs—a landowning upper caste—and Kolis—a numerically large but upwardly mobile lower caste who earlier used to be predominantly tenants. It is estimated that about 40 per cent of the total population of Gujarat claims Kshatriya status. By joining hands these two castes had formed the Kshatriya Sabha, a reform-oriented organization that played a decisive role in the 1962 assembly election. Both these castes have had been at loggerheads with the Patidars, a dominant caste in Gujarat. To understand the formation of this group and their political mobilization as well as for other relevant details see Myron Weiner (1967) especially the section 5 of Part II (The Participation Crisis, pp. 92–110).

2. The 'Patidars' are described basically as an enterprising peasant caste, a forward looking (middle) peasant community that had taken up cultivation of cash crops (cotton and tobacco) besides traditional crops like bajra in the late nineteenth century. Traditionally, the Patidars came from a farming community called the Kunbis—a peasant community from Maharashtra. Interestingly, 'Kunbi' is considered to be a variant of 'Kurmi'. The latter is the name of a peasant proprietor cultivating caste of the Gangetic plains (central and eastern Uttar Pradesh as well as Bihar). Historian Hardiman says that during the Mughal period some Kunbis, who 'organized themselves into coherent communities of village rulers' later came to be known as Patidars. Earlier the Kunbis and Patidars were differentiated on the basis of wealth and social status, but after 1931, this distinction was blurred and the peasant community, irrespective of its land holdings, as a whole is known as Patidars in Gujarat. However, the 'Kunbis' as a peasant caste do have a seizable presence in neighbouring Maharashtra, where they are clubbed with Marathas. Again, in Maharashtra also, the essential difference between the Marathas and Kunbis is that of their status (Pocock 1972: 1; Hardiman 1981: 37, 42; Bhat 1971: 310).

   To this enterprising caste, Gujarat owes for its widely acclaimed dairy cooperatives. In fact, it was the Patidars of the Kheda district in Central Gujarat who launched the dairy cooperatives following the advent of railways and cream separating machines. Anand town became a major dairy centre in early twentieth century itself. By 1918, the net worth of dairy exports, Rs. 24 lakhs, had excceeded the total revenue of Kheda district (Hardiman 1981: 261–2).

   The *Gazetter of Bombay Presidency* (vol. III, 1879) described the Patidars 'as the best farmers in the district, sober, quite industrious and except on such special occasions as marriage, thrifty [as cited by Weiner 1967: 75].

   Patidars are in popular perception shrewd, frugal and hardworking. In the modern Gujarat, they claim to be Vaishyas and interestingly, are acknowledged as such by others (Shah 1991: 60) For the business acumen of Patidar castes and their pioneering role in dairy cooperatives in Gujarat see also Baviskar et al. 1997, vol. 4: 96–111.
3. It was in late nineteenth and early twentieth century that Patels (Patidars) began emigrating to east Africa, where they worked in the railways. Historian David Pocock has indicated that it was the spectre of famine and plague that forced them to move to distant shores. See Patel and Rutten 1999, pp. 952–4.

In a micro study of Kheda district, Myron Weiner (1967: 75) also notes: 'At the turn of the century many Patidar families migrated to East and South Africa as result of famine in Kaira (Kheda) district. Many of the schools and clock towers found in the villages of Kaira were financed by the money sent home by Patidars in Africa. The readiness of Patidars to move outside their district and indeed outside the country to maximize their prosperity is a mark of their extraordinary mobility and enterprise. For reasons which, incidentally, have never been studied, the Patidar community is characterized by the Protestant spirit so often described as one of the conditions necessary for entrepreneurship.' Weiner has also observed that besides being economically enterprising, Patidars also happen to be political 'organizers, leaders, and followers of the nationalist movement in Kaira district'.

The emigration of Patidars has continued all along. For instance, during a field study conducted in 1987, information was collected from a retired principal of a local high school about the numbers of households of Patidars in village Kansia (Kheda district). About two decades ago there were 90, but the number had dropped to 80 at the time of the study. The pace of emigration further accelerated, with 'one or two Patidar houses permanently closed every year. A.S. Patel 1996: 266.

4. Perhaps it had roots in the Vaishnavite and Jain religious traditions, which in first place had inspired Gandhiji. His notions about non-violence to a large extent were based on these traditions; this also explains why it was Gujaratis who found Gandhi's ideas most appealing. People in Gujarat in fact found these ideas 'compatible with both their religious and political sentiments. Gandhi's constructive work programme, for example, was enthusiastically adopted by Gujratis. In the early twenties young villagers and townsmen, generally from more prosperous and educated families, flocked to the Gandhian banner and began to organize peasants, students, and factory workers. The Congress organization in Gujarat became on of the best organized and most effective nationalist units in the country.' Weiner (1967: 73)
5. *Patel Bandhu*, a journal of the Patidar caste, had long back asserted that 'all agricultural communities of India were Patidars' and also called for forming an organization to bring them together. The call was given to Marathas of Maharashtra, Vokaligas of Mysore, Reddis of Andhra, and Naidus of Madras suggesting that all these communities were essentially Patidars. For details, see Bhat (1971: 310).
6. Weiner's study (1967: 74–91) of the recruitment, functional approach

of party workers and formal institutions linked to the Congress party in Kheda district in particular and Gujarat in general shows the dominance of Patidars in politics and economy of the district. It also illustrates as how the political parties and the social system affect each other.

7. The founder chairman of Amul dairy kept this milk cooperative away from politics during his entire tenure, his own political persona notwithstanding. He never allowed politicians to interfere in the affairs of the milk cooperative union and he shielded the technocrats, to whom he had given a free hand, from any kind of political pressure. This was in contrast to the prevailing scenario in Maharashtra where state politics were intertwined with the cooperatives. Also, the chairmen and boards of directors of sugar cooperatives had a major say in running the affairs of cooperatives.

Was it an altruistic policy extraordinarily pursued by the chairman of Amul? Parhaps not. A perceptive observer of the Gujarat cooperatives says that this phenomenon—a technocrat having the upper hand—has its roots in the political rivalry between the two numerically large caste groups, Patidars and Bariyas, in the district. Amul was created by Patidars, who had always held the offices of chairman and directors. By the end of 1950s when the capacity of the dairy was under expansion, 'the Union's need to feed this capacity forced it to expand its area of operation to distant villages in the district. Most of the villages were Baria dominanted. Being mostly small landholders and agricultural labourers the Barias are poorer than Patidars but numerically stronger. They represent 45 per cent of district's population as against 14 per cent of Patidars.' Prior to that, the Baria caste were already holding the chairmanship of more than half the village level cooperative societies, against 37 per cent of Patidars. Since Patidars were already losing to numerically large Barias in other power structures such as the zilla panchayat and state assembly, they knew that an open political contest would lead to factionalism, and they would be the ultimate losers. (In Maharashtra, on the other hand, the dominant Maratha caste, being numerically strong, could afford to politicize the sugar cooperatives, since whichever faction won, the Marathas could continue to control the sugar cooperatives). Thus to avoid open political contest with Barias, the Patidars 'deliberately projected the managers and technocrats as real men of power to make the positions of chairman and directors less attractive'.

That apart, Amul dairy was a model of rural development, a show piece exhibited to visiting dignitaries from abroad, and there was tremendous pressure on the authorities to maintain the image of Amul as a 'true benefactor of the poor', free from political rivalries.

For details, see Sujata Patel (1984) and also for the comments of Baviskar (1997) on milk cooperatives in Gujarat, pp. 104–11.

8. There are several case studies of cooperatives and panchayats confirming the dominance of Patidars. For instance, let us take two case studies of oilseed and cotton cooperatives. The Ghadia (a village in Kheda district) Oilseed Growers' Cooperative Society (OGCS) had 129 members, of which three-fourths were Patidars, as compared to 7 per cent Kshatriyas. Again, out of 9 executive committee members, 5 were Patidars and both the key positions, chairman and secretary, were held by Patidars. Although Patidars constituted just 30 per cent of the total village population, they owned 65 per cent of the total cultivable land. The Kshatriyas, making 38 per cent of the total population, owned one-fifth of the total cultivable land.

Another OGCS in Kansia village (Khambhat taluka in Kheda district) had altogether 92 members (in 1987, when the study was conducted) but almost half (52) were Patidars, followed by Kshatriyas, (27). It should be noted that of total 365 households in the village, Patidars comprise only 22 per cent, as against 45 per cent Kshatriyas. The Patidars own about 70 per cent of the cultivable land as compared to 15 per cent owned by Kshatriyas. No wonder that of the 9 executive committee members, 5 were Patidars, whereas Kshatriyas, Brahmins, Banias and Scheduled Castes had each one as executive member. And the chairman was also a Patidar.

At the same time, in the panchayat of this village, the majority of elected members were Kshatriyas while the sarpanch was a Patidar. Two important observations made in this study are worth quoting. One, the Patidars were aware of the numerical strength of the Kshatriyas and thus avoided contesting open elections for the managing committee of the OGCS. Two, given the rising aspirations of upwardly mobile Bariyas (one of the sub-caste of Kolis), the Patidars had started realizing that their days were numbered. In fact, the then sarpanch of Kansia village panchayat had gone on record to say that the chances of another Patidar becoming sarpanch was remote (Patel 1996: 269).

There is yet another study, of a federation of cotton cooperatives at the district level named Shri Madhya Gujarat Cooperative Cotton Marketing Union (MGCCU) that also confirms the pattern of Patidar dominance. The study, conducted in 1992, reveals that not only MGCCU based at Baroda rather the Cotton Cooperative Unions in other Central Gujarat districts, namely, Surat, Bharuch, Ahmedabad and Sabarkantha, were also dominated by rich Patidars. All the 15 board members, out of total 25, interviewed in the course of the study, were big farmers, though there were four businessmen among them.

The study highlights the dominance of big farmers and rich and influential Patidars, at the district level. Not totally immune from factional rivalry, Patidars, never allowed their rivalries to place 'obstacles in the function of Cooperatives . . . or political differences hampering their goal of augmenting their wealth.' They run cooperatives on business lines. The study also underlines the linkages between the cooperative leaders, panchayat leaders and state politicians.

Over the years the profiles of cooperative leaders have also undergone changes. In the past, these were essentially enterprising farmers, but leaders who never appreciated 'extravagance' and had an antipathy for ostentation. But the leaders of 1990s are different. 'Some of them are flamboyant. Some of the leaders of village level cooperatives are businessmen (for instance, civil contractors)' and 'so in the 1990s we find Patidar farmers who are businessmen in one sphere and cooperative leaders in another and also politically active and weighty' (Rajaram 1999: 2102).

The Patidars are a factor in the success of cooperatives which in turn helped them to extend their influence and control over other power structures. This has been explained in detail by T.T. Catanach (1970), Shanti George (1985), K.L. Gillon (1968), Kusum Nair (1961). The latest studies, including that of Rajaram (1999), show the perpetuation of Patidar control over cooperatives. But, Patidars have, over the years, given way to numerically large Kshatriyas in both urban and rural local bodies as well as in state politics. These power structures are no longer the exclusive preserve of the Patidars.

9. Since the early 1970s, Indira Gandhi, emerging as the most powerful leader of the country, introduced a different kind of politics, defined by as 'plebiscitary politics'. This is characterized by the presence of supreme charismatic leaders at the top, who in no way would be dependent upon the organizational network of their party. Instead, the party would be dependent on the charisma of the leader for electoral victory. This kind of politics, therefore, does not leave any scope for any other leaders emerging from the organization. The supreme leader would nominate/anoint as Chief Minister one who would be holding that office at her pleasure. (Following her death, Rajiv Gandhi also adopted this style of his with mother.) For a detailed discussion on

plebiscitary politics, see Loyd I. Rudolf and Susane H. Rudolf, 1990, pp. 85–103.

10. For a brief description of the rule of the RJP governments led by Vaghela and Dilip Parikh, see Priyavandan Patel (1999).
11. For a chronology of events following the return of Keshubhai Patel to power, see two issue of *Frontline*, 18 June (pp. 42–3) and 10 September (pp. 117–19). Both these indicate the overconcentration of power in Keshubhai Patel's hand, and the growing alienation of his ministerial colleagues and MLAs.
12. The total number of zilla panchayats in Gujarat now is 25. The Vaghela government added 4 new districts to the existing 19, and 2 more were created by the BJP government.
13. The Rashtriya Swayamsevak Sangh (RSS) is officially described as a cultural organization but it is known for jingoistic views on both domestic and foreign affairs. The BJP is considered as a poitical arm of this organization. All the important leaders of the BJP, at least the old ones who are at the helm of affairs, had started their political career within the folds of the RSS.
14. During the recent riots a former member of the Parliament made repeated phone calls to police control room to save him from the mob but nobody came to his rescue. He was brutally killed. A sitting judge of the state High Court was evacuated but house of another judge was set to fire. Shops located just opposite the office of the Police Commissioner were burned down. Even, two top ranking Muslim police officers were targeted. In fact, arsonists were so emboldened that they even burnt the offices of a couple of Muslim organizations housed in the secretariat building. The complicity of police forces in the riots was too glaring to be ignored. Several fact finding committees, including that of the National Human Right's Commission highlighted this fact.

    Apart from the newspapers, the recent Gujarat riots was extensively convered by popular weeklies and journals. For instance, see the issues of *EPW*, 16 March, 6 April, and 27 April, and also *Frontline*, 29 March, 26 April, 24 May 2002.
15. In order to reap electoral gains out of communal conflagration, Narendra Modi dissolved the state assembly and insisted that election be held at the earliest, presumably in October. This proposal was turned down by the Election Commission (EC) on the grounds of abnormal situation in the state. Not to be deterred by this decision of the EC, the powerful supporters of Modi in the central government arranged a

presidential reference to the Supreme Court on the issue of deferring polls in Gujarat. Interestingly, the Supreme Court uphold the competence of the EC in this regard. Finally, the EC announced that the election would be held on 12 December 2002.

16. The BJP government had earlier postponed gram panchayat elections twice, due since May–June 2000. Later in September 2000 when elections to taluka and zilla panchayats were held, the BJP turned out to be a loser. Since then on some pretext or the other it had put gram panchayat elections to hold. In fact, given the state of turmoil in the state in the month of April, elections to even local bodies was the last thing anybody could have expected. Yet in a dramatic manner elections were conducted in 1,600 villages. The total number of the gram panchayats in the state is 13,316. The GP elections, in any case, are held in phases. Hence it takes more than a year to cover all the villages. See *Indian Express*, 17 June 2002.
17. The proposed *rath yatra* was postponed when the National Human Rights Commission had apprehended that the *rath yatra* could aggravate the law and order situation. Later, Modi embarked upon a statewide *gaurav yatra* as a prelude to (election) campaign in the state.
18. The survey was conducted as part of the a broader national election study undertaken by the Centre for the Study of Developing Societies in 1996. In the survey about 500 voters, selected on the basis of stratified random sampling, were interviewed in Gujarat about various issues related to democratic politics and social change. The survey analysis including the Gujarat chapter, were published as special articles in *EPW* (1999), nos. 34–5, 21 August and 3 September.

Three

Empowering People or the Party?: Panchayati Raj in West Bengal

Factional rivalry had been an important feature of the Congress party of West Bengal. The two major factions operating within the party in the 1930s and the 1940s were known as the Anushilan and the Jugantar groups.[1] Even stalwarts like Subhas Chandra Bose and J.M. Sengupta could not free themselves from factional rivalry within the provincial Congress of undivided Bengal.[2]

Another important characteristic of the Bengal Congress was that it did not always toe the line of the central leadership of the party. In 1920 the leadership of the Indian National Congress passed to Gandhi, who became the moving spirit behind the freedom struggle. The leaders of the Bengal Congress, who came mostly from the English-educated urban middle class, had difficulty in accepting either the Gandhian world-view or Gandhian political idioms. Consequently, Gandhi had very few followers within the Bengal Congress.

1947–1967

With several factions fighting with each other, the Congress party on the eve of Independence was suffering from a leadership crisis. Expulsion of Subhas Chandra Bose from the party in 1939 was a severe blow from which Bengal Congress could not fully recover. With no single group in control of the party's state unit, the Congress High Command backed Prafulla Chandra Ghosh, a Gandhian and a member of the Congress working Committee, to form the first Congress government of West Bengal. The Gandhians being a minority force in the party, Ghosh had a tough time running the government. The state could not come to terms with the ravages of the famine (1943), in which nearly a million people had died, and Partition, that forced millions of refugees to cross the border. Inside the party, the faction known as the Hooghly group led by Atulya Ghosh was gradually establishing its authority, marginalizing the other important factions.

P.C. Ghosh resigned in December 1947 and B.C. Roy, a doctor by profession and Congress leader not aligned to any particular faction, assumed office as Chief Minister in January 1948.[3] Within the party, Atulya Ghosh established his authority. Thus began an era during which (until the death of Roy in 1962), the Roy-Ghosh combine established a new pattern of relationship between the leaders of the government and those of the party. This ensured a very fruitful division of functional responsibility: Roy was free to run the government and Ghosh devoted his energy to building the party. Even after Roy's death in 1962, this arrangement worked. P.C. Sen, the new Chief Minister, ran the government, leaving the affairs of the party to Ghosh.

Ghosh, in his turn, gradually transformed the Congress organization into an efficient machine.[4] It had units spread over districts and even at levels below the district. The leaders of the units at each level would act as linkmen between the electorate and the administration at that level. In rural areas, the link with the masses was established, not through extensive mobilization of the people at the lower level, but through 'key men'. These 'key men' were people in the 'higher levels of local stratification system' and influential in local areas. In rural areas, they would belong to the landed gentry on whom the sharecroppers or landless labourers depended for livelihood; or the village *mahajan* or moneylender; or leaders of dominant castes in the local area; or leaders of village factions. These locally influential persons would support the Congress party with the hope of gaining patronage. Such patronage would come in various forms, ranging from accessing state aid under various development programmes to getting protection from strict application of law that would hurt their interest. The most glaring example of the latter is retention of large quantities of land by the big landowners beyond the ceiling imposed by the Land Reform Act.

These key men could exert influence over the masses of their localities. By drawing them into the fold of the Congress, the party ensured two things: first, the persons occupying the existing power centres in society were neutralized; and second, such persons could serve as a medium for reaching the party to the masses and to enlist their electoral support.

Apart from politicizing the traditional power structures, the party's strategy included capturing power centres created through modernization processes initiated by the state. Thus, the local Congress leaders or workers would be encouraged to occupy the membership of governing bodies of schools or colleges, offices of cooperative societies and positions in various bodies created by the state such as the regional transport authority and local government institutions like the union board, district board, and municipality. Very often, the local key men themselves would be recruited in the party and offered such positions.

If the hold over the traditional power structures removed hostility of the locally influential persons to the government, control over the modern power-centres gave the party ample scope to distribute state largesse. In fact, intervention in the distribution of state largesse became a major preoccupation with the local Congress workers or leaders. Such intervention could be direct through the control over modern power-centres, or indirect, by influencing the bureaucracy. Thus, the local Congressmen would be mediators between the people and the state. At the local level, the bureaucracy practically represented the state and, hence, forging a link with the bureaucracy became an important task for Congressmen. As the state's functions increased with the introduction of Five Year Plans, the mediatory role became all the more important.

Thus the Congress organization built by Atulya Ghosh developed a 'system of close constituent-party-administration ties'.[5] The party itself tried to accommodate all types of interests, its major objective being to remain in power within the parliamentary system of government. As a result, the party developed by Ghosh turned out to be a 'political machine' in the sense that its organization was 'held together and motivated by the desire for personal gain rather than by political principle or ideology'

(Banfield 1961 qouted in Franda 1971: 90). Such an organization was bound to have internal factions. Factional disputes were managed by compromise and adjustment through informal procedures. The desire for 'personal gain' was fulfilled through distribution of patronage and ties between the party and the administration helped the process.

This style of politics had obvious limitations. Frequent recourse to adjustment and compromise with various conflicting groups circumscribed any government policies 'that would go against the wishes of those influential in the system' (Franda 1971: 75). The excessive importance given to the narrow objective of accommodating the desire for personal gain of the supporters and party workers/leaders over ideology and principles, is a political strategy that maintains a delicate balance. Surprisingly, it worked for a long time and paid rich dividends for the Congress. In three successive elections after Independence, the party achieved remarkable success, retaining not only more than 60 per cent of the Assembly seats, but also increasing its share of votes from one election to the other (see Table 3.1).

One of the reasons for this may be the overwhelming presence of the Congress party all over the state, in contrast to the feeble presence of the opposition parties. The main opposition in the first three elections was the Communist Party of India (CPI), which was steadily increasing its influence, gaining 10.76 per cent, 17.82 per cent and 24.96 per cent of the votes in the Assembly elections of 1952, 1957 and 1962 respectively. But its influence was restricted to urban areas, especially in industrial areas. Despite the activities of its front organization, the Krishak Sabha, the CPI

TABLE 3.1: STRENGTH OF CONGRESS PARTY IN THE WEST BENGAL LEGISLATIVE ASSEMBLY ELECTIONS 1952 TO 1962

Year	Strength of Assembly	Seats won by Congress	% of total votes polled by Congress
1952	238	151 (63)	38.2
1957	252	151 (60)	46.1
1962	252	157 (63)	45.4

Note: Figures in brackets indicate percentages.

did not have roots in rural West Bengal to enable it to mobilise the people left practically untouched by the political machine of the Congress.

The success of the Congress in the first two decades after Independence cannot, however, be fully explained by the weakness of opposition parties. Other factors also contributed to this success. First, there was a well-knit party organization that provided stability of government at a time when the planning regime was going through its golden period, enabling the state to make substantial investment in the public sector. Second, there was stability of leadership both in the party and in the government, and a viable division of labour between the party chief and Chief Minister. Third, there was the existence of a disciplined political organization that kept a constant vigil over the electoral interest of the party. Fourth, the Congress of that period inherited the image the party had acquired during the freedom movement. During the 1950s and early 1960s, the Congress could boast of many freedom fighters. In spite of the fact that the party became a haven of self-seekers, its top leaders like Atulya Ghosh or P.C. Sen, along with many other less-known veterans were honest people, with deep faith in parliamentary democracy and an abhorrence for violence. Last but not least, the political machine of the Congress was not an unmixed evil. It fulfilled certain essential social functions. Acting as a mediator between the people and the faceless bureaucracy, the party made governance somewhat humane. Through the network of its units, the party became a vehicle of interest articulation, even though such interests more often than not reflected the needs of those who possessed social or economic power. The party also provided an opportunity for 'social mobility in a society where social mobiles are frequently frustrated' (Franda 1971: 90).

1967–1977: The Decade of Chaos

The political machine of the Congress developed cracks in the mid-1960s, due to internal and external factors. Internally, a factional dispute turned into a crisis and then into a split in the party. In 1965, Ajoy Mukherjee, a veteran party leader from

Medinipur, was president of West Bengal Pradesh Congress Committee (WBPCC). Mukherjee was respected as a freedom fighter and an honest leader who preferred to lead an austere life even after enjoying ministerial office in state government for several years. But he was a lightweight in the power structure of the Congress organization. As president of WBPCC he was overshadowed by other office-bearers, particularly Nirmalendu Dey, the nephew and a trusted lieutenant of Atulya Ghosh. Mukherjee felt uncomfortable when he found Dey openly violating his instructions. In September 1965, Mukherjee took the drastic step of removing Dey from the position of General Secretary of the party. This action of Mukherjee was considered as an open revolt against the leadership of Atulya Ghosh and P.C. Sen. Within a few days, the WBPCC, which was under the complete control of Ghosh and other leaders loyal to him, held a requisition meeting and removed Mukherjee from the presidential chair of the committee (Sengupta 1985: 35).

Mukherjee refused to take the affront lightly. He started a state-wide campaign among the Congress workers against what he termed 'coterie rule'. In February 1966, he even held a conference in Calcutta where speakers expressed concern over the fact that 'a group . . . had emerged within the party, which sought to realize its vested interest at the cost of party's interest' (ibid.: 36).

As noted earlier, the Congress machine had a well-established procedure of conflict management. But this procedure went haywire as a result of Mukherjee's open revolt against the leadership. The inevitable outcome was his expulsion from the party in June 1966.

Elections to the Legislative Assembly were due in 1967. Mukherjee lost no time to form a separate party called the 'Bangla Congress'. In 1950, P.C. Ghosh, along with some of his Gandhian followers, had defected to form the Krishak Majdoor Party. That split did not pose any threat to the electoral prospects of the Congress, but the 1965 split, leading to the formation of Bangla Congress, dealt a severe blow to the party from which it never recovered fully. The 1967 elections, as we shall see later, brought the downfall of the Congress and marked the beginning of a decade characterized by violence, chaos and crisis in governability.

The failure of Congress in the 1967 elections cannot be attributed to the split within the party alone. Certain external factors also worked against it soon after the death of B.C. Roy in 1962. Armed conflict with China (1962) and Pakistan (1965) created inflationary pressures and hardship to the people, particularly the urban middle class. An industrial recession in the mid-1960s brought in its wake large-scale lay off or closures in the factories leading to great industrial unrest. In terms of food production, West Bengal was a deficit state. Droughts in two consecutive years (1964 and 1965) created acute shortages of food and other essential commodities. P. C. Sen, the Chief Minister, adopted a plethora of regulatory measures and imposed a levy on foodgrains both at the level of large farmers as well as mill owners in order to run the public distribution system.

Even though Sen's food policy was well directed, it failed to produce results. The consumers, especially urban consumers, were unhappy as the public distribution system failed to meet their requirements and food prices in the open market soared. The large producers, traders and rice mill owners felt aggrieved because of the procurement policy. The discontent was fully exploited by the leftists led by the Communist Party of India, Marxist [CPI(M)]. It was in 1964 that the split in the communist party took place, giving birth to the CPI(M). The radical elements of CPI along with others that might be called 'centrist' joined the new party. The communist leaders who were arrested following the Chinese aggression were released in 1964. All of them were part of the CPI(M). Inflation, industrial recession and food problems provided a very favourable ground for the radical elements of the new Communist Party to launch militant movements. Processions, *bandhs*, large-scale arson—all these extra-parliamentary methods of registering protest and discontent were the characteristic features of the movements organized by the left parties. The government used force leading to police firing in some places to restore order. This further aggravated the situation.

Given this background, the Congress went to the polls in

February 1967. What was so long considered to be impossible took place in this election. The hegemony of Congress was lost. What is more, the party stalwart, Atulya Ghosh, lost a parliamentary seat and P.C. Sen, the Chief Minister, lost the Assembly seat in his home-town Arambagh, to the rebel congress leader, Ajoy Mukherjee.

The five years that followed were marked by events that had profound influence upon the course of future politics in the state. The most distinguishing features of this period are: (i) the collapse of the Congress machine created by Atulya Ghosh; (ii) expansion of the influence of the CPI(M), despite a split within the party; (iii) split in Indian National Congress and the rise of Indira Gandhi on the national political scene, marginalizing old stalwarts like Atulya Ghosh; (iv) unsuccessful experiments with coalition ministry-making; (v) rise of militant agrarian movements in Naxalbari and other areas and emergence of politics of violence; (vi) breakdown of democratic institutions and unprecedented use of force by the state in the name of curbing Naxalite influence.

The chaotic political situation of the period will be evident from the fact that in the course of five years, the state witnessed four coalition ministries and nearly three years of President's rule in three spells (Table 3.2).

The 1967 election was a triangular contest. While Congress fought alone, the opposition parties organized themselves in two fronts. The United Left Front (ULF) was led by CPI(M) and included some leftist parties. The Peoples' United Left Front (PULF), on the other hand, was a combination of CPI, Bangla Congress, and some other parties including some left parties. Congress for the first time failed to secure an absolute majority, winning 127 out of 280 seats. Neither of the two combinations, however, could individually claim majority support, but the combined strength of the two fronts was enough to form a ministry. The prospect of forming the first non-Congress ministry in the state prompted them to unite and a United Front of thirteen parties was born with Ajoy Mukherjee of the Bangla Congress as the leader.

TABLE 3.2: MINISTRIES AND PRESIDENT'S RULE IN WEST BENGAL DURING 1967–72

Period	Political Parties in Power	Chief Minister
2 March to 20 Nov. 1967	United Front	Ajoy Mukherjee (B.C.)
21 Nov. 1967 to 19 Feb. 1968	Progressive Democratic Front with Congress support	P. C. Ghosh (PDF)
20 February 1968 to 24 February 1969: President's rule		
25 Feb. 1969 to 15 March 1970	United Front	Ajoy Mukherjee (B.C.)
16 March 1970 to 1 April 1971: President's rule		
2 April 1971 to 25 June 1971	ULDF—Congress	Ajoy Mukherjee (B.C.)
26 June 1971 to 19 March 1972: President's rule		

The first United Front ministry suffered from three kinds of threats. First, there was intense inter-party rivalry within the U.F., making the concept of collective responsibility unworkable. Ajoy Mukherjee himself criticized the CPI(M) openly for its alleged encouragement to lawlessness. Second, the extremists within the CPI(M) commenced an armed agrarian revolt in Naxalbari of Darjeeling district against the official policy of the party. Even though the ministry resorted to strong-arm tactics to quell the disturbance and the CPI(M) expelled from the party its extremist leaders, the Naxalbari uprising set in motion a series of events that ultimately led to the formation of the third Communist Party, namely Communist Party of India (Marxist-Leninist) in May 1969. This party claimed to follow the Maoist strategy to usher in an agrarian revolution. The militant movements of Naxalites and their consequences have been documented elsewhere.[6] For the present purpose, it is necessary to remember that with the Naxalite movement a decade began which was characterized by the politics of violence and undermining of democratic institutions. Last, ever since a non-Congress ministry with substantial presence of leftists came to power in the state, it suffered from a constant threat of dismissal by the central government. In fact, the first UF ministry was dismissed in November 1967 by the then Governor, Dharma Vira, in a manner that disregarded all constitutional norms.

A few defectors from the UF formed a new group called the Progressive Democratic Front (PDF) under the leadership of P.C. Ghosh, who had left the Congress in 1950 to form a new party. This small group (having only 17 MLAs) formed the ministry with Congress support after the first UF government was dismissed. The ministry died a natural death within barely three months after it failed to hold the assembly session,[7] as a result of which President's rule was imposed. In the interim election held in February 1969, the United Front proved its supremacy by returning 214 MLAs in a House of 280. CPI(M) increased its own strength considerably from 43 in 1967 election to 80 in 1969, while the Congress was further marginalized, its strength being reduced by more than half from 127 in 1967 to 55 in 1969. Despite the fact that the CPI(M) was the dominant party within the UF, it allowed Ajoy Mukherjee to lead the second UF ministry also. Jyoti Basu, the CPI(M) leader, became the Deputy Chief Minister.

The second UF government, like its predecessor, demonstrated lack of capacity to govern and West Bengal became a scene of chaos and lawlessness. The parties within the UF were ideologically poles apart, 'nearly as wary of each other as they were of Congress. They spent considerable energy devising political strategy that could help transform their temporary hold on government into an expanded political base' (Kohli 1991: 277). Of all the parties, the CPI(M) went ahead of others in spreading its influence in rural as well as urban areas.

On the positive side, the CPI(M) Land Reform Minister, Harekrishna Konar, adopted a policy of unearthing *benami* land (land held clandestinely over the ceiling limit through registration under false names) and vesting the same to the government under the Land Reform Act for distribution to the landless.

Konar's policy was to identify *benami* land through the members of the party's peasant wing, using the official machinery to vest the identified *benami* land in the government and to encourage the peasantry to occupy the vested land (Bandyopadhyay 1994: 307–10). This policy made the state bureaucracy 'a slightly better instrument for carrying out a programme of social interventionist action'. Besides, 'through the vesting of land, and even more so through the occupation of such vested land as a consequence of peasant initiative, the left parties (and in particular the CPI(M) were able to penetrate deep into rural West Bengal' (ibid.: 308).

However, there was also a negative aspect to the UF's agrarian programme. All parties within the UF fought for 'occupation' of parcels of vested land. Overzealous party workers even went to the extent of occupying *benami* land before it was officially vested. This was against Konar's policy, but he was unable to restrain even his own party workers. Besides, there was intense competition among the partners of the UF to steal the show in the land-grab movement. This led to a situation of lawlessness and chaos in rural areas. In the later period (1972–7) the Congress government took full advantage of this to suppress peasant movements.

In the urban areas, the leftists, particularly the CPI(M), pursued a policy of militant trade unionism in industry and other spheres of organized sector. This created havoc for the industrial sector, already facing numerous problems brought by recession. Trade union activities also adversely affected the functioning of government offices and educational institutions. Educational institutions particularly were targets of the CPI(M)'s Student Federation of India (SFI), of the Naxalites's union, as also the Congress student wing, Chhatra Parishad, which during the period 1969–72 and thereafter assumed an increasingly militant character.

With the intensification of internecine conflict within the UF, it became difficult to run the government. Ultimately, Ajoy Mukherjee resigned in March 1970 and with his resignation the second UF experiment ended.

The period of the second UF government was politically significant. The May day of 1969 witnessed the emergence of CPI(ML), the third communist party. Again, this was the year when the Indian National Congress was split into two. In West Bengal, stalwarts like Atulya Ghosh and P.C. Sen joined the Congress (O).

When elections were held in 1971, the Congress fought as two separate parties. The Congress (R) led by Indira Gandhi saved the Indian National Congress from a complete rout, securing 105 seats, while Congress (O) managed to win only 2 seats. The CPI(M) further improved its position, winning 111 seats, and the Bangla Congress was routed, managing to retain only five seats. There was a hung Assembly, with no single party or single electoral combination of like-minded parties being in a position to form the ministry. A coalition ministry was sworn-in with Ajoy Mukherjee once again as Chief Minister. It was a coalition of minor parties and the Congress with some left parties supporting from outside. What unified these parties was the desire to keep the CPI(M) out. 'Ideologically divergent political parties had formed the earlier UF government, only to keep the Congress out of power' (Basu Raychaudhury 1976: 397). No negative factor can keep divergent parties together for long. The third Ajoy Mukherjee government broke down within three months of assumption of power, preparing the ground for the imposition of President's rule for the third term in five years.

The turmoil and chaos in the parties and administration of West Bengal during 1967–72 reflected the passing away of an old order and the struggle of new forces to fill the vacuum. The 1967 election marked the beginning of the end of the political machine of Atulya Ghosh. Interestingly, the failure to ensure electoral victory for the Congress in 1967 was due to inner party contradictions, and not the expansion of influence of the communists/leftists, who later became the most important contenders for power. The crucial factor in the 1967 defeat of the Congress was the emergence of the Bangla Congress, which gained 10.4 per cent of votes and 34 Assembly seats. The Bangla Congress could register such impressive electoral results because well-to-do farmers and traders in the major rice producing districts felt aggrieved by P.C. Sen's food policy. The intention of the policy, as was noted earlier, was to provide relief to consumers through a public distribution system. Despite excesses committed in its implementation, the policy was definitely pro-people. Such a pro-people policy worked against the logic of the Congress politics, based as it was on the support of the local notables.

Participation in two UF governments provided the leftists, particularly the CPI(M), an opportunity to expand their base in rural West Bengal. Harekrishna Konar's land reform policy brought a new opportunity for mobilizing the poor peasantry.

The 1969 split of the Congress led to the rise of a new party. The new Congress party introduced what has been termed as 'plebiscitery politics'. Henceforth, the party would fight the elections not on the strength of its organization network, but by utilizing the charisma of Indira Gandhi. The entire power of the party would be centralized in her hands. Chief Ministers and the party leaders of the states would not emerge through the natural process within the party, but would be nominated by the leader. Indira Gandhi, after splitting the party, had introduced and perfected this new style.

In order to pursue 'plebiscitary politics', Indira Gandhi needed a pro-people image. Hence, from 1969 onwards, she consciously took a left-of-the-centre stance. Banks were nationalized, privileges of the former princes were curbed, and an Indo-Soviet Peace Treaty was signed. Her *Garibi Hotao* slogan promising land reform and many other relief measures for the poor electrified the nation. In the 1971 parliamentary elections, the electorate gave her overwhelming support, marginalizing the Congress (O) and its leaders. The verdict of 1971 was so decisive that the uncrowned king of West Bengal, Atulya Ghosh retired from politics.

Given this backdrop, West Bengal went to the polls once again in 1972 to constitute its Legislative Assembly. The election did not disappoint Ms. Gandhi. The Congress led by her captured 216 of the 280 Assembly seats, reducing the strength of the CPI(M) (which had been improving its position from one election to another and had emerged as the largest party in the election only a year ago) to mere 14 seats. There was widespread rigging in the election, and CPI(M) cadres were subjected to violent repression by the state machinery, aided by the youth leaders of Congress (R) during President's rule preceding the election. Yet, the sweeping victory of congress (R) cannot be wholly attributed to these factors. The charisma of Indira Gandhi and the experience of unstable governments in the last five years had their effect upon the electorate.

The new incarnation of the Congress, which ruled the state from 1972 to 1977, was radically different. Sidhartha Shankar Ray occupied the top position in the ministry, because Indira Gandhi gave him total support. He had no base either in the party or among the people. His source of power was the confidence Ms. Gandhi had in him. This enabled him to become leader in the government as well as in the party.

Even though there were some leaders who enjoyed considerable popular support in their respective districts, the main strength of Congress (R) was provided by the student and youth leaders who joined politics in the 1967–71 period. It is significant that there were 134 Chhatra Parishad and Youth Congress members among the 216 MLAs, five of them ministers (Basu Raychaudhury 1976: 401). They had no training in constructive politics. They were baptized into politics only to combat the left forces. The militancy shown by them in their movements against the left during 1967–71 was not matched by their commitment for any ideology. They tasted power too early in their political career and this made them greedy for more. Very soon, they were divided into factions. S.S. Ray, under constant threat from the militant youth leaders, fomented these factions to keep his position intact. He also devised a 'carrot and stick' policy to consolidate his position as leader. Disregarding all norms of public appointment, he devised a scheme under which Class III and Class IV posts of government would be filled from panels prepared by MLAs. Each MLA was empowered to recommend 30 persons from his constituency for appointment to such posts.

Thus, distribution of patronage was institutionalized. On the other hand, Ray took an unprecedented step in instituting a commission of inquiry to probe into the allegations of corruption against some ministers of his own cabinet.

The manner in which Ray exercised his authority left the party in shambles, but fitted well with Ms. Gandhi's style of functioning, because well-organized party machinery might give rise to leaders with mass base, which she discouraged. The gap in solid party work to expand its base was sought to be filled with political rhetoric. It was during S.S. Ray's regime that progressive amendments were made in the Land Reform Act and a new legislation was enacted to introduce a three-tier panchayat system. None of these, however, were implemented. Even the existing urban local government institutions remained superseded.

Ray, however, excelled in unleashing state terror against Naxalites and the CPI(M). Atrocities of the state machinery against the Naxalites started in 1971 when Ray was a Central Minister-in-Charge of West Bengal affairs and continued during the entire period of his Chief Ministership. How many Naxalites were killed or maimed by the police under his regime will never be known. After the 1972 election, a large number of CPI(M) leaders and cadres had to go underground to avoid repression by police and Youth Congress workers. During the Emergency (1975–6) even journalists of repute were imprisoned. This excessive use of force by the state machinery is a clear indication of what Kohli (1991) terms the 'governability crisis'.

After 1977: Restoration of Order

The events that led to the installation of first non-Congress government at the Centre in 1977, following the lifting of Emergency are too well known to be repeated here. The five-year rule of the S.S. Ray-led Congress government came to an end when the assembly election of June 1977 firmly established the Left Front led by the CPI(M) in the seat of power, reducing the strength of the Congress to only 20 seats in a House of 294. The CPI(M) alone gained absolute majority, winning 177 seats.

In five successive elections held thereafter, the Left Front repeated the performance of 1977, creating a record of sorts in the parliamentary history of the country. What is special about the CPI(M) which has not only kept the left forces united, but also has been instrumental in its victory in the six successive Assembly elections in the state?

Even though CPI(M) has continued to win absolute majority in all the Assembly elections, excepting the election of 2001, it has never tried to form government alone. The party fought all the elections as senior partner of Left Front and the ministries in West Bengal have been those of the front. By maintaining the unity of the Left in the bi-polar electoral scenario of West Bengal, the CPI(M) has been able to marginalize the Congress. Even though the Congress has considerable presence in the state, its performance in terms of number of seats has remained dismal. Non-splitting of leftist vote bank in the first-past-the-post electoral system is one of the reasons for its poor show. The factional squabbles within the Congress (I) which intensified after the party's 1972 electoral victory and have remained a permanent feature during the last three decades, ultimately leading to the emergence of a separate party called Trinamul Congress, have also contributed to its misery in fair measure.

However, the electoral success of the CPI(M) cannot be explained by negative factors alone. The most significant achievement of the Left Front government was restoration of order. From 1967 onwards militancy acquired an aura among the cadres of the CPI(M). The leadership itself fanned militancy, because the new party had to prove its revolutionary credentials in comparison with the CPI which was termed as revisionist. Besides, the party had to come to terms with its radical elements that spearheaded a peasant insurrection in Naxalbari of Darjeeling district and declared that the objective conditions of the country called for starting a Maoist type of revolutionary struggle. In such an environment, pure constitutionalism was an anathema for the Marxists. Yet, the party had to justify its involvement with electoral politics. This they did by advancing the theory that the United Front was a strategy for isolation of 'the main party of the bourgeoisie, advancing the ideology of the party, releasing the people and the working class from the grip of bourgeois ideology' (B.T. Ranadive quoted in Mukhopadhyay 1985: 85). The front was also considered a weapon of mass struggle. It provided an opportunity to 'tell the masses of the impossibility of such governments developing themselves into the media of basic social transformation' (Mukhopadhyay 1985: 85). Time and again, the CPI(M) leaders—both in the government and in the party—declared that the UF government would not allow use of police to suppress the democratic and legitimate struggle of the people.

There was an inherent contradiction between running a government and leading a militant struggle, but the force of circumstances and its own political line led the CPI(M) to accomplish such an incredible two-in-one feat. Add to this the movements led by the Naxalites for whom the 1970s held promise for liberation from all kinds of 'exploitation'. The result was chaos on all fronts. In the villages, different leftist parties vied with each other in land-grab movements. In the cities and towns, trade unions resorted to *gherao* to press for workers' demands. Students in colleges and universities started flouting all norms throwing discipline to the winds. The political parties demonstrated their strength by rallies/processions or calling 24-hour or even 48-hour *bandhs*, suspending normal activities.

The CPI(M) learnt at great cost the futility of such politics when it went out of power in 1970. Repressive measures taken by the state first under President's rule and then under Congress rule was an eye opener. The Emergency probably taught the party the value of an open and democratic environment.

Hence, after coming to power, the party laid stress on law and order. The natural urge of the CPI(M) cadres to indulge in political vendetta against those elements of Congress who were responsible for their suffering during 1972–7, was admirably restrained by the leadership of the party. The trade unions in industry were instructed to eschew avoidable militancy in their confrontation with capital. The violence that characterized politics of the past decade (1967–77), was put to an end, thanks to the determined efforts of the CPI(M), which utilized both the party machinery and the state apparatus to restore order.

On the positive side, the Left Front ministry undertook several reform measures. With determination, it formulated and implemented a land reform policy. The most spectacular part of this was *operation barga*—a novel tenancy reform programme to get the *bargadars* (sharecroppers) registered, so that they had protection from eviction and could obtain their due share of produce as prescribed under the Land Reform Act. This programme which has been documented extensively (Bandyopadhyay 1980, 1994; Kohli 1983, 1987) was unique on several counts. First, the programme needed deployment of a large land reform bureaucracy on a war footing continuously for a period of about four years. Second, implementation of the programme required mobilization of the sharecroppers—a task that could be accomplished only with the support of the political party in power. This was a programme that demanded concerted efforts on the part of the bureaucracy as well as the party to motivate sharecroppers to get them registered, overcoming the resistance of the vested landed interests. By all standards, the programme was a success.

Simultaneously with the launching of *operation barga* and other land reform measures, the government gave high priority to the panchayati raj system. Within a year of its coming to power, the new government held elections to all the three tiers of panchayat. In doing so, the front broke new ground. For the first time in the country, political parties directly participated in the panchayat elections in all the three tiers. After elected panchayat bodies took position, the state government endowed these bodies with the powers and responsibilities for performing various rural development programmes. The first major responsibility shared by the newly-elected panchayats was massive relief operations for the victims of the devastating flood of 1978. Thereafter, panchayats have been gradually required to shoulder the ever-increasing responsibility for various rural development functions, particularly the centrally-sponsored poverty alleviation programmes. Unlike any other state governments, the Left Front government of West Bengal made the institution of panchayats the main plank of its rural development strategy. Elections have been regularly held to these bodies and they have never suffered from lack of funds, because the major poverty alleviation programmes like Food for Work, NREP or JRY/IRDP have been executed through them.

Apart from tenancy reforms and establishing panchayat democracy, the first Left Front government of 1977–82 took several other measures which made the lower level government employees, school and college teachers as well as sections of middle classes feel that the government was sensitive to their sufferings. Even though the benefits that accrued from such measures were not substantial, these measures, along with the political rhetoric voiced by the numerous party units and their front organizations, bolstered the image of the CPI(M) and its allies as champions of distributive justice.

It will be apparent from the above that after coming to power in 1977, the CPI(M) adopted a stance qualitatively different from the one pursued by it in the late 1960s. In 1977, 'it had moved away from a revolutionary inclination [of the 1960s] to a reformist orientation' (Kohli 1991: 287), and ever since, the party has carefully avoided any political action that could offend the norms of the Constitution. All the reform measures it has initiated have been strictly confined within the constitutional and legal framework. Such 'parliamentary communism' or 'reform communism' (Kohli 1983, 1990) has been the most striking feature of the post-1977 political strategy of the CPI(M). Accordingly, electoral politics has been a matter of greatest importance to the party. Compulsions of electoral politics have prompted the party to try to expand its support-base quickly, especially in rural areas where it was weak. These compulsions again forced the party to form a broad alliance of people representing different economic interests. Thus, the CPI(M)'s support base included not only agricultural labourers, sharecroppers and other categories of the poor in rural areas, but also the middle peasantry, the professional classes, and business men—practically everybody except the big land-owning *jotedar* classes.

The necessity of forging such a broad support base has forced the party to shift emphasis from the mobilization of the propertyless for militant mass struggle to providing relief to them within the legal and constitutional framework. Accordingly, the party laid emphasis on reaching the benefits of the poverty alleviation programmes to the rural poor. Popularly elected panchayati raj bodies and disciplined party machinery proved to be of great help to the CPI(M) in this respect. The state's record in reaching the benefits of poverty alleviation programmes to the target group has been better than that of most other states (Kohli 1987). Thus the strategy of the CPI(M) has enabled it to reach the rural poor without the mediation of landed gentry or local influentials, and this constitutes the most distinguishing difference between the communist politics and the erstwhile Congress politics of the state.

The upshot of the above discussion is that phenomenal electoral success of the Left in post-1977 period is due to several factors:

(a) unity within the non-Congress left parties;
(b) adoption of reformist orientation by the CPI(M);
(c) endeavour to forge a broad support base of CPI(M);
(d) capacity to reach the rural poor without the mediation of locally influential people and landed gentry;
(e) a disciplined party organization to generate political capacity of the government to implement modest measures of poverty alleviation and distributive justice;
(f) utilization of PRIs to translate government policies into action.

Panchayat System in West Bengal

At Independence, West Bengal had a network of rural local governments in the form of union boards, constituted under the Village Self-Government Act of 1919. The union board was a group of villages corresponding to 'gram' under the present-day Panchayat Act. During the British days, the union boards performed two types of functions: providing civic amenities and maintenance of *chowkidars* and *dafadars*. The *chowkidars* and *dafadars* were mostly utilized for performing odd jobs of local police and local administration and were of little use for the common people. The union boards were crippled by acute shortage of funds. 'Local taxation for local purposes' being the British policy with regard to the local government institutions, the union boards had to depend entirely on internal resources for discharging their statutory functions. With an inadequate tax base, internal resource generation could not have been impressive. Besides, the maintenance of *chowkidars* and *dafadars*, being the first charge of the union board fund, consumed more than 50 per cent of the meagre resources generated, leaving an insignificant amount for civic functions.

Even though, in terms of providing services, the performance of the union boards was far from satisfactory, this institution came to occupy a vital position in local administration. It provided a link between the people and the government and rendered assistance to the district administration in matters where local information and contact were necessary or in functions where the bureaucracy needed public cooperation. The pre-Independence union boards were, thus, in a sense, part of the *Raj* and the presidents/vice-presidents of these boards enjoyed prestige and had considerable influence in the local area. In most cases, the office-bearers of the union boards belonged to the elite groups drawn from amongst the *zamindars* or other land owning classes. After Independence, the Congress took care to fill the electoral posts of the union boards with its own men. This fitted well with the politics of extending influence of the party through the locally influential people. The union boards were convenient institutions for distribution of patronage, a necessary ingredient for the politics of Congress.

With a poor resource base, lack of autonomous functional jurisdiction beyond rudimentary civic services, absence of accountability to the people, the board members being elected by a restricted electorate, the union boards were nothing but a caricature of local government. Yet, no attempt to reform these institutions was made until 1964.

Immediately after Independence, some state governments

enacted legislation to form gram panchayats, as use of Gandhian idioms in the Congress politics of those days was necessary to earn credibility. The West Bengal Congress, as mentioned earlier, had no such necessity. Gandhians had practically no influence either in the party or in the government of the state. During the freedom struggle, Atulya Ghosh was a constructive Gandhian worker and, so was P.C. Sen, who came to be known as Gandhi of Arambagh (Sen's home-town). But the politics that Ghosh introduced had no place for Gandhian principles. Sen, on the other hand; concentrated on his ministerial work in the cabinet led by B.C. Roy who was a modernizer *par excellence* and had little regard for Gandhian ideas.

In such a political ambience, replacement of union boards by panchayats based on Gandhian principles was inconceivable. Yet, one of the Directive Principles of State Policy in the Constitution (Article 40) relates to the formation of gram panchayats as institutions of self-government. At the national level, the Congress party also adopted resolutions to form panchayats. Probably these factors led the Congress in Bengal to enact a panchayat legislation in 1957 to replace the Village Self-Government Act of 1917. The 1957 Act was a clever device to fulfil the obligation of Article 40 of the Constitution without disturbing the old institutional set-up of the union board.

The 1957 Act divided the erstwhile unions into two parts, *gram* and *anchal*. For each *gram* with a population of roughly 1,000 voters, there would be a gram panchayat elected directly by the people on the basis of adult suffrage. For *anchal*, there was an anchal panchayat consisting of all chairpersons of gram panchayats and one or two members from all the gram panchayats. The gram panchayats were empowered to undertake a large number of functions. Most of these were not different from those earmarked for the erstwhile union boards. However, in view of the changed context, some items related to rural development were added to the list of functions. Even though the gram panchayats had functions, the power to raise resources through taxes, fees and tolls was given to the anchal panchayat. The scheme of the 1957 Act envisaged that anchal panchayats would levy taxes (on land

and buildings), tolls and fees or receive government grants if any, and distribute the fund among the gram panchayats under its jurisdiction after deducting expenses of its own establishment and that of *chowkidars* and *dafadars*. The revenue raising power of the anchal panchayat was not very different from that of the erstwhile union boards. Hence, as before, the anchal panchayat had little to distribute to the gram panchayats for development functions. The two-tier panchayats at the village level had thus nothing new to offer in terms of decentralization of functions of the state government. It was the same old wine in a new bottle. The change in nomenclature of the institutions satisfied the 'letter' of Article 40, but not its 'spirit'. In fact, the government thought it unnecessary to make a sharp departure from the traditions built up by the institution of union boards.

It is necessary to note that the report of the study team of the Government of India headed by Balwantrai Mehta was published in 1957, the year in which the West Bengal Panchayat Act was passed. As is well known, the Mehta team had recommended a three-tier panchayat system for village, block and district level and endowment of power and responsibilities to the panchayats to enable them to take charge of the community development programme, the most important rural development programme of the contemporary period. There was enthusiastic acceptance of the report by a large number of states. At the instance of Jawarharlal Nehru, the recommendations of the Mehta team were accepted as official policy by the Congress party and the Government of India. For Nehru, introduction of the panchayat system was 'the most revolutionary and historical step in the context of new India'. Despite this euphoria, West Bengal preferred to ignore the committee's recommendations. The state did not show any inclination to go beyond what was provided in the 1957 Act. The implementation of the Act too was extremely slow. Conversion of the union boards into gram and anchal panchayats after holding elections was progressing at a snail's pace. This position continued to 1962.

In May, 1962, B.C. Roy died and P.C. Sen took over as Chief Minister. The lackadaisical attitude towards panchayats probably disturbed Sen, whose inclination for Gandhian idioms stood in sharp contrast to his celebrated predecessor. It is because of his initiative that in 1963, the West Bengal Zilla Parishad Act was passed, introducing the anchalik parishad at the block level and zilla parishad at the district level. The latter body was to replace the archaic district board, constituted under the Bengal Local Self-Government Act of 1885. Like the anchal panchayat, members of both the anchalik parishad and zilla parishad were either *ex-officio* members or elected indirectly. Since the 1963 Act did not disturb the 1957 Act, West Bengal was to have a four-tier panchayat system with the gram and anchal panchayat at the lowest level and the anchalik parishad and zilla parishad at the intermediate and district levels respectively.

Along with enacting the legislation, Sen took measures to constitute all the panchayat bodies within a short time. Thus, on 2 October 1964, the entire state of West Bengal was covered by duly elected panchayat bodies at the village, block and district levels. After the formation of these bodies, the state government took steps to provide funds and assign execution of some development programmes to them. Even though the schemes assigned to the panchayat bodies were minor in nature, the gesture indicated the honest intention to decentralize some governmental functions through panchayat institutions. The government also appointed an official committee to suggest measures for strengthening these grass roots democratic bodies.

However, Sen chose a bad time to introduce the panchayat system. At the national level, after Nehru's death, the panchayat movement lost active support. Nehru's successors had no faith in panchayat democracy (Dey 1986). At the state level, as mentioned, several factors combined to create acute crisis in governability. The government led by Sen became so preoccupied with combating the pressing problems facing it that no determined policy to infuse life into the nascent panchayat bodies could be formulated, and in 1967 the government went out of power.

The first United Front government, which came to power in 1967, did not see eye to eye with the panchayat system introduced by the Congress government. Promising fresh elections to the panchayat bodies, the new government announced that new legislation would be introduced to remodel the panchayat system. Pending introduction of new legislation, the anchalik parishads and zilla parishads were superseded. The first United Front ministry was dismissed before concrete action for reorganization could be taken, but during its second term in 1969–70, the second ministry introduced a comprehensive Panchayat Bill to replace the 1957 and 1963 Acts. Again, the ministry went out of office before the Bill could be passed.

The period following the exit of the second United Front ministry witnessed breakdown of order and acute political instability. In the midst of this turmoil anything other than restoration of order became a non-issue.

Mention has been made of the Congress government that was in power during 1972–7. It was also mentioned that a comprehensive panchayat legislation was enacted by this government in 1973. This Act of 1973 was modelled on the recommendations of Balwantrai Mehta Committee. It envisaged a three-tier panchayat system. At the lowest level, the two-tier system of gram and anchal panchayat was replaced by a single unit, the gram panchayat, the jurisdiction of which coincided with the erstwhile anchal panchayat. The intermediate and district level panchayats remained unaltered, with the difference that anchalik parishad at the block level was renamed the panchayat samiti.

The Congress enacted the legislation but did not hold any election to constitute the panchayat bodies under the new Act. As a result, when this government went out of power in 1977, the panchayat system of the state lay moribund. The intermediate and district level panchayats remained superseded and the lower level panchayats were on their deathbed, since for a period of fifteen years no election had been held to these bodies.

Things took an abrupt turn when the leftists assumed office in 1977. The ministry made some amendments to the Panchayat Act of 1973, the most important of which was provision for direct election to all the three tiers of panchayats. This was a departure from the normal pattern, since the general practice followed in other states was to provide for direct election only to the gram panchayats and indirect election to the intermediate level panchayat and the zilla parishad. The Left Front lost no time in holding elections to all the three tiers of panchayats under the 1973 Act as amended. Elections were held in June 1978 and in this election political parties were allowed to contest openly. The June 1978 election to the West Bengal's panchayats happened to be the first panchayat election in the country in which open participation of political parties was allowed. Hence the panchayats that were constituted in West Bengal after the 1978 election were 'political panchayats'—a species unknown to the first-generation panchayats of the early 1960s. The Asoka Mehta Committee had also recommended participation of political parties in panchayat elections. West Bengal put the concept into practice even before that report was submitted.

For the Left Front, panchayats were not just showpieces. Gradually, the government started assigning various functions to these grass roots democratic institutions. The first was rescue and relief operation after the devastating flood of 1978 and the reconstruction work that followed. The panchayats plunged into this work and earned credibility in the eyes of the people. Thereafter, the state government was emboldened to entrust to these bodies the responsibility of executing major poverty alleviation programmes and other welfare and developmental programmes. Today, these institutions are executing various types of rural development programmes. In fact, at present, there is hardly any programme of rural development with which panchayats are not associated directly or indirectly. The state government has also ensured that the panchayats do not suffer from lack of funds. The entire establishment expenditure of all the three tiers is met by the state government. Besides, they receive funds against schemes assigned to them.

In order to ensure cooperation of the bureaucracy with the panchayats, several steps were taken. First, the District Magistrate was made the Executive Officer of the zilla parishad and the Block Development Officer was appointed Chief Executive of the panchayat samiti. Second, officers of line departments were made *ex-officio* members of the standing committees of the zilla parishads and panchayat samitis. Third, the zilla parishad chairperson was made the chairperson of the District Rural Development Agency (DRDA). In various district level coordination committees, where chairperson of zilla parishad and the collector were members, the former was made the chairman. Last, in all kinds of target group-oriented schemes of various departments, responsibility for beneficiary selection had been given exclusively to the panchayats. Hence it becomes difficult for different development departments to execute schemes bypassing the panchayats.

Since 1978, panchayat elections have been held regularly at intervals of five years. If not anything else, regular elections are the outstanding achievement of West Bengal, when one considers records of other states. The institution has taken deep roots and for the common people in the rural areas it is this institution, and not the field level bureaucracy that represents the state (Kumar and Ghosh 1996; Williams 1999).

What has happened with regard to institutionalization of panchayats in the state within a short period after 1978, did not happen earlier. What are the political variables that have led to the institutionalization of panchayats during the left front regime? And how does one account for non-performance of other regimes? To these, we shall now turn our attention.

Regime Character, Ideology and Governability

1947–1967

The Congress ruled West Bengal uninterruptedly for two decades from (1947–67). The story of this period has already been described in detail. It had been noted that the politics of the Congress at that time did not require direct contact with the common people, because the social base of the party in the countryside was restricted to the affluent sections mostly the landed gentry, the professional classes and the traders of the rural areas. Electoral support of the masses was secured through locally influential people and distribution of benefits of modest reform measures through them. Weak organizational strength of the communists or other left parties in rural West Bengal allowed the Congress to remain complacent about the fact that it did not have any direct base among the lower middle class or the poor. The party was quite satisfied with its political strategy in which support of the local influentials was of utmost importance. So long as the opposition remained virtually absent from the rural field, the necessity of broad basing the grass roots level local government institutions in order to spread the party's roots among the masses was not felt by the party. This explains why the West Bengal Congress showed scant interest in the Balwantrai Mehta Report.

Secondly, most of this period saw B.C. Roy as the Chief Minister and Atulya Ghosh as the party president, Roy enjoying considerable independence in determining government's development policies. From the point of view of development, this was the most productive period of the state. Under the stewardship of Roy, who was a visionary, the government initiated a large number of development projects (Basu Raychaudhury 1976: 387–8). Despite his brilliance, integrity, and enviable administrative competence, Roy demonstrated an urban bias in his development ideology. He had scant respect for the Gandhian model of rural reconstruction. He did not share Nehru's enthusiasm for either the community development programme or panchayati raj. This does not mean that he had no interest in rural areas, but for him rural development meant modernization of the social or economic infrastructure in terms of more schools and colleges with facilities for modern education, more hospitals, improved communication, large irrigation projects, etc. The human side of development as embodied in the concepts of community development or panchayati raj, never appealed to Roy. He had little understanding of rural society and lacked sensitivity to agrarian problems. His concern for making the bureaucracy work was not matched by an enthusiasm for village democracy. This explains partly the lukewarm attitude of his government towards panchayats. For Roy, the functions of a democratic body at the grass roots level was to provide rudimentary civic services only and for this purpose the union boards were good enough.

This period, it should be noted, was marked by remarkable political stability. The government had to handle the tremendous problem of rehabilitating millions of refugees from East Pakistan. This was also the period when the leftists were consolidating their position. They stepped up many movements against the government on various issues, but none of these could create any crisis for governance. Governability was not in doubt. Perhaps all this created a sense of complacency in the party. It was not understood that the democratic aspirations of people in the rural areas were rising and could not be accommodated within the framework of the 'political machine' introduced by Congress. Common people outside the power structure needed some forum to ventilate their grievances. Broad-based local government institutions could have provided such a forum. The party also could have acquired a capacity to establish direct contact with the masses through such institutions without the mediation of local notables. This opportunity was lost, since the party could not assess the need for broadening its social base. Clearly, the utility of Congress politics was wearing out and the party failed to notice it.

Things changed, somewhat, after P.C. Sen became Chief Minister. Unlike Roy, Sen had roots in rural West Bengal. Throughout the freedom struggle, he had worked as a Gandhian in Arambagh subdivision of Hooghly district. It seems that he had an ideological commitment towards panchayati raj as conceived by Balwantrai Mehta team. Besides, adopting a policy that could be interpreted as Gandhian was probably necessary for him to earn legitimacy. His insistence that political parties should not contest panchayat elections, and his decision to introduce the four-tier panchayat system in West Bengal on the birthday of Mahatma Gandhi in 1964 indicate that he was articulating a political idiom associated with Gandhism. He did not face any opposition from the party because of his association with Atulya Ghosh, but more importantly, because it did not pose threat to Congress politics in the state. However, he could pursue a pro-panchayat policy for a very short period. As described earlier, from 1965 onwards, Sen's government faced a tremendous crisis, leading it to use force to quell disturbances. Nurturing new democratic institutions was not possible during this period. The first serious attempt to institutionalize panchayats in the state, thus, ended in a failure.

1967–1972

The first United Front ministry (1967) immediately after assuming office, superseded the anchalik and the zilla parishads—the two most powerful tiers of the four-tier panchayat system introduced by Sen—because these bodies were controlled by the Congress. The second UF ministry (1969–70) would perhaps have gone for fresh panchayat elections, had the new Panchayat Bill introduced by it been enacted. Conditions for winning these elections were favourable for the parties within the front. The fall of this ministry before the enactment of the Bill put an end to this possibility. The political situation during 1970–2 did not permit further progress on the matter.

The New Congress (1972–1977)

The new Congress, which formed the ministry under the leadership of S.S. Ray in 1972, gave West Bengal a stable government for five years, but, as explained earlier, introduced a new kind of politics under which party organization was not considered important. In fact, during this time the organization of the party was completely destroyed. In the state, S.S. Ray tried to imitate Indira Gandhi's style of functioning, but ended up creating innumerable factions within the party and the government. He could never set his house in order and his response to the prevailing chaos, dissent or discontent was the use of coercive force. There was however no dearth of rhetoric, which found expression in the enactment of progressive legislation for restructuring the land owning pattern or reforming rural local governments. But Ray's government did not have any ideological commitment to these. Also, it did not have political capacity to implement progressive policies, because the Congress was faction-ridden and without an organizational base. Besides, the state leaders of Congress functioning within the framework of 'plebiscitery politics' were busy in guarding their respective positions in the party, and had little time for serious development work. This explains why the Ray ministry did not try to hold panchayat elections, despite the fact that a comprehensive legislation to set-up a three-tier panchayat system was enacted within a year of its assumption of office.

The Left Front Regime (1977–)

The Left Front's unique contribution to the growth of panchayati raj system in the state has already been highlighted. It is admitted by all that among the second-generation panchayats (that is, the panchayats that emerged after the Asoka Mehta Committee Report), West Bengal's panchayat system is the most successful. This is the only state where panchayat elections have been held regularly at intervals of five years and where substantial functions of the state government have been assigned to the panchayats. Institutionalization of the panchayat system is generally considered the most significant contribution of the CPI(M)-led rule in West Bengal. What has prompted the CPI(M) to attach such high priority to the panchayats as its political and developmental policy? Is the party ideologically committed to panchayati raj?

Among the CPI(M) leaders, only E.M.S. Namboodiripad evinced a clear perception about the need for restructuring the Indian polity on the principle of the widest decentralization of state power.[8] In his note of dissent to the Asoka Mehta Committee Report (GOI 1978), he made the following observations.

> What is required is that, while certain definite fields of administration like defence, foreign affairs, currency, communication etc., should rest with the Centre, all the rest should be transferred to the states and *from there to the districts and lower levels of elected administrative bodies.* (emphasis added)

Writing about the same time, B.T. Ranadive, another prominent leader of the CPI(M), on the other hand, appeared to be more concerned with the 'autonomy of states', rather than revitalization of panchayats. He criticized the Janata Party's 1977 election manifesto emphasizing the need for revitalization of panchayats and municipalities and vesting in these bodies 'larger power and responsibility'. 'It is strange', he said, 'that while the manifesto speaks about strengthening the power of the panchayats and municipalities, it does not mention the need to strengthen the autonomy of the states.' According to him, increased power to local bodies should be considered, 'instruments of democratic advance and struggle, but cannot be described as decentralization of political power in scientific terms' (1977). Viewing panchayats principally as a means of organizing struggle, seemed to be the explanation for encouraging the growth of the institution, and this fitted well with the revolutionary credentials of the party. Echoing Ranadive's views, an article published in *Peoples' Democracy* on the eve of the first panchayat elections in West Bengal, argued,

> Through the panchayats, the left front intends to unleash the initiative of the rural masses and inculcate in them a spirit of self-confidence, so that *a mass movement is gradually built up against the age-old exploitation.* The more they are involved in the socio-economic affairs of the village, the greater would be their realisation of the problems created by the present bourgeois-landlord structure of our society and the way to solve them. (Pal 1978)

Whatever may be the theoretical formulation, even scholars sympathetic to the CPI(M) admit that, 'over the years, the panchayats have become less the nodal point of rural mobilization, but their pivotal role in rural development management has increased' (Lieten 1992: 103). It was mentioned above that the post-1977 CPI(M) moved away from the path of extra-parliamentary revolutionary struggle to overthrow the so-called 'bourgeois landlord' state system. It was more inclined to utilize existing constitutional institutions. That explains why panchayats ceased to be 'nodal point of rural mobilization' for class struggle, but does not explain why the panchayat system was revitalized to play a pivotal role in rural development management during the Left Front regime.

To answer the last question, one has to take into account the perception of the CPI(M) and the Left parties about the politico-administrative realities facing them in 1977. First, the fear of arbitrary imposition of Article 356 to dislodge the constitutionally elected state government was there, as the memories of the 1960s were still fresh in the minds of the CPI(M) leaders. In such an eventuality, perhaps they thought they would still be able to wield power, if they could capture the local government institutions. Second, the CPI(M) was ever sceptical of the bureaucracy, particularly those belonging to the all-India services. In the 32-point programme of the second UF government (1969–70), it was declared that the government would 'endeavour to change the rules governing the services of ICS, IAS and IPS cadres with a view to maintain effective control of the state government over them'. In the memorandum on centre-state relations issued in 1978, the Left Front even went as far as recommending abolition of the all-India services. There was a lurking suspicion among the left parties that they would not get enough cooperation from the bureaucracy. That is why, during the initial years, the Left leaders harped on the theme that the Left Front government, would not govern only through the bureaucracy, but would take into confidence the mass organizations of the people. Third and most important, the left did not have a political base in the rural areas. It was during the tenure of the UF governments, that they could penetrate the villages in a significant manner for the first time. But they did not find time to consolidate their rural base. Moreover, during Congress rule in the 1970s, it was not possible for the CPI(M) to pursue its normal political activity. After gaining a surprising electoral victory in 1977, the immediate political task of the CPI(M) was to consolidate its organizational base quickly in the rural areas.

It was one of those rare occasions for a political party in power that one single solution would provide a clue for facing a chain of seemingly unrelated political or administrative problems. After assuming power in 1977, the CPI(M) found in the growth of the panchayat system, an instrument to face all the above-mentioned politico-administrative problems confronting it. It would be unrealistic to assume that the picture was quite clear to the CPI(M) in the beginning. The party seemed to have discovered, as it were, the potentialities of the institution of panchayats gradually after they registered a landslide victory in the first panchayat election.

Even at the time of Assembly elections in 1977, the CPI(M) was not quite sure of its electoral support base in the rural areas. The party was ready to concede at that time quite a few seats to the Janata Party with which it fought parliamentary elections together. The negotiations broke down, because the Janata Party wanted more seats than the Left could concede. In the election that followed, the Janata Party was wiped out completely and the Left Front swept the polls, with the CPI(M) alone, gaining absolute majority. The result surprised even the CPI(M). It was therefore quite natural for CPI(M) to expect that it would be able to capture the panchayats, if elections were held when the conditions were in their favour. Accordingly, the Front went for panchayat polls within one year of assumption of office. But, before that, the Front took two major decisions. First, the Panchayat Act was amended to make room for direct elections to all the three tiers of panchayat in place of direct elections to the lowest tier and indirect election to the other two tiers. It is interesting to note that the 36-point programme of the Left Front in the 1977 assembly election stated that 'elections to panchayats, municipalities, corporations and other local bodies should be held immediately under the *system of proportional representation*'. A shift in the stand taken on the manner of election, preferring first-past-the-post electoral system in place of the system of proportional representation, had evidently taken place after the prospects of winning local body elections were carefully assessed. The second important decision taken by the Left Front related to the amendments in panchayat election rules, permitting political parties to contest the elections directly with party symbols. Considering the practice followed until that time throughout the country, both were unconventional decisions, but they suited the political purpose of the left.

Panchayat elections in 1978 therefore served the most important political purpose of the CPI(M), namely, building its base in rural areas. Kohli (1987) has rightly pointed out that 'the CPI(M) had two options: rapid expansion of the party or restructuring of the local government. The communist leaders of Bengal . . . probably knew well that rapid expansion would destroy the party as a cohesive and disciplined force.' The CPI(M) therefore had to choose the second option, namely restructuring local government. The strategy was to 'control the panchayat through CPM sympathizers, while leaving the disciplined party cadres to play the crucial supervisory role over the local governmental institutions' (Kohli 1987).

It is, therefore, the perception of a political necessity rather than commitment to the ideology of decentralized governance that motivated the CPI(M) to build a strong panchayat system. Having occupied the panchayats in 1978, the communists found that an organizational base had been created from which it would be possible to

> resist . . . central government repression in future. Decentralizing the administrative apparatus would make it more difficult for the central government to impose President's Rule effectively. . . . As control of the village meant effective control of the state in electoral terms, no party could rule democratically without eliminating the communist organization in the villages. (Mallik 1993: 136)

It also became apparent gradually that panchayats offered an opportunity to the Left to reduce total dependence upon the bureaucracy to distribute patronage, so necessary for pursuing electoral politics. Channelling of the funds of poverty alleviation programmes through panchayats has helped the CPI(M) establish its political authority firmly. Glyn Williams (1999: 229–30) in his study of three villages in the district of Birbhum, notes as follows:

> The control of development funds for JRY and IRDP schemes gave [panchayat] members a degree of economic influence . . . [A]ny development work a member undertook became highly personalised: rather than fulfilment of an objective set of criteria, it was seen by potential beneficiaries as 'help' . . . especially by those amongst the labouring classes, . . . [R]ather than being an institution in which [people] actively participate, it is seen [by them] as a distributor of personalised benefits.

In the same study, Williams noted that such 'personalized benefits' were, no doubt, going to the poor, but to those among them who were 'politically well connected'. Distribution of patronage through panchayats is, therefore, handy in increasing influence of the party. The panchayat members were also found to be playing 'a role in the village similar to a village headman. [They] were expected to sort out a whole variety of "non political" disputes' (ibid.: 235).

In running a government within the parliamentary framework, the CPI(M) faced a crucial problem. It is a party of the dispossessed class. Yet, in the parliamentary system, it needed a broad alliance of all classes in order to come to power and retain it through elections. It had to accommodate the conflicting interests of the propertied and the propertyless. How this paradox was resolved is not the concern of the present study,[9] but, what is important to note is that the panchayats gave an excellent platform to the party to form a broad alliance of classes incorporating the poor and the well off, landless labourers and the middle as well as the rich peasantry. The poor benefited from the poverty alleviation programmes and from land reforms in both of which panchayats had a role to play. The rising middle peasantry as well as the rural literate sections—mostly teachers of primary and secondary schools—found in the panchayats a space for political participation and an opportunity to articulate their demands and voice their grievances. It is significant that most of the panchayat leaders as well as those of the party come from the middle class.

Thus, the institution has helped it to consolidate its position in the rural areas and expand its support base. It will, therefore, not be wrong to assert that the motive behind CPI(M)'s pro-panchayat policy is political and electoral interests and not ideology. The fact that the party was not enamoured of the concept of decentralization or local democracy before it came to power is revealed in evidence of other kinds. In the 18-point programme of the UF in 1967, the 32-point programme of the second UF government in 1969, and the 36-point programme of the Left Front in 1977, panchayats received nothing more than a cursory reference. Even in 1977, the CPI(M) was not quite sure about the importance that the panchayats would acquire in future and as such, treated the subject as a minor portfolio to be allotted to an ally in the Left Front. Accordingly, the RSP, a minor party, held the portfolio between 1977 and 1982. Thereafter, the CPI(M) seems to have realized the crucial importance of panchayat in achieving the electoral objectives of the party, and claimed it. Since then, the portfolio has remained in the hands of CPI(M). Last, the same government that took pride in holding local government elections regularly, allowed the Calcutta Corporation to remain superseded for eight long years, up to 1985. Election to the Corporation was announced in 1986 after ensuring victory of the Left Front through the amalgamation of some suburban municipalities where the CPI(M) had considerable influence, with the Calcutta corporation.

Thus, the institution of panchayats was promoted and given continuous support because it served the political objectives of CPI(M). If this is true it is also necessary to show that the party has devetoped a mechanism to ensure that the institution does not pose a threat to party's design of operation, but serves what Mallik calls 'party political objectives' (1993: 214). For, autonomous and empowered institution of local government is a two-edged sword. It may help consolidate the party's organization and its support base. But it also promotes the growth of grass roots leaders who may not give unqualified support to the central directives of the party. They may also be emboldened to articulate the 'will' of the local community challenging the rationale of the policies and programmes of the government of the day. Such problems may emanate not only from those local bodies held by the opposition, but also from those captured by the ruling party. What strategy the party adopts to avoid such contingency? How the party retains its control over panchayats?

First, it is necessary to point out that West Bengal's panchayats have not yet been allowed to grow as institutions of self-government. In the absence of devolution of functions from state to the local government institutions, untied funding and support of the services of local bureaucracy, panchayats of the state had to remain satisfied with the execution of the poverty alleviation schemes. In a report prepared for the government of West Bengal, Mukarji and Bandyopadhyay (1993) had observed: 'Wherever we went and whichever panchayat level we met, we were only told of activities undertaken under the Jawahar Rojgar Yojana (JRY).

So pervasive is the JRY fixation that in the event of the scheme being withdrawn, the panchayats will have little to do and may have to fold up.' The concept of self-government, the authors observed, was as yet totally unknown. The position did not change even after the 73rd Constitution Amendment, which expressed the intention that the respective state Acts should endow panchayats with such power and responsibilities as would enable them to function as institutions of self-government. Even the recommendations of the first state finance commission to provide untied funds to the panchayats and to transfer to them local-level functions of the line departments were put in cold storage for about four years, and then implemented only partially.

The policy of denying autonomy to the panchayats and treating them as 'agencies' of the state government has been pursued consistently by the state government. The constitutional amendment also could not change this policy. CPI(M) seems to think that 'controlled' local government institutions will be a better instrument for pursuing its political objectives. To enable them to function as 'institution of self-government', as envisaged in the Constitution, will be a risky proposition.

Even in its restrictive domain, West Bengal's panchayats has a significant role to play in respect of distribution of benefits of government programmes. They execute a plethora of centrally sponsored poverty alleviation and welfare programmes. In other words they are power centres of considerable importance in rural areas. If panchayats have to serve party's interests, then the party has to develop a mechanism to control them.

In a well researched work using empirical as well as archival data consisting of inner-party documents, Harihar Bhattacharyya (1998) has shown that the local organizations of the CPI(M) retain total control over the panchayats. Bhattacharyya observes,

> . . . panchayats of West Bengal since 1978 happen to be politicized. . . . The whole operations of panchayats in the state have been heavily determined and conditioned by the political design of the party. . . . *The crux of the design is the party's control over panchayats.* . . . The party sources clearly establish the fact that as the centre for decision-making at the grassroots, panchayats are emptied of all real content, as the important decisions are taken at the

level of the PSC [Panchayat subcommittee of the local party unit]. . . . *The party's basic attitude towards panchayats is instrumental and manipulative: it wants to control . . . and utilise them.* Nowhere in the party's design is it even mentioned that the institutions of panchayats themselves are important and have even to be developed from within. Panchayats are thus typically subjugated to the authority of the party. . . . The sanctity of the platform of the panchayat is not to be used for itself, but for the party. (Bhattacharyya 1998: 113–14, emphasis added)

Bhattacharyya gives adequate empirical and archival evidence of the manner in which the party units at different levels of panchayats control elected members. His findings are corroborated by another empirical work on West Bengal's panchayats (Bhattacharya 2002). Relying on the evidence of the respondents of her survey, Moitree Bhattacharya observes that the elected representatives do not express their individual views on matters decided in the 'panchayat meetings'. Real authority lies with the leaders of the appropriate party unit. It is they who take decisions, the elected representative endorse and implement them. 'According to the CPI(M) guidelines, the activities of the zilla parishads are controlled by the party's district committees, panchayat samitis by the zonal committees and gram panchayats by the local committees of the party (ibid.: 168). The party has built up an elaborate organization starting with the gram committee at the village level. Then there are local, zonal and district committees. The PRIs are 'controlled' through this network of party organization.

In effect, what exists as panchayats in West Bengal, at least in those places where the CPI(M) dominates, is a façade behind which lies the panchayat sub-committee of the local party unit which takes all the major decisions. If this is the position of the elected members, what about the empowerment of the masses which panchayati raj is supposed to bring about? It is no wonder that people's participation in panchayat's activities has always remained a casualty (Bhattacharyya 1998; Kumar and Ghosh 1995).

In the orthodox ideology of the communist party, the institutions of liberal democracy have no value in themselves. For it, the party is supreme and remains the only agent of social change. CPI(M) is a Leninist-Stalinist party. Its organization principle is democratic centralism, even though 'democracy' and 'centralism' are contradiction in terms. The political ethos of this principle is centralization and the authority-structure of the party is hierarchic. It was unusual for the party to strive for decentralization in governance. The circumstances under which it promoted decentralization in West Bengal have been described. Developing self-governing institution was not on its agenda. Hence, the party allowed the government to develop the institution, but imposed a strict though covert control. Panchayats helped the party expand its support base and to brighten its electoral prospects, and the party retained and supported these institutions. But it did not allow the panchayats to emerge as self-governing institutions. It denied them autonomy and exercised strict party control over them.

This design is in operation for about twenty-five years. Does future hold any promise for change? Is CPI(M) of West Bengal prepared to strengthen the process of democratic decentralization abandoning its manipulative attitude to the panchayats?

It is necessary to point out that the policy of the same party in Kerala on decentralization has been refreshingly different. Under Namboodiripad's leadership, Kerala CPI(M) had consistently given support to local democracy. In his dissenting note to the Asoka Mehta Committee Report, Namboodiripad went beyond the orthodox Communist ideology and argued that 'defence of parliamentary democracy at the central and state level (where it exists but is very often threatened by the authoritarian forces) and its expansion to the lower levels as envisaged in the four pillar democracy is . . . of extreme importance in the advance of Indian society' (quoted in Isaac with Franke 2000: 35). According to him, democratic decentralization serves the cause of class struggle, as it helps the working people to rise against oppression and exploitation. Based on this theoretical formulation, it was easy for the Kerala CPI(M) to argue that 'principle of party organization should be distinguished from the principles for . . . government administration'. Democratic centralism is the principle of organizing Communist Party, while 'democratic decentralization is the principle of governance' (Isaac with Franke 2000: 34–5). Obviously, this is a departure from the orthodox ideology of the party inasmuch as reliance is placed on the institutions of liberal democracy as agents of social change. Also, there is implicit recognition in this policy of the fact that the party's vanguard-of-the-working-class-role should not eclipse community initiatives in local development. The party should tolerate a political space where common people may directly interact with the state's democratic institutions without its mediation.

In 1996, the Left Democratic Front (LDF) led by CPI(M) came to power in Kerala. Immediately thereafter, the state government launched a radical decentralization programme. Popularly known as People's campaign for decentralized planning, the programme envisaged devolution of powers, functions and resources to the panchayats and municipalities on the basis of the principle of subsidiarity and institutionalization of decentralized planning in a transparent and participatory manner. By any standard this was the boldest experiment in local democracy.[10]

The Kerala experiment seems to have created an impact upon West Bengal. Attempts were being made from mid-1990s to empower the gram sansads (ward level assembly of all adult people) and to enlist people's participation. Drawing lessons from the Kerala model, the government drew up an action plan in 1999 to introduce participatory planning at the gram panchayat level, with gram sansad as the starting point of the planning process. Pilot projects were started in four Blocks (Ghatak and Ghatak 2002). Later, in 2001–2 the government decided to extend participatory planning process in all the gram panchayats in a phased manner.

These initiatives indicate that there is awareness about the urgent need of reforming the state's PRIs. Till now, however, the reform measures have not met with success. Small number of gram panchayats has opted for participatory planning process. The kind of seriousness with which Kerala government executed People's Plan Campaign is not noticeable in West Bengal to implement the new reform policy.

Why Kerala was successful in carrying out a radical decentralization programme faster than that of West Bengal, despite the fact that CPI(M) was in power in both the states? It is argued that

Kerala was facing a crisis in economic sphere and decentralization was seen as a means of overcoming such crisis. In contrast, West Bengal witnessed a rapid economic growth in rural areas and 'this has tempered popular demand for further reform' (Ghatak and Ghatak 2002). This explanation does not seem satisfactory, for there is no evidence that people do not demand transparent, accountable and participatory local government institutions or more devolution of functions and resources to these bodies. Same authors have also identified certain political factors responsible for the difference, which merit attention. First, Kerala's political environment is very different. Here opposition is very strong and the Left operates in a competitive political field. In such a political environment, the 'big bang' approach to panchayat reform was considered as a rational political move to gain electoral advantage. The Left in West Bengal did not feel such necessity, as they monopolise the political space of the state. Second, in West Bengal the rural middle class has 'emerged as an important power base in the party' and this class resists empowerment of the masses through participatory governance at the local level (ibid.).

Concluding Remarks

For long 25 years, the CPI(M) of West Bengal has pursued the strategy of establishing hegemonic control over all political and civil society institutions. Those who have benefited from this resist any reform that disturbs the status quo. Consequently the regime's capacity to govern has been reduced. As already noted, there is awareness about the need for changing the policy of 'limited decentralization' with party's control over panchayats, but the determination to carry out the reform measures is not in sight. It seems that the party has to cross many hurdles within its own turf, if it desires to implement a radical programme of democratic decentralization that allows more democracy at the local level and empowers the masses. To what extent the CPI(M) can change its strategy of establishing complete control over the representative institutions at the grass roots in order to pursue the ideal of local democracy remains to be seen.

NOTES

1. Founded in the early part of the twentieth century, Anushilan and Jugantar groups were extremist organizations. They joined the mainstream national movement later and operated from the Congress platform. Though not strong numerically, they had considerable influence in the Bengal politics of late 1920s and 1930s.
2. For this aspect of Bengal politics, see Chatterjee 1969.
3. Though not a full-time politician, B.C. Roy was an important factor in the pre-Independence Congress. He was a member of the so-called 'big five', a creation of C.R. Das. Other leaders in this group were N.C. Chunder, N.R. Sarkar, Sarat Chandra Bose and Tulsi Goswami.
4. For an analysis of Ghosh's political style, see Franda, 'The Political Idioms of Atulya Ghosh', in *Asian Survey*, August 1966; reprinted in Franda 1971.
5. See Franda 1971:75. Analysis of Congress politics in West Bengal during 1950s and 1960s is based principally on Franda.
6. See Banerjee 1980 and Ghosh 1974.
7. P. C. Ghosh was prevented from proving majority of his ministry in the Assembly, because 'the speaker Bijoy Banerjee had created history by twice declaring the appointment of Dr. Ghosh as Chief Minister and the summoning of the session of the State Assembly on his advice, as unconstitutional' (see Basu Raychaudhury 1976: 395). The role of the Governor, Dharma Vira, in dismissing the first UF government has been highly criticized. At the same time, the ruling of the speaker Bijoy Banerjee in not allowing the Assembly to function, reflected a narrow partisan attitude in dealing with a purely constitutional question.
8. As early as 1958, while leading the first Communist ministry in the state of Kerala, E.M.S. Namboodiripad introduced a Bill to empower the panchayats/municipalities and to form a District Council. These bodies were to have sufficient power and autonomy in respect of the subjects transferred to them. The Bill could not be passed, as the ministry was dismissed much before the expiry of its term. At his initiative, the leftist governments of the state made repeated attempts to introduce democratic decentralization in 1967, 1969 and 1991. Namboodiripad was also the moving spirit behind the massive decentralization programme undertaken in the state under the banner of people's campaign for decentralized planning in 1996. See Namboodiripad 1995; Issaac with Franke 2000.
9. For an understanding of this aspect of CPI(M) politics in West Bengal, see Dwaipayan Bhattacharya 1999.
10. For a comprehensive account of Kerala's People's Plan campaign, see Isaac with Franke 2000.

Four

Panchayats in Bihar: The Story of a Non-Performer

Bihar,[1] the poorest and the second most populous state of India,[2] represents a picture of chaos on all fronts. Intense caste and class conflict, decay of political institutions, breakdown of governmental machinery, near-destruction of educational system, extreme poverty, and stagnation in economy characterize Bihar although it is blessed with enviable natural resources for the growth of agriculture as well as industry. Since Independence, and particularly from 1967, no government in Bihar has been able to formulate and pursue any long-term developmental policy. The situation has gone from bad to worse creating in the process acute crisis in governability. To capture what lies at the root of this crisis, it is necessary to grasp Bihar's political system in the context of the society and the economy of the state.

Caste and Class

Bihar has an extremely rigid caste structure so that caste identity occupies predominant position in its social or political discourse. It is estimated that 13 per cent of the population belongs to the upper castes. Within this are included Brahmins, Rajputs and Bhumihars, followed by Kayasthas. Around 51 per cent of the population comes under the category of backward castes, but all backward castes are not equals. The Yadav (or Ahir), Kurmi and Koeri castes along with the Bania are grouped in the category of, 'upper backward', because of their higher social and economic position. They together contribute around one-fifth of the total population and a little over a third of backward castes.

Others in the backward category belong to various types of Shudra castes. The SCs, who are also Shudras, constitute 14 per cent. Besides, there are Muslims and ST people constituting 12.5 per cent and 4.1 per cent of the total population respectively (Table 4.1).

TABLE 4.1: MAJOR CASTE GROUPS OF BIHAR

Category	Caste Group	Percentage of Total Population
Upper Castes	Brahmin	4.7
	Bhumihar	2.9
	Rajput	4.2
	Kayasthas	1.2
	Total	*13.0*
Upper Backwards	Bania	0.6
	Yadav	11.0
	Kurmi	3.6
	Koeri	4.1
	Total	*19.3*
Lower Backwards	Badhi	1.0
	Dr....	1.8
	Hajjam	1.4
	Kahar	1.7
	Kanu	1.6
	Kumhar	1.3
	Lohar	1.3
	Mallah	1.5
	Tatwa	1.6
	Teli	2.8
	Other Shudras	16.0
	Total	*32.0*
Total Backwards		51.3
Muslims		12.5
Scheduled Caste		14.4
Scheduled Tribe		4.1
Total		100

Source: Blair 1980. This table was constructed on the basis of 1931 census data for Hindu castes and 1961 census data for all others. Bengali speakers who constituted 2.4 per cent of the population have not been shown as a different caste group.

In a caste-dominated society the prominence of upper caste is sustained not only by their position in the ritual hierarchy, but also by their superior economic strength. Bihar offers a typical example of this. Hence, inter and intra-caste relations in the state cannot be fully understood without placing it in the background of class relations.

In pre-Independence days, Bihar's agrarian sector was feudal. The Permanent Settlement introduced in the state during the eighteenth and nineteenth century brought new kinds of zamindars, and soon rural society was stratified in terms of type of control one had over land. At the top of the pyramid there were zamindars paying rent directly to the government. Below them there were tenants paying rent to the zamindars. Sub-tenants held land under tenants. Many tenants and sub-tenants used to lease out land to the sharecroppers. (Thus rent was the dominant mode of extraction of surplus for all those classes of people who had control over land.) At the bottom of the pyramid, there were agricultural labourers and poor peasants. Abolition of the zamindari system after Independence brought about some changes in the agrarian sector, but for a variety of reasons, it could not totally eliminate the feudal character of rural society. Even as late as the 1980s, it was found that tenancy and usury were dominant modes of appropriation and along with these there was widespread prevalence of bonded agricultural labour as well as various non-economic forms of extraction from the poor peasants (Prasad 1987).

A survey done in the early part of 1980s revealed that as many as 41 per cent of agriculturist households were leasing-in land out of whom 77 per cent were sharecroppers and another 10 per cent wre paying rent in kind. Nearly 12 per cent of the households got land for cultivation under labour service terms. In the case of sharecroppers, the landowners extracted 50 per cent of the produce, but around 90 per cent of them did not supply any input. Besides, bulk of leasing-in involved very small areas (one acre or less) and fragmented holdings (ibid.). Another feature of the exploitative character of the rural economy was heavy indebtedness of the poor peasants. Of the 97 per cent direct producers representing 67 per cent of the rural households in the sample villages of the survey referred to above were found to be indebted to the traditional sources—the moneylenders, the landlords and the employers. Average rate of interest was as high as 48.79 per cent. About one-third of the agricultural labourers were attached to their employers. They were compelled to work in their employers' lands on priority basis. Any default on their part would lead to various kinds of punishments—loss of wage, termination of sharecropping rights or other kinds of social repression. Wage rate of agricultural labourers were found to be varying not only from village to village and from season to season, but also from person to person indicating 'absence of capitalist labour market'. A familiar method of non-economic coercion was to implicate the attached labourers in criminal cases like theft, dacoity or extortion (ibid.).

Bihar has a dismal record in the area of land reform. Even though within four months of Independence (December 1947) the state government introduced a Bill for zamindari abolition, it was not before five years that the government could begin preparation for the implementation. The intervening years were spent on negotiations over compensation and litigation in High Court and Supreme Court. Besides, it took seven long years from 1955 to 1962 before a Bill for fixing the upper ceiling of land and acquisition of surplus land by the state could be enacted. Another three years passed before the notices to enforce the 1962 Act could be issued (Frankel 1989: 90–1). The big landlords could have enough time (ten years) to hide their ceiling-surplus land through various illegal or fake transfers. Over and above this, there were the usual loopholes to benefit the large landowners.

Failure and neglect in implementing even a modest measure of land reform resulted in an extremely skewed pattern of ownership of agricultural holdings in Bihar. As of 1980–1, nearly 76 per cent of operational holdings were in the hands of marginal farmers owning land up to 2.5 acres. Together they had under their control barely 27 per cent of total agricultural land. On the other hand, only 4.8 per cent of operational holdings were owned by the big farmers having land of 10 acres and above, but they had under their control as much as 35 per cent of the agricultural land of the state. Small farmers owning between 2.5 and 5 acres constituted around 4 per cent of the farmers and cultivated 15 per cent of the total area. Like the big farmers, the middle farmers having holdings between 5 and 10 acres owned land disproportionate to their size. There were only 8.5 per cent of such holdings, but such holdings together covered nearly one-fourth of the agricultural area. Thus a small group of around 13 per cent farmers was controlling 50 to 80 per cent of agricultural land (ibid.: 93).

To add to this extreme inequality in land-owing pattern, there was the spectacle of growing de-peasantization. Extreme indebtedness and poverty among the smallest landowners led them to sell their tiny plots and join the swelling ranks of agricultural labourers (ibid.).

How does the class division fit in with the caste hierarchy of Bihar's rural society? Previously, the Brahmins, Bhumihars and Rajputs were the zamindars and the intermediaries as well as big ryots. Middle peasant households who hire labour for conducting farming activities as well as poor-middle peasant households who employ only the labour of the family for cultivating their lands were drawn mostly from the upper backward castes of Yadavs, Kurmis and Koeris. Poor peasants and agricultural labourers were found mostly among the STs/SCs as well as among the backward castes. True, one could find instances of variation in such caste-class identity. Some zamindars, for example, came from outside the upper caste. However, for the most part, caste coincided with class (Prasad 1979; Blair 1980).

After abolition of zamindari, there was a change. Most of the big peasants are now of upper castes (Brahmin, Rajput or Bhumihar), and the bulk of agricultural labourers and poor peasants come from the SCs. It is the backward castes, particularly the upper backwards, who have made some progress. Some surplus land sold by ex-landlords or big peasants went to the upcoming upper backward castes. It is estimated that at least 10 per cent of agricultural land passed in this way into the hands of the middle peasantry (Prasad 1979). Besides, some backward caste tenants of

Muslim zamindars became landowners after the former left the country following Partition (Kohli 1991).

This is not to say, however, that all upward backward caste people have sizeable lands. The same is true of the upper caste people also. Pressure of population on land and division of holding through inheritance had its effect on upper and backward castes. Thus, there are many middle and small peasants among the upper as well as backward castes (Kohli 1991). It is, however, true that marginal farmers are more among the backward caste landowners and most of the landless labourers come from the SCs and STs.

Inequality and caste-class configuration reveal one aspect of Bihar's society. Its significance will not be understood fully, unless features of the state's economy and the semi-feudal elements influencing inter-personal behaviour of people are fully grasped.

With 829.79 lakh people as per 2001 census, present Bihar is the third most populous state in India. What is worrying is that density of population of the state is increasing, indicating growing pressure upon land and other natural resources. Today Bihar is a densely populated state next only to West Bengal. Accompanied by the spectacle of over population, Bihar represents an impoverished rural economy, as will be evident from the economic indicators given in Table 4.2.

What is revealing in Table 4.2 is the fact that Bihar is one of the worst performing states in the country in all aspects. First, in all the six indicators, its performance is below the national average. Second, it is the poorest state in India. It has not only the lowest per capita rural income, but also the lowest per capita state income. Its growth rate of SDP is second lowest among that of the major states. Third, its land-man ratio—0.14 ha per person—is the lowest in the country, indicating high pressure of population on land or lack of utilization of all cultivable land or both. Fourth, its per capita food grain production is 40 per cent below the national average, though foodgrains happen to be the main agricultural crop of the state. Even though Bihar's rate of growth of production of foodgrains in the 1980s was better than that of some other states, it was below the national average.

TABLE 4.2: SOME ECONOMIC INDICATORS: BIHAR AND THE NATIONAL AVERAGE

	Unit	Bihar	All-India
1. Gross cropped area of rural population (1987–90)	Hc.	0.14	0.29
2. Per capita food grains production (average for 1990–1 to 1992–3)	Kg.	121	201
3. Per capita rural income (average for 1987–90)	Rs.	948	1522
4. Real per capita state income (average for 1990–1 to 1992–3)	Rs.	1,150	2,219
5. Growth rate of per capita SDP, 1992–3 to 1998–9	%	1.6	4.4
6. Poverty indices 1993–4 (head count ratio)			
Rural	%	49	33
Urban	%	27	18
Combined	%	46	29

Sources: For sl. 1 to 4, CMIE (1994) and for sl. 5 and 6, Dreze and Sen (2002).

Lastly, with 35 per cent of female literacy and 62 per cent male literacy as of 2001, present Bihar is the least literate state in India. About 93 per cent of SC women and 85 per cent of ST women were illiterate as of 1991. Bihar's female-male ratio (926) was below the national average (933) in 2001.

The undivided Bihar had a fairly strong industrial base with two steel plants, mining, heavy engineering, fertilizer and metal-based industries. But this industrial base did not spearhead the process of industrialization. As of 1991, 81 per cent of Bihar's main workers were engaged in the primary sector activities. Thus the state remained an agriculutre-based economy. But unlike many other states of India the green revolution bypassed it, except in some districts of its central area. It is only here that attempts to improve productivity through the use of ground water irrigation and hybrid seeds are noticeable. But even here the progress is not phenomenal compared to the productivity of the advanced states.

It is therefore easy to see why the number of the poor is so high in the state. Extreme inequality in the land ownership pattern, existence of semi-feudal production relations as evidenced in the widespread prevalence of sharecropping, usury, bonded labour and coercion of marginalized people through non-economic methods stand in the way of Bihar's development.

No amount of hard data is enough to describe the lack of social opportunities of the common people, unless one has an idea of the caste-mediated social relations. Even in the recent past, the low caste people used to be treated with contempt. They were not supposed to argue with the upper caste persons. Even casting vote during elections was an upper caste prerogative. The village of S.N. Sinha, who was a Chief Minister, had never seen a Dalit inside the polling booth. It was inconceivable for an upper caste voter to stand in the same queue with a lower caste person (Bharti 1990). In the villages, residential quarters of the SCs or the lower backward caste people will invariably be at the outskirts and at a distance from the place where the upper caste families live. Das (1992) reports that a rustic Dalit has no right to a comfortable seat inside a bus even if he pays the full fare. He will invariably be asked to sit elsewhere or even at the roof of the bus to make room for persons with higher social status. The upper caste and the upper backward caste rich landowners have private armies and they terrorize the rural poor (Das 1992). Even though a wind of change is blowing, the Brahminical social order has not yet disappeared totally in this state.

POLITICS OF BIHAR

Bihar's politics may be divided into two phases. In the first phase, which extends up to the 1960s, it is principally a story of the use of political power by the upper castes to retain their social domination. The second phase that began from 1967 is marked by the rise of upper backward caste people as major contenders of state power and forceful protest movements of the marginalized Dalits and neglected tribals.

Pre-Independence Period

Bihar was a late entrant in the political movements of pre-Independent India. One of the reasons for this was the absence of a sizeable middle class exposed to modern education. Until 1900, there were only a handful of Biharis who had imbibed modern ideas through English education (Frankel 1989: 63–9). Among those who received modern education, Kayasthas and upper class Muslims for outnumbered others. The Kayasthas formed the first Caste Association and it was this Association, which was responsible for launching the first political movement for a separate province of Bihar (ibid.).

It was only in 1908 that the Congress established its provincial branch in Patna. The party, however, had no full-time political workers and practically no programme or movement. Yet Gandhiji chose Champaran district of Bihar as the place for his first experiment of civil disobedience on Indian soil, when he took up the cause of cultivators against the exploitation of indigo-planters in 1917–18. During this historic mission, Gandhiji did not find any active organization of the Congress to help him. The organization began to grow from around 1920 onwards when committees were set-up in districts and talukas (Frankel 1989: 69–73).

Two important characteristics of the nationalist movement under the auspices of the Bihar Congress, which had a bearing even upon its post-Independence activities, require to be noted. Firstly the leadership of the party was drawn exclusively from among the upper castes, initially from among the Kayasthas and later other twice-born castes (Bhumihars, Rajputs and Brahmins). The lower castes, SC and tribals were practically kept out from the leadership. The leaders of the party belonged to the landed families of moderate to well-to-do means in villages and middle-class professionals and merchants of towns (ibid.: 73). Second, the leadership had all along been conservative and averse to any kind of change in the social order. Accordingly, there has been no attempt to attack the rigidity of caste institutions. More important, the Congress remained insensitive to the oppression of the poor peasantry under the zamindari system. In its political discourse, any radical agenda of agrarian reforms was conspicuously absent. This is evident in the conciliatory attitude the Congress took towards the zamindars, and the lack of concern it displayed towards exploitation of the peasantry and the peasant movement.

The caste and class bias of the pre-Independence Congress leadership was more clearly evident in its attitude to the movements of the Kisan Sabha led by Swami Sahajanand Saraswati. With a modest beginning in 1927, the Bihar Pradesh Kisan Sabha was established in 1929. From then to the early 1940s, Sahajanand added a new dimension to the struggle of the peasantry of Bihar. He conducted the peasant movement purely on the basis of class, cutting across caste divisions. Naturally, the movement turned against the zamindari system. Ultimately, in its third conference held at Hazipur in November 1935, the Bihar provincial Kisan conference passed a resolution on the abolition of zamindari (Mundargi 1990). At any stage, the Congress could not take any step that would alienate zamindars and big ryots. Hence, even though Kisan Sabha had extended its full cooperation to the activities of the Congress,[3] it was difficult for the Congress leadership to tolerate the radical programme of the Sabha.

Towards the end of 1937, a Zamindar Sabha of Muzaffarpur district accused the Kisan Sabha for creating an anarchic situation in the villages and urged the Congress leaders to look into the same. The Congress in its turn asked its district committees to watch the activities of the Kisan Sabha. Soon thereafter, the District Congress Committees of Champaran, Monghyr and Saran issued directions to their members not to take part in the tours of Sahajanand (ibid.). Thus started the process of alienation of Sahajanand, the moving spirit of Kisan Sabha movements, from the mainstream of the Congress. By 1942, he became completely isolated and the Kisan Sabha he led, disintegrated.

The Post-Independence Period

At Independence, Congress was in control of the state government. The party retained absolute control over government uninterruptedly for two decades after 1947. The same leadership, which was at the helm of affairs during the nationalist movement, guided the destiny of this caste-ridden, semi-feudal and impoverished state during this period. Apart from stability of government, there is nothing that can be cited as its positive contribution to development. Rather, the seeds of anomie that characterize Bihar's present political scenario were sown during this very period.

In 1946, a Congress ministry headed by the veteran Shrikrishna Sinha came to power in Bihar. Sinha continued as Chief Minister until his death in 1961. There is a general consensus that the period 1947 to 1961 is the brightest in Bihar's post-Independence politics, because the government was stable and effective under a mature leadership. Facts do not, however, substantiate this assessment. First, little could be expected from the old leadership that had led the nationalist movement. They were conservative and biased towards the upper castes and the landed gentry. Nothing that would disturb the status quo could be expected from them. Secondly, steeped in casteism, they themselves were involved in narrow inter-caste conflict. Thirdly being status quoists at heart, they sought to build their support base through mobilization of people of their own caste and by co-opting other castes. With multifarious developmental and welfare programmes under the Nehruvian planning regime, access to state power became an extremely important objective to pursue for the elite of all castes, for it is only through such power that one could get a share of the largesse provided by the state. In the traditional society of Bihar, it is only the caste idiom that worked in politics. Hence, the caste structure became increasingly politicized, leading to intense inter-caste conflicts.

It was noted earlier, how the pre-Independence Congress forged a link with the zamindars and the landed gentry. It is this class bias of the Bihar Congress that delayed zamindari abolition and prevented the government from introducing even a modicum of land reforms.

Remaining within the same party and government, the heavyweight Rajput leader, A.N. Sinha, was constantly at loggerheads with the Bhumihar Chief Minister Shrikrishna Sinha until his death. The leadership struggle did not confine itself only to the top. It percolated down to all levels. This inter- and intra-caste rivalry among the Congress leadership, which was the exclusive domain of the upper-caste, became more intense after the death of Sinha in 1961. B.N. Jha, a Brahmin, K.B. Sahay, a Kayastha and M.P. Sinha, a Bhumihar, fought among themselves for leadership. 'Each drew support from a few caste-based factions, but none of them was tall enough to mobilize wide support cutting [across] the intra-party factions' (Prasad 1976: 53). This was the beginning of the period of unstable governments and growing crisis in governability. Between 1962 and 1990, no Chief Minister of the state has been able to complete a full term of five years (see Table 4.3).

The first chink in the armour of the Congress surfaced in the period from 1962 to 1967. First, the rising aspirations of the backward castes were making it difficult for the upper-caste Congress leadership to monopolize state power. K.B. Sahay, the Chief Minister, had to increase the representation of backward castes in his cabinet by curtailing the number of ministerial positions for the upper castes. Second, because of the dependence of Sahay on political concessions to various factions, he failed to stop the abuse of power by faction leaders occupying ministerial positions (Frankel, 1989: 87–8). Third, the droughts of 1965 and 1966 brought the state to the brink of a famine.

All this made the government extremely unpopular. Unable to check the tide of extreme unpopularity expressed through demonstrations, strikes and *bandhs*, the government resorted to the use of force, which culminated in police firing in August 1966.

So, when the elections were held in 1967, the Congress for the first time found itself dislodged from power. None of the opposition parties was in a position to form a government on its own strength. The result was the emergence of coalition politics based on narrow political gains of various factions. Between 1967 and 1972, Bihar had nine Chief Ministers, three separate spells of President's rule, and one mid-term election.

Some new features in state politics came to surface during this period. The backward castes began to make their presence felt

TABLE 4.3: MINISTRIES IN BIHAR: 1947 TO 2000

Period	Party in Power	Chief Minister
1947–61	Congress	Shri Krishna Sinha
1961–2	Do	B.N. Jha
1963–7	Do	K.B. Sahay
1967–9	Three coalition ministries of Opposition parties One ministry backed by Congress which was in power for four days	Mahamaya P. Sinha S.P. Singh B.P. Mandal B.P. Shastri
1969–71	Five coalition ministries in two of which mainstream Congress, i.e. Congress (R) was a partner	Harihar Singh B.P. Shastri Daroga Rai Karpoori Thakur B.P. Shastri
1972–3	Congress	Kedar Pandey
1973–5	Do	Abdul Ghafoor
1975–7	Do	Jagannath Mishra
1977–9	Janata	Karpoori Thakur
1979–80	Do	Ramsundar Das
1980–3	Congress	Jagannath Mishra
1983–5	Do	Chandrasekhar Singh
1985–90	Do	Bindeshwari Dubey Bhagwat Jha Azad Jagannath Mishra
1990–5	Janata Dal Supported by some non-Congress parties	Laloo Prasad Yadav
1995	Janata Dal Later Rashtriya Janata Dal	Laloo Prasad Yadav/ Rabri Devi
2000	RJD supported by Congress and other minor parties	Rabri Devi

Sources: For 1967–72, Prasad (1976);
for others up to 1985, Frankel (1993)

in the legislature and the government. Even while distributing tickets for 1967 election, the Congress party itself—which was previously almost monopolized by the upper castes—had to make major concessions for backward castes. It is not a coincidence that out of nine governments formed during this period, seven were led by men of the backward or Harijan castes (Prasad 1976: 66). Articulation of Bihar politics in terms of backward versus upper castes started in this period. Secondly, it was in 1969 that Congress split occurred. Prominent Congress leaders of Bihar joined the new Congress led by Indira Gandhi. Third, in the midst of extremely unstable politics, emerged the new phenomenon of rigged elections. Henceforth, booth-capturing and other forms of rigging became a normal feature of Bihar elections.

In the 1972 elections, the Congress came back to power. Even though the party was dislodged after five years, it bounced back in 1980 and retained power till 1990. But during its fifteen-year rule—five years in the 1970s and for a full decade in the 1980s—the style of functioning of the party had undergone a fundamental change. Power was centralized in the hands of the Prime Minister. Party leadership would not emerge through the normal process, but would be appointed by the Prime Minister or her coterie. None of the Congress Chief Ministers of Bihar during this period had any mass base. They derived their power from the Prime Minister and could retain the same, so long as their loyalty was not questioned. The shaky power base of such Chief Ministers prompted them to adopt short-cuts which ruined whatever remained in the organization of the state Congress party, weakened the bureaucracy and intensified all-round criminalization of electoral politics. The use of force and booth capturing and other forms of rigging became the normal features of Bihar elections. Corruption in public life became the order of the day.

It has been observed that, the 'criminalization of politics intensified during Jagannath Mishra's regime as Chief Minister' (Kohli 1991: 218). Picked up by Sanjay Gandhi, this university teacher became Chief Minister during the Emergency in 1975. 'One of the strategies adopted by Mishra and by nearly all subsequent leaders was to consolidate control by appointing ministers, civil servants and police officers who were loyal. Thus the competence of the ruling elite declined further' (ibid.: 216). The arming of private militias of landowners, the entry of criminals into electoral politics, corruption, and the erosion of the effectiveness of bureaucracy and police, all intensified during his regime. Later, these became normal features of the politics of Bihar. Mishra's political fortunes fluctuated after the defeat of the Congress in 1977, but he managed to become Chief Minister twice thereafter, in the 1980s.

In the 1977 elections, a strong anti-Congress reaction to the Emergency brought the Janata Party—a party formed by the merger of Samyukta Socialist, Jana Sangh and Congress (O)—to power with overwhelming majority. Karpoori Thakur, a long-standing socialist leader, became Chief Minister. Earlier in the 1967–72 period too, he led a coalition ministry of non-Congress parties, for a span of only 163 days.

Thakur's 1977 ministry was remarkable, because for the first time in the history of Bihar a non-Congress party came to power with a two-thirds majority. Its tenure, however, was short. Widespread public discontent over the reservation policy and internal dissension within the party forced Thakur to resign in 1979. The Janata Party split into two during the mid-term parliamentary election of 1980 and then into three during the assembly election held shortly thereafter.

The 1990 election brought Congress rule to an end once again when Janata Dal had emerged as the largest party, but failed to achieve absolute majority. With the backing of other minor parties like the CPI and CPI(M) Laloo Prasad Yadav formed a Janata Party cabinet and completed a full term as Chief Minister for the first time since the days of Shrikrishna Sinha. Yadav led the party to victory once again in the polls of 1995, winning 169 seats in the 324-member assembly.

Laloo Prasad Yadav brought much needed political stability to the state of Bihar. He achieved remarkable success in winning the confidence of the Muslims. His dramatic decision to arrest BJP leader L.K. Advani during his *rath-yatra* in 1990, and subsequent steps taken to arrest communal disturbances, had endeared him to the Muslims and marginalized the BJP (Jha 1995: 38). Second, he projected himself as a fighter for the cause of social justice, and for the dignity of the backward sections. In the process he gained the confidence of the Dalits, Backward Castes, Scheduled Castes, tribal people, Muslims, and the poor. They backed the Janata Dal in the 1995 elections. The impressive Janata victory in the 1995 polls was not the result of a mere Yadav-Muslim alliance as is commonly believed, but the alliance of the poor, irrespective of caste and creed (Chaudhuri 1995: 18). Third, Laloo Prasad Yadav was successful in positioning himself as the undisputed leader within the Bihar Janata Dal, eliminating the rise of intra-party factions. This was not an easy task, for at the beginning he had two other contenders for the top post. He could outmanoeuver others primarily because of the support he received from the MLAs of his own caste (*India Today* 31 March 1990). He took no time to consolidate his own power within the party by creating an image for himself among the masses as well as by distribution of patronage to aspiring legislators and partymen.

Why did the poor vote for Yadav's party? This government did nothing to provide economic justice to the deprived. The government took no action for land reform. Even the mention of the latter is absent in the Janata Dal's election manifesto. The bulk of funds for poverty alleviation continued to be pocketed by the vested interests (Gupta 1995: 790). Agricultural labourers did not get even the prescribed minimum wage and there was no attempt to break existing semi-feudal tenancy relations. Instead of solving the basic problems of the poor peasantry that led them to mount violent movements in central Bihar under the Naxalite banner Yadav had resorted to strong tactics to suppress peasant uprisings (Chaitanya 1991: 2612).

While Yadav gave nothing concrete to the poor, he accomplished an outstanding feat. He projected himself as the Messiah of the poor. He is an extraordinary communicator, 'with a mastery over folk language'. He talks to the masses in their language and presents himself as one who has risen from humble origins, but has reached the top position from among themselves. He has relentlessly sought to establish his pro-poor credentials in hundreds of mass meetings (Gupta 1995: 790). This strategy worked. The poor stood solidly behind Yadav during elections.

After the 1995 assembly election, Laloo Prasad Yadav was bubbling with confidence. It seemed that so long as he led the Janata Dal, it would remain invincible in Bihar. However, he soon had to face disappointments. In 1996, he was involved in the so-called fodder scam and the CBI registered corruption cases against him. In the Lok Sabha elections that year, the Opposition parties carried a virulent campaign against the scam and the Janata Dal was put on the defensive. In 1995, the Janata Dal was weakened by a split. A separate party, the Samata Party, emerged on the national scene. Nitish Kumar, a prominent leader of Bihar and with large following among the Kurmi caste, joined this party and offered a challenge to Yadav's leadership. This party gave a poor show in the 1995 assembly election. In the 1996 Lok Sabha poll, it entered into an alliance with the BJP. The strategy had worked. Contrary to expectations, the Janata Dal won only 22 Lok Sabha seats, compared to 33 seats in the 1991 elections. From this period, Yadav has been going through difficult situations. In 1998, he was chargesheeted in a number of corruption cases. The national leadership of the party found it difficult to retain him as its president, and Yadav responded by breaking away. He floated a new party, the Rashtriya Janata Dal (RJD), and resigned from the post of Chief Minister after installing his wife, Rabri Devi, in the chair. From that time, Yadav has remained proxy Chief Minister of Bihar, leaving the official position to his wife. The election of 2000 returned a hung assembly, but Yadav's RJD emerged as the single largest party winning 123 out of the total of 324 seats. With support from the congress and other parties, RJD could form the government, again with Rabri Devi as Chief Minister.

The assertion of backward castes is an important feature of Bihar politics in the 1990s. The party or parties claiming to look after their interest have gradually increased their strength in the State Assembly. In 1990, they won 124 seats; in 1995, 170 (JD 164 and Samata 6). In 2000, it was 178 seats (RJD 123, JD(U) 21 and Samata 34).

An analysis of the voting trend in the decade 1989–99 indicates that there has been steady rise in the vote base of the parties representing the backward castes. Starting with 36 per cent in

1989, it went up to 46.25 per cent in 1996 (JD plus Samata), 51 per cent in 1998 (RJD plus Samata plus JD) and 50 per cent in 1999 (RJD plus JD(U) (Sinha 1999). No aspiring political party can now expect to expand their support base without giving political representation to the backwards. Even BJP could increase their influence after enlisting the suppot of Kurmis and Koeris (Kumar 1999). However, the benefits of political representation of the backward castes have remained confined to a section among them: Yadavs, Kurmis, Koeris and Vaisyas. 'The most backward castes, which constitute about 30 per cent of Bihar's population, have not found sufficient representation. . . . They have been used as vote banks by almost all parties' (Louis 1999). But the most backward castes, Dalit sub-castes and the backward Muslims are coming under one platform. There are indications that this forum is getting strengthened. Probably 'Bihar is once again showing the way for alternative assertions' (ibid.).

Another trend of the post-1995 period is the steady erosion of the charisma of Laloo Prasad Yadav. First the upwardly moving backward castes, especially the Kurmis, became disillusioned for several reasons: the 'Yadavization' phenomenon whereby undue favour had been given to a particular caste, systematic deterioration of law and order, and utter neglect of development work. Second, the most backward castes and Dalit are also disenchanted as the government has shown little concern for their basic social and economic problems (Hauser 1997). All this and the tactful electoral alliance of the Opposition parties affected Yadav's electroal prospects. In the 1996 Lok Sabha election, Yadav was expecting a landslide victory for the Janata Dal, but he managed to win only 22 out of 44 seats it contested. In the next two elections of 1998 and 1999, his RJD got 17 and 7 seats respectively. A comparison of 1996 and 1998 Lok Sabha polls shows that OBCs in general, and lower OBCs and Dalits in particular, are shifting away from the party under his leadership: JD in 1996 and RJD in 1998 (Kumar 1999). It is true that in the assembly election of 2000, RJD emerged as the single largest party, but it failed to get absolute majority. This shows that Yadav is still a big factor in Bihar politics, but his influence has certainly diminished.

Non-Mainstream Politics

The description of Bihar politics will remain incomplete without mention of two other important political struggles, those carried out by poor peasants, and those of the ethnic minorities.

Drawing inspiration from the Naxalite movement of West Bengal, the Bihar unit of the Communist Party of India (Marxist-Leninist) (CPI-ML) launched class-based peasant struggle in the late 1960s. However, because of the lack of a cohesive ideology and strategy, the party soon slipped into acts of adventurism, anarchy and mindless violence. Many splinter groups arose within the party, each following its own programme. It did not take much time for the state machinery to suppress the movement by the mid-1970s.

Resurgence of the activities of these radical Marxists started in 1977, following the release of many erstwhile Naxalite leaders.[4] From the early 1980s onwards, at least three groups of CPI-ML were active in several districts of central Bihar: the CPI (ML) Liberation group, the CPI (ML) Party Unity and the Maoist Communist Centre (MCC). Popularly labelled as 'Naxalities' or 'extremists', the militant movements led by them spread over 197 villages in the districts of Patna, Gaya, Aurangabad, Bhojpur, Rohtas and Nalanda, according to one official estimate of the late 1980s (Chaudhry 1988: 51).

The struggles of the peasants appear to revolve around three issues, fair wages for labour, seizure of surplus lands in the occupation of rich peasants and its distribution among the landless, and the restoration of social dignity to the Dalits (Das 1992: 114–15). However, these have very often taken the form of armed confrontation against either the state machinery or the private armies of the rich peasants, or both. Organized strictly along class-lines—a feature unknown to the caste-ridden mainstream politics of Bihar—these movements are showing remarkable staying power, creating acute problems for the ruling party.

For a long time, the tribal people of south Bihar were engaged in a movement demanding a separate state for themselves. Though Jharkhand, the state they carved out for themselves, included parts of West Bengal, Madhya Pradesh and Orissa, the political movement they carried on was concentrated in Bihar. Protest movements of south Bihar tribes against economic exploitation and cultural homogenization are quite old. As early as 1937, Jaipal Singh had established a Jharkhand party. The Jharkhand movement had seen many vicissitudes since then. It is not necessary to go into the details of the same. What is important for us to note is that the movement assumed the character of a storm in recent times. In 1995, governments at the centre and the states made some concessions. An antonomous council was established. But without funds and real transfer of power, the council failed to satisfy the leaders of the movement. Ultimately a new state was created in the year 2000 by splitting Bihar into two parts. The tribal districts in the south of the undivided Bihar comprise the present state of Jharkhand.

Panchayats in Bihar

Even though Bihar is criticized for its utter neglect of the development of panchayats, it is an irony of history that it is among those very few states of India which enacted a panchayati raj legislation as early as 1947, only within a few months of achieving independence. Gram panchayats and gram kutcheris, their judicial arm, started functioning under this Act in 1948. In appearance, this action of the Bihar government could be shown as fulfilment of a commitment to the Gandhian principle of *gram swaraj*. It is necessary to remember that the greatest Congress leader of Bihar—Rajendra Prasad—was a loyal disciple of Gandhi. Besides, Gandhiji's towering image had mass appeal, cutting across the social cleavages, especially in Bihar. In such an ambience, any proof of commitment to Gandhian principles was a forceful means to acquire legitimacy. However, panchayats under the Bihar Panchayati Raj Act of 1947 had nothing to do with Gandhi's gram swaraj. In substance, the two structures of gram panchayat and gram kutcheri were meant to perpetuate the existing feudal social order in the villages. While both were elected bodies, in gram panchayats—the executive body—the mukhiya was the chief executive and he was directly elected by the people. Along with him, four other members would also be elected. The mukhiya had the prerogative to select four other members, thus forming a nine-member executive committee including himself. For the judicial branch, the sarpanch or head of the gram kutcheri was elected along with four other members.

The functions of these two structures were minimal. The kutcheri was to mediate in local disputes or to administer justice in petty cases. In a feudal rural society marked by wide caste and class divisions, intra and inter-caste rivalry and factions, there was little chance for the marginalized people to get justice from a gram kutcheri. Yet the system functioned until the early 1960s.

A more important structure for local democracy was the institution of gram panchyat, but it had meagre power, and few resources. Hence, in terms of village development, its role was negligible. But the then Congress government was careful to protect the interest of superior castes and classes through this institution, and one of its important functions was to organize a village volunteer force to protect the village and to combat emergency situations like fire and epidemic. All able-bodied persons in the age group of 18–30 were to become members of this force. Soon it was found that in the name of village protection, the poor and the propertyless were being used as night watchmen, free of cost, and very few from the rich families offered such voluntary service. Night patrolling was more essential for the rich. It meant nothing to the property-less people.

Without financial resources and without any transfer of governmental functions to the panchayats, these institutions of the 1947 Act were poles apart from Gandhi's *gram swaraj*. When the Community Development Programme began in 1952, real powers in respect of rural development passed on to the newly-created bureaucratic structure, the Block Development Office. In order to give popular content to the community development programme, mukhiyas were made members first of the advisory committees at the block level in 1955, and then of the Block Development Committee in 1958. Though the latter had some executive power, in essence the entire programme was run by the block officials with little involvement of panchayats. Such an arrangement continued up to the 1960s.

Thus, between 1947 and 1961, Bihar had panchayats in its villages, though in terms of decentralization of governmental functions, these institution were of little significance. However, locally the institution had prestige and authority. But as is natural for a semi-feudal society, such institutions served basically as allies of the dominant power structure of the respective areas. Mukhiyas and other members invariably belonged to the dominant castes or classes. The power to nominate a member to the executive committee was an additional instrument for caste or class supremacy. Common people had little chance to contribute to these bodies. There was a provision of direct democracy in the institution of the gram sabha, in which all adult persons of the village were members. But meetings of that body were never held and the provision for direct democracy remained a cruel joke.

And these were the only institutions of village democracy. Even this modicum of democracy, however was allowed to exist only up to the mid-1960s. It goes to the credit of the then governments that between 1952 and 1964, elections to the panchayat bodies were held at a regular intervals in 1952, 1955, 1958, 1961 and 1964. Between 1964 and 2000, panchayat elections had taken place only twice—in 1971 and in 1978–80, both during the Chief Ministership of Karpoori Thakur.

At the all-India level, panchayati raj assumed almost the character of a movement, following the report of the Balwantrai Mehta Committee (GOI 1957). In the late 1950s, under the vigorous patronage of Nehru, establishment of three-tier panchayats at the village, block and district level became the official policy of both the Government of India and the Congress party. Jayaprakash Narayan, then a Sarvodaya leader, gave full-fledged ideological support to this policy. Apart from Congress, the Socialists hailed the system. Accordingly, it became necessary for the Bihar Government to respond to this policy. A state which went ahead of others to establish village panchayats was found this time to be reluctant to broadbase and empower the system. But this was the time when state after state enacted new panchayat legislations, held elections, and set-up a three-tier system. Power to the people was the new political rhetoric of Congressmen, but Bihar was found to drag its feet on the issue.

In 1961 Bihar enacted the Panchayat Samiti and Zilla Parishad Act which received the Governor's assent in 1962. This, together with the 1947 Act, was to be the basis of three-tier panchayat at the village, block and district levels.

When one looks at the 1961 Act, it becomes clear that the framers of the Act did not want the new structures of panchayat samiti and zilla parishads to become power-bases of local politicians. For in none of these bodies were there provisions of direct election. Panchayat samitis were staffed by ex-officio members (mukhiyas and chairmen of municipalities), nominated members (representatives of cooperative societies) and co-opted members. Similarly, the zilla parishad consisted of ex-officio members (pramukhs of panchayat samitis and MLA/MP/MLCs) and three members elected indirectly from the electoral college of commissioners of municipalities. But the government seemed to be afraid of setting up even these sanitized institutions of local government. Between 1962 and 1980, during a period of 18 years, panchayat samitis and zilla parishads were established in only 8 out of a total of 32 districts.

Panchayat elections were last held in 1978. Thereafter no election took place till 2001. After the expiry of the five-year term, the term of the office of mukhiya of a gram panchayat and pramukh of a panchayat samiti continued to be extended by the government every six month. Zilla parishads were superseded in 1981. Thus, what remained of the panchayat structure of Bihar till the end of the last century, was a skeleton of mukhiyas and pramukhs of 1978 vintage. When deaths of such persons created vacancies, the government promptly filled the vacuum by nomination. In fact, the task of nominating mukhias and pramukhs became a full-time job of a deputy director in the directorate of panchayats. However under an order of the Supreme Court in 1997, all the elected members in office since 1978 were dismissed and their powers were passed over to the officials (Kumar 2001).

The Karpoori Thakur Interlude

In the long barren period extending from the early 1960s to the end of the 1990s, Karpoori Thakur's rule in 1971 and then in 1977–8 provide a remarkable departure insofar as panchayat democracy is concerned. He was Chief Minister of a coalition ministry for only 163 days from 22 December 1970 to 1 June 1971. As noted, this was a period of great confusion, when Bihar was governed by as many as nine Chief Ministers and President's rule was invoked thrice during 1967–72. Yet, within five and a half months during which he was in office, the Thakur cabinet ordered a panchayat election. When Thakur became Chief Minister once again in 1977, he conducted elections to the panchayati raj bodies, despite objections from all quarters, including his own party. For the first time, he initiated the process of implementing the 1961 Act in totality in all districts. It is because of his actions that Bihar acquired a full-fledged three-tier panchayat system in all its districts by 1980.

Why did Thakur give panchayats such high priority? The common explanation is that he wanted to 'consolidate the Janata Party base' (Sinha 1978: 982). But this explanation is not fully satisfactory, for it does not say anything about the social base which Thakur targeted for consolidation of his party's power base. Contrary to the Congress politics of retaining political power through the key men of the upper castes, Karpoori Thakur wanted to build a mass base. This required mobilization of the underdog of the SC, ST and backward caste categories. For this, Thakur took two steps. First, he adopted a reservation policy for government posts for SC, ST, backward castes as well as women and the poor, irrespective of caste. Second, he ordered panchayat elections for all the three tiers. The reservation policy was meant to prove his government's credentials as the champion of the oppressed. The objective of the panchayat policy was to extend the influence of his party by creating a political space for those whom he wanted to mobilize.

It seems that Thakur was moderately successful in his objective. A large-scale displacement of the old office-bearers of panchayats took place after the panchayat election, and it was believed that those who came were supporters of Karpoori Thakur (Blair 1980: 72). However, he did not find time to consolidate the panchayati raj system. In 1979, Thakur had to resign and in 1980, the Janata Party itself went out of power. By 1981, the zilla parishads were superseded and no elections to the lower bodies were held after their five-year term expired.

Thakur did not get much time to pursue his objective of institutionalization of the support base for his party. Yet, whatever he could do had yielded results. Analysing the performance of various parties in the Assembly and Parliamentary elections held between 1980 and 1985, Blair noted that it was only Karpoori Thakur's Lok Dal—a fragment of the old Janata—which 'managed to institutionalize itself with popular support base' (ibid.: 133). This institutionalization of the party as a strategy for mobilization is what distinguishes Thakur's politics from others in Bihar. The priority attached to panchayats in his agenda stems in all probability from his anxiety to institutionalize the power-base of rainbow coalition of backward groups that he was attempting.

Panchayats under Laloo Prasad Yadav

The ideology of panchayati raj received shabby treatment at the hands of Laloo Prasad Yadav. It was during his first term as Chief Minister that the 73rd Amendment of the Constitution was passed. This amendment made it mandatory for all state governments to bring state legislation on panchyats at par with the constitutional requirement by 24 April 1994, and to hold panchayat elections immediately thereafter. All that the Yadav regime did was to amend the law within the stipulated date. But in doing so, it had ensured two things. First, the Act provided precious little in terms of devolution of administrative and financial powers to the panchayats, but contained many provisions to strengthen state government control over these bodies. In this respect, the Janata Dal led by Yadav seemed to be in complete agreement with Jagannath Mishra of the Congress. 'Both were seen to be equally disinterested in granting any real administrative or financial power to the panchayats' (Gupta 1993: 1568). Secondly, Yadav made elaborate provisions for reservation of seats for the backward castes. In this, he made no distinction between the upper and lower sections, obviously to allow the upper crust of backward groups (mostly Yadavs) to reap the benefits of reservation. He made a quick census for this and fixed the quotas for backward, SC and ST sections. As a result, much more than 50 per cent of seats on an average went in favour of the backward sections.

Even after all this, Yadav was reluctant to hold panchayat elections. But he needed an alibi to hide his real intention. He found one soon. For the purpose of fixing quotas of backward castes, a census was necessary, as reliable data on OBC population are not available. The government asked the District Magistrates to conduct the census in one week. Everybody knew that such a casual approach to caste census would invite litigation. This is what happened. Aggrieved persons went to the High Court. In its judgement delivered in March 1996, Patna High Court declared, *inter alia*, that the reservation provisions for OBCs were unconstitutional. The state government promptly filed a special leave petition (SLP) to the Supreme Court against the judgement. Even though the SLP was admitted, it did not come up for hearing in the apex Court. But Yadav was totally unconcerned about it. In a state level conference of mukhias and pramukhs held on 18 February 1997, Yadav assured that his government would try utmost to obtain appropriate orders of the Court, so that panchayat elections could be held quickly (Kumar 2001). The state government did nothing. And they took the plea that the election notification could not be issued, because the matter was subjudice. In reality there was no bar in holding the election. This became clear when the Patna High Court, in response to a petition filed before it, directed the state governemnt in April 2000 to conduct panchayat election, as there was no stay of the apex Court against its judgement. Instead of taking further steps in terms of this direction, Bihar Government took the matter again to the Supreme Court. In August 2000, the Supreme Court confirmed the order of the High Court and asked the state government to hold election, 'subject to the final verdict on its special leave petition' (ibid.). After this, elections were held in April 2001.

Even though Yadav had to succumb ultimately, he managed to postpone the panchayat elections for over seven years. His undemocratic and unconstitutional posture came in for harsh criticism not only in Bihar, but also in other parts of the country. But he stuck to his position. Whether the empowerment of grass roots leaders elected to the PRIs will have impact upon Yadav's style of politics is for the future to tell. Some observers are optimistic. With 8,412 mukhias and 1.16 lkahs of elected members including 40,000 women, political space of the common people have widened. For the first time villagers will be able to contact holders of political power 'without any intermediary'. Above all, there is the institution of gram sabha, which will provide an opportunity to the people to know how the development funds are being utilized (Kumar 2001). Besides it is significant that the lower backward caste candidates captured some posts of zilla parishad chairpersons and nearly 4 per cent of mukhia's posts. At least 1.06 per cent of mukhias belong to the SC. All of them were returned from unreserved seats, as there was no reservation in the chairpersons' posts in the last election. The success of these subaltern groups may not be spectacular. (In fact, the upper backward groups have captured most of the posts of charpersons in different tiers.) What is important is that the presence of the most neglected groups in the power structure has, at least, become noticeable. This indicates a change in the politics of Bihar (Gupta 2001).

Regime Character, Governability and Panchayats

For almost half a century after Independence, panchayats could exist only during the first phase of Congress rule and in the short periods of SSP or Janata regime headed by Karpoori Thakur. Both in the later period of Congress (1962 to 1967, 1972 to 1977 and 1980 to 1990) and during the Janata Dal (and RJD) regime of Laloo Prasad Yadav (1990 onwards) panchayats ceased to exist.

What are the deterrent factors that forced different regimes of Bihar to centralize power and neglect creation of decentralized power structures in the form of rural local government? We shall examine this in the light of the political history of Bihar.

First phase of Congress Rule (1947–1961)

Until 1961, when Shrikrishna Sinha died, the Congress was the dominant party in Bihar and in the country. The Opposition was weak. Social domination of the upper castes was matched by their total control over the political system. Leaders were veterans of the nationalist movement, which provided enviable political capital to the party. The Congress had its network of organization from the national to the district level. The patronage system linked the local leaders of the upper castes with the organizational network of the party. There was some discipline within the party and the top echelons could resolve conflict at lower levels either by writ or persuasion and conciliation. At the same time, the lower level organizations had some political space of their own. Of course, there were factions. Conflict between the Bhumihar Shrikrishna Sinha and the Rajput A.N. Sinha within the cabinet, were well known. Similar cleavages were there throughout the party. Yet, everybody maintained a semblance of discipline and even A.N. Sinha, after he lost the leadership battle in the 1957 election, did not do anything that could break the party. At the socio-economic level, there was not much turmoil. The upper-caste supremacy went almost unchallenged.

Thus, up to the early 1960s, the government did not face any crisis. There was stability and political institutions were functioning. The party remained cohesive. Democratic norms were observed, even though this democracy was restricted to the upper caste and class. As a result, despite tension underneath, there was a kind of political equilibrium on the surface.

In addition, the Congress of those days took the posture of a party with an ideological basis. It was a confused ideology, no doubt, given the objective of the party to include all kinds of interest groups, classes and castes under one umbrella. Nevertheless, Congressmen and women of those days never ceased to air precepts and rhetoric reflecting such diverse world-views as Gandhism, socialism and liberal democracy.

It is because of projections of the Congress government as one wedded to the Gandhian principle that village panchayats were introduced in Bihar as early as 1947–8. It is the caste and class bias of the then ruling party that forced these panchayats to remain as showpieces and protectors of the existing social and economic order of the agrarian sector. The institution fitted well with the patronage linkage system under which the mukhiyas became a link between the government and the people. Since, mukhiyas also came from the socially dominant segments, there was no chance of the political equilibrium being disturbed.

This explains why village panchayats functioned without interruption throughout the 1950s. Between 1952 and 1961, panchayat elections were held with exemplary regularity. At the same time, it should be noted that no attempt was made during this period to go in for either strengthening these institutions with greater devolution of power and resources, or for extending democracy to the lower castes/classes through active participation in panchayats. The compulsion of taking the Gandhian posture forced the ruling party to establish and sustain panchayats. But, their caste/class bias as well as their political strategy to retain state power with the help of the landed gentry and dominant castes prevented them from taking any radical step to deepen local democracy. So long as the strategy worked without creating any problem of governance, panchayats were allowed to exist.

The Transition Period (1961–1967)

As noted earlier, the situation took a turn after the death of Shrikrishna Sinha. First, factional rivalry within the Congress increased considerably, setting in motion an organizational disintegration. Second, this was the time when advanced sections of the backward castes began to make their presence felt. This was expected, given the modernizing influence of better communication, large-scale state intervention in the socio-economic fields and more importantly, adult suffrage. K.B. Sahay, who became Chief Minister in 1963 was found making concessions to the 'upper backwards' whose voice had been practically throttled in the earlier period. His public speech referring to Sushil Kumar Bage, a Scheduled Tribe MLA as 'my right hand', and to Ram Lakhan Singh Yadav as 'my left hand' was significant in traditional Bihar politics (Frankel 1989: 87).

The internal factions within the Congress party, demands of the better-off among the backward castes for greater political power, growing discontent of the have-nots in the villages, and the extraordinary food crisis of the mid-1960s, worked against the Sahay government and completely destabilized the political equilibrium of the Shrikrishna Sinha era. The ruling party faced for the first time a crisis in governability. Judging by the three indicators mentioned by Kohli (1991: 383–4) to evaluate governability of a regime or the capacity of the regime to govern, the Sahay government faced tremendous problems in respect of legitimacy, its capacity to promote socio-economic development, and to maintain order without coercion. Thus it is easy to explain why restructuring of the panchayat system on the lines of the Balwantrai Mehta Committee Report did not take place, despite the fact that it was the official policy of Congress and Nehru himself was providing leadership to the panchayati raj movement of those days. It is true that the village panchayat elections were duly held in 1964. But this event should be seen as a routine function of a state government which had got used to such elections at regular intervals of three years ever since 1952.

Second Phase of Congress Rule (1972–1977 and 1980–1990)

The fifteen-year rule of the Congress during the 1970s and the 1980s is qualitatively different from its fourteen-year continuous rule immediately after Independence. In the second phase, certain developments took place, which together weakened the government to such an extent that it seemed to have withered away in this state.

After the split of 1969, especially from 1971 onwards, Indira Gandhi introduced her 'plebisicitary politics'. The organization of the Congress in the past, provided space for politics to be mediated through the national, state and local party organizations. Indira Gandhi put an end to it. The party was centralized and power concentrated in the hands of the Prime Minister who was also the party president. In the states the party leaders and Chief Ministers of the state would not emerge from within the party organizations, but would be selected by the leader or the coterie around that leader. A typical example of this is the rather sudden appearance of Jagannath Mishra in Bihar's politics. His only qualification to become Chief Minister was that Sanjay Gandhi liked him. It is necessary to mention that Indira Gandhi's politics that led to the centralization of power of the state and the party in the hands of the Prime Minister at the cost of the party organization, was followed without much variation by her son Rajiv Gandhi. Thus, during that era the Congress party was reduced to a shambles. The Bihar Congress became the hunting ground of the corrupt, of self-seekers, opportunists and even criminals. The entire institutional order, party organization, legislature, bureaucracy, parastatal organizations and educational institutions broke down. The regime lost its capcity to govern.

It is not a coincidence that putrefaction of state politics was accompanied by acceleration of violence. On the one hand, private armies of the rural rich proliferated and received patronage from the police, and, on the other hand, poor peasants started organized protest movements under the leadership of the radical Marxists. Very often they would clash with the musclemen of the rich. It goes to the credit of the peasants that, from the late 1960s they have not allowed the movement to subside, even though their influence hardly crosses central Bihar. The ethnic minorities also gradually intensified their movement leading ultimately to the creation of a separate state of Jharkhand in the year 2000. Thus, discontent, disorder and violence were all-pervasive in Bihar, making the state extremely difficult to govern.

It has been argued that centralization of power and absence of party organization in a democracy with a fragmented society render a regime powerless, and limit its capacity to perform (Kohli 1994: 98–9). Revival of panchayats was the least that could be expected from such a regime. Besides, local democracy goes against the logic of 'plebiscitary politics', as the former creates space for grass roots leadership with popular support to flourish. This explains why it was not possible for the Congress regimes of the period under consideration to support, and then to implement, the policy of democratic decentralization.

Laloo Prasad Yadav's Regime (1990 onwards)

Laloo Prasad Yadav also has been pursuing the same plebiscitary politics introduced by Indira Gandhi. For Yadav, the party is a one-man show. It is he who stands between the party and the masses. Authoritarian in style, Yadav's political capital is his own image as deliverer of the oppressed, and not the political organization of the castes and classes he professes to mobilize.

A good number of neo-rich have emerged in recent times from amongst the backward groups such as Yadavs and Kurmis. They now seek to become a part of the patronage network for siphoning off the developmental funds being pumped into the villages under the anti-poverty programmes and other schemes, by playing middlemen roles between the masses and the government (Gupta 1993a: 1568). Previously, only upper-caste people had that prerogative. The neo-rich among the backward want to replace them. This also suits Yadav's purpose for mobilizing the backward groups without decentralization of either state or political power. MLAs also have a big hand in deciding the manner in which development funds will be spent in the districts. Thus, neither the MLAs nor the local influential people, a large number of whom lend support to Yadav for the sole purpose of misappropriating government resources, are interested in changing the status quo.

More importantly, 'some genuine power to the panchayats may indeed lead to the emergence of alternative power centres' (Gupta 1993a: 1568). Yadav cannot risk this, for he does not have the party organization to contain the challenges that may come from such power centres. Moreover, 'giving more power to the panchayats is also wrought with grave consequences (from the ruling party's point of view), considering the growing spread of rural people's struggle in large parts of rural Bihar' (ibid.).

Yadav, however, knew that sooner or later he would have to hold panchayat elections, because this was a constitutional duty. That is why he took care to make block reservation without making a distinction between the upper and the lower echelons. He also used to talk of partyless panchayat polls, because he had not built up any party structure. Even after all this, he did not muster enough courage to hold panchayat elections until 2001 when the elections had to be held under the direction of the Supreme Court.

The Karpoori Thakur Regime

It was mentioned earlier that in his twenty-two month rule in 1977–9, Karpoori Thakur gave importance to the setting up of the panchayat system. And this he did, despite protests of many within his government. We tried to show that it was the character of his politics and the social base of his party that prompted him to give high priority to the panchayats. From pre-Independence days, Thakur was a Socialist and he remained a Socialist all through. Accordingly, the social base of his party was the poor. He wanted to create opportunity for them to participate in democracy. Since panchayats are capable of creating some space for the backward to participate, he wanted to revitalize the system.

Secondly, Thakur was a man of organization. He had no inclination towards the plebiscitary politics of the Gandhis or Yadav. The party to which he belonged was subjected to many splits. But he always tried to avoid splits. Paul Brass has concluded that Thakur pursued consistently the goal of socialist unity (Brass 1984: 180–1). So, after coming to power, he was anxious to enhance the organizational strength of his party. The panchayat seemed to be a convenient instrument for this. It is significant that around the same time the CPI(M) in West Bengal followed the same strategy to expand its party base.

Concluding Remarks

The bottom line of the foregoing discussion is that the sustenance and growth of the panchayat system within a state in India are dependent on certain social and political variables, which are not necessarily independent of one another. Attempts have been made to identify the political variables from Bihar's political history, even though the social realities of Bihar had to be kept in mind in order to appreciate the political facts in perspective. The burden of the discussion is that Bihar's failure to institutionalize panchayats has to be located in the character of the successive regimes of the state, social base of the ruling parties, style and strategy of these parties in enlisting the support of the electorate and last, but not the least, in the crisis of governability that every regime in Bihar has been facing for a long time.

NOTES

1. Unless specifically mentioned, Bihar includes the new state of Jharkhand.
2. As of 2001, combined population of Bihar (8.29 crores) and Jharkhand (2.69 crores) is nearly 11 crores, next only to present Uttar Pradesh (16.60 crores). With 880 persons per square kilometre, present Bihar is the second most densely populated among the major states of India.
3. During the civil disobedience movement (1930–3), Kisan Sabha suspended its activities to give full support to the political movement of the Congress.
4. For a review of the developments in the Naxalite movement of Bihar, see Gupta (1993b).

Conclusion

The Quest for Local Democracy

Panchayati raj is essentially a project of enriching the practice of democracy. Democracy enriches the lives of citizens in three different ways. First, it widens the scope of social and political participation. Therefore it has an *intrinsic* value. Second, it has an *instrumental* role, because it enables people to express what they value and to demand that political attention be paid to it. Third, by guaranteeing discussions, debates and exchange of views in the public sphere, democracy plays a crucial role in the formation of values and determining social or economic priorities. Thus it has also a *constructive* role to play (Sen 1999; Dreze and Sen 2002).

To what extent these roles can be played by a democracy depends upon its 'content' and not only in its 'form'. In other words, usual attributes of a democratic polity such as representative government, universal suffrage, freedom of expression, right to form associations, separation of powers, rule of law, etc., do not by themselves guarantee that the practice of democracy will be qualitatively rich automatically. The essence of democracy lies in political and social participation of citizens and the corresponding responsiveness and accountability of the authority structures of the state. The problem of democratization of the polity is more acute in a society where gross inequality exists in terms of class, caste and gender and rural-urban divide.

Local democracy can play a crucial role in enriching the practice of democracy. It makes the democratic system relatively accessible to the disadvantaged, and thus expands the scope of social and political participation of the common people. Political freedom is never safe in the hands of a centralized government. The local government is the bulwark against centralization of state power. Second, it makes government more responsive, transparent and accountable. It also ensures efficient and prompt service delivery especially, in the fields of elementary education, health care, local infrastructure, environmental conservation and so on. Third, it gives an opportunity to the ordinary citizens to learn the art of collective decision-making and to influence through public discussion formation of values, fixing social priorities and determination of public policy. Thus by ensuring more democracy at the levels of village communities, panchayati raj can significantly contribute in 'transforming the practice and quality of democracy' (Dreze and Sen 2002).

Our study of the four states show that the state governments have, by and large, shown reluctance in institutionalizing a third stratum of government at the local level. It is true that some regimes showed more interest than others did in allowing alternative centres of political power structures to grow at the community levels. But even such regimes stopped short of conferring autonomy to the rural local government institutions. Others have not tolerated even the existence of such institutions. The case studies have tried to identify the political variables that can explain the stance taken by the different political regimes of the concerned states towards institutionalization of local democracy. Expressed in the form of a set of explanatory hypotheses, they are as follows.

First, those parties that seek to infiltrate rural areas and expand their party organizations, would be inclined to create panchayat structures. Second, the regime that seeks to retain power through 'plebiscitary politics' alone will not be interested in creating and empowering the organization of the party, and by the same logic will be averse to the panchayat institution. Third, the social base of the party plays an important role in determining the attitude that the regime would take towards panchayats. The more a regime seeks to identify itself with the groups excluded from the traditional power structure, the more it feels inclined towards panchayats, unless it seeks to stay in power through 'plebiscitary politics'. Fourth, ideology as expressed through the political idioms used by a political party in power may enforce it to take a pro-panchayat stance. But if that party has no intention to disturb the existing power relations, then it would tolerate panchayats, so long as they do not pose any threat to such relations. Last, when a regime faces crisis in governability, it would depend more on the state's bureaucratic machinery and consequently would oppose decentralization.

The case studies also show that the political parties are not interested in genuine decentralization. Even when a certain regime takes a pro-panchayat stance, it stops short of devolution type of decentralization that might enable the local government institutions to function autonomously. Thus even the regimes that are apparently panchayat-friendly are averse to the concept of decentralization of governance and direct participation of people in decision-making without the mediation of the political or social elite.

This does not augur well for the future of Indian democracy. It shows that the country's political system is monopolized by the political actors who do not want to share power that they may acquire by accessing the state's power structures through the electoral system. Electoral victory accordingly acquires supreme importance in their scheme of things. In the first-past-the-post electoral system, this requires creation of 'vote banks'. Again to create 'vote banks' the political parties spend their energy to invent appropriate slogans that may appeal to the targeted voters. But they scrupulously avoid articulation of political programmes that could make democracy meaningful for the ordinary people. For political parties following the strategy of 'plebiscitary politics', such behaviour is understandable. They cannot exist in a system that permits and encourages cooperative decision-making. Unfortunately parties with such inclination are increasing.

What is intriguing is the behaviour of the political parties who profess to subscribe to well-defined pro-people ideologies and believe in conducting political activities through their party organizations in order to realize their stated objectives of social transformation. Even they seem to be afraid of political participation of the common people. Is electoral politics responsible for putting ideology in the back burner leading to what can be called 'displacement of goals' of these parties? Or is it the case that the project of democratization did never have high priority in their agenda, because they want to establish strict party control over the entire political space? This study indicates that answers to both the questions are in the affirmative.

Another disquieting feature is the tendency of the political parties to create a patron-client relationship between the political elite and the masses. This is evident in the pattern of distribution of the largess of the state, inclination of the groups of people to cling to the ruling party to derive favour, reckless misuse of public fund to satisfy the targeted voters and so on. The whole concept of creating 'vote bank' is rooted in developing a patron-client relationship within the political system. What was a particular feature in human relationship within India's rural society seems to have been replicated in the political system. No wonder that the political elite discourages decentralization that facilitates empowerment of the masses through political and social participation.

The present study, thus, has brought to the surface a grim reality. The agenda of widening and deepening democracy has no priority in the programmes of political parties. Given to them it is unlikely that they will pursue the project of local democracy to its logical extent.

What, then, should be the future route of carrying forward this project? Fortunately the sites of public action are not confined to the political system only. There is the domain of what is called civil society. People can participate in social actions through the non-political and non-market institutions of various kinds. Community groups at the grass roots levels, the non-governmental organizations, the media and the academic and research institutions—all can play useful role in the task of transformation of society. It is in such sites that the struggle for local democracy has to be intensified. There are many instances where the initiatives taken by the civil society institutions have influenced public policy. To make democracy work for the common people is too precious an objective to be ignored by the civil society institutions engaged in the task of social transformation.

References

AVARD, *Panchayati Raj as the Basis of Indian polity*, New Delhi: Association of Voluntary Agencies for Rural Development, 1962.

Bandyopadhyay, D., 'Reflections on Land Reforms in India, Since Independence', in *Political Discourse in India*, vol. II, ed. T.V. Satyamurthy, New Delhi: OUP, 1994, pp. 301–22.

———, 'Responsive governance', *Mainstream*, vol. XXXIX, no. 32, 28 July 2001, pp. 21–7.

———, *Land Reforms in West Bengal*, Calcutta: Government of West Bengal, 1980.

Banerjee, Sumanta, *In the Wake of Naxalbari*, Calcutta: Subarnarekha, 1980.

Banfield, C. Edward, ed., *Urban Government: A Reader in Administration and Politics*, Glenco: The Free Press, 1961.

Basu Raychaudhury, Nirmal Chandra, 'West Bengal: Vortex of Ideological Politics', in *State Politics in India*, ed. Iqbal Narain, Delhi: Meenakshi Prakashan, 1976.

Bavadam, L., 'Battle for survival', *Frontline*, 24 September 1999, pp. 12–14.

———, 'A BJP debacle in Gujarat', *Frontline*, 27 October 2000, pp. 113–14.

Baviskar, B.S., 'Milk and Sugar: A Comparative Analysis of Cooperative Politics', in *Social Structure and Change*, vol. 4, *Development and Ethnicity*, ed. A.M. Shah et al., New Delhi: Sage, 1997, pp. 89–114.

———, 'Factional Conflict and the Congress Dilemma in Rural Maharashtra (1952–75)', in *Diversity and Dominance in Indian Politics: Changing Bases of Congress Support*, vol. I, ed. Richard Sisson and Ramashray Roy, New Delhi: Sage, 1990.

———, *The Politics of Development: Sugar Cooperatives in Rural Maharashtra*, New Delhi: OUP, 1980.

———, 'Cooperative and Politics', *EPW*, 23 March 1968, pp. 490–5.

———, 'Faction and Party Politics: General Elections in an Assembly Constituency in Maharashtra', *Sociological Bulletin*, vol. XX, no. 1, 1971, pp. 54–77.

Baviskar, B.S. and D.W. Attwood, *Finding the Middle Path: The Political Economy of Cooperation in Rural India*, New Delhi: Vistaar, 1996.

Bharti, Indu, 'Dalits gain New Ijjat', *EPW*, 5–12 May 1990.

Bhatt, A., 'Caste and Political Mobilisation in a Gujarat District', in *Caste in Indian Politics*, ed. Rajni Kothari, New Delhi: Orient Longman, 1970, pp. 299–339.

Bhattacharyya, Harihar, *Micro Foundation of Bengal Communism*, New Delhi: Ajanta, 1998.

Bhattacharya, Dwaipayan, 'Politics of Middleness: The Changing Character of the Communist Party of India (Marxist)', in Ben Rogaly, Barbara Harris-White and Sugata Bose, *Sonar Bangla? Agricultural Growth and Agrarian Change in West Bengal and Bangladesh*, New Delhi: Sage, 1999.

Bhattacharya, Moitree, *Panchayati Raj in West Bengal: Democratic Decentralization or Democratic Centralism*, New Delhi: Manak Publication, 2002.

Blair, Harry W., 'Rising Kulaks and Backward Classes in Bihar', *EPW*, vol. XV, no. 2, 12 January 1980, pp. 64–74.

———, 'Electoral Support and Party Institutionalisation in Bihar: Congress and the Opposition, 1977-85', in *Diversity and Dominance in Indian Politics*, vol. 1, ed. Richard Sisson and Ramashray Roy, New Delhi: Sage, 1990.

Bose, Nirmal Kumar, ed., *Selection from Gandhi*, Ahemadabad: Navajivan Publishing House, 1957.

Brass, Paul L., *Caste Factions and Party in Indian Politics*, Delhi: Chanakya, 1984.

Carras, Mary C., *The Dynamics of Indian Political Factions: A Study of District Council in the State of Maharashtra*, Cambridge: Cambridge University Press, 1972.

Catanach, I.J., *Rural Credit in Western India 1875–1930: Rural Credit and the Co-operative Movement in the Bombay Presidency*, Berkeley: University of California Press, 1970.

Centre for Monitoring Indian Economy, *Basic Statistics Relating to States of India*, September 1994.

Chaitanya, Krishna, 'Social Justice, Bihar Style', in *EPW*, vol. XXVI, no. 46, 16 November 1991, p. 2612.

Chakravarthy, G. and S. Pal, *Human Development Profile of the Indian States*, Delhi: NCAER, 1995.

Chatterjee, Bhola, *Aspects of Bengal Politics in the early Nineteen Thirties*, Calcutta: World Press, 1969.

Chaudhry, Praveen K., 'Agrarian Unrest in Bihar: a case study of Patna district 1960–1984', *EPW*, 2–9 January 1988.

Chaudhuri, Kalyan, 'Signals from Bihar', *Frontline*, 5 May 1995.

Cowlagi, V.R.S. and S.S. Mehta, 'Lessons from Panchayati Raj in Gujarat', in Amitava Mukherjee (ed.), *Decentralisation: Panchayats in the Nineties*, New Delhi: Vikas, 1994, pp. 211–14.

Das, Arvind N., *The Republic of Bihar*, Delhi: Penguin India, 1992.

Dey, S.K., 'Panchayati Raj in Independent India', in *Panchayati Raj in Karnataka Today: Its National Dimensions*, ed. George Mathew, New Delhi: Institute of Social Sciences and Concept Publishing House, 1986.

Dreze, Jean and Amartya Sen, *India: Development and Participation*, New Delhi: OUP, 2002.

Franda, Marcus F., *Political Development and Political Decay in Bengal*, Calcutta: Firma KLM, 1971.

Frankel, Francine R., 'Caste, Land and Dominance in Bihar: Breakdown of the Brahmanical Social Order', in *Dominance and State Power in Modern India*, vol. 1, ed. Francine R. Frankel and M.S.A. Rao, New Delhi: OUP, 1989.

Ghatak, Maitreesh and Maitreya Ghatak, 'Recent Reforms in the Panchayat System in West Bengal: Towards Greater Participatory Governance?', *EPW*, vol. XXXVII, no. 1, 5 January 2002, pp. 45–58.

George, Shanti, *Operation Flood: An Appraisal of India's current Dairy Policy*, New Delhi: OUP, 1985.

Ghosh, Buddhadeb, *Panchayati Raj: Evolution of the Concept*, New Delhi: Institute of Social Sciences, Occasional paper series 25, 2000.

———, 'A Study of Panchayats of West Bengal', Report prepared for the Institute of Social Sciences, New Delhi, Mimeo, 1996.

Ghosh, Sankar, *The Naxalite Movement*, Calcutta: Firma KLM, 1974.

Gillon, K.L., *Ahemadabad: A study in Indian Urban History*, Berkeley: University of California Press, 1968.

Godbole, Madhav, 'Cooperative Sugar Factories in Maharashtra: Case for a Fresh Hook', *EPW*, vol. XXXV, no. 6, 5 February 2000, pp. 420–4.

Government of India (GOI), *Report of the Team for the Study of Community Projects and National Extension Services*, Delhi: National Development Council, Committee on Plan Projects, 1957.

———, *Report of the Committee on Panchayati Raj Institutions*, Ministry of Agriculture and Irrigation, Department of Rural Development, 1978.

Government of Maharashtra, *Report of the Committee on Democratic Decentralisation* (V.P. Naik Committee), Bombay: Cooperation and Rural Development Department, 1961.

———, *Panchayat Raj Evaluation Committee Report* (P.B. Patil Committee), Bombay, 1986.

Gupta, Saibal, 'New Panchayats and Subaltern Resurgence', *EPW*, vol. XXXVI, no. 29, 21 July 2001, pp. 2742–4.

Gupta, Tilak D., 'Partyless to Powerless Panchayats', *EPW*, vol. XXVIII, no. 31, 31 July 1993 (a), pp. 1567–9.

———, 'Recent Developments in Naxalite Movement', *Monthly Review*, vol. 45, no. 4, September 1993 (b), pp. 8–24.

——— , 'Election with a Difference', *EPW*, vol. XXX, no. 15, 15 April 1995, pp. 789–92.

———, 'Gujarat: Cosmetic Makeover', *EPW,* vol. XXXVI, no. 40, 2001, p. 3797.

Harris, John, 'Comparing political regimes across Indian states', *EPW,* vol. XXXIV, no. 48, 27 November 1999, pp. 3367–77.

Hauser, Walter, 'General Elections 1996 in Bihar: Politics, Adminstrative Atrophy and Anarchy', *EPW*, vol. XXXII, nos. 44–5, 1997.

Inamdar, N.R., 'Maharashtra', in *Patterns of Panchayati Raj in India*, ed. G. Ram Reddy, Delhi: Macmillan, 1977.

India Today, 31 March 1990.

Issac, T.H. Thomas with Richard Franke, *Local Democracy and Development: People's Campaign for Decentralized Planning in Kerala*, New Delhi: Left-Word Books, 2000.

Jha, Ajit Kumar, 'Choices out of Anarchy', *Frontline*, 24 March 1995.

Jones, Dawn E. and Rodney W. Jones, 'Urban Upheaval in India: The 1974 Navnirman Riots in Gujarat', *Asian Survey*, vol. XVI, no. 11, 1975.

Joshi, Satyakam, 'Congress Debacle in Panchayat Poll', *Mainstream*, 23 September 1995.

Kaviraj, Sudipta, *Politics in India*, New Delhi: OUP, 2000.

Karve, I., 'Maharashtra: Land and Its People', in *Maharashtra State Gazetter*, Bombay, 1968.

Kohli, Atul, 'Parliamentary Communism and Agrarian Reforms: The Evidence from India's Bengal', *Asian Survey*, vol. XXII, no. 7, 1983, pp. 783–809.

———, 'From Elite Activism to Democratic Consolidation: The Rise of Reform Communism in West Bengal', in *Dominance and State Power in India: Decline of Social Order*, vol. II, ed. Francine R. Frankel and M.S.A. Rao, New Delhi: OUP, 1990.

——— , *Democracy and Discontent: India's Growing Crisis of Governability*, Cambridge: Cambridge University Press, 1991.

————, *The State and Poverty in India: The Politics of Reform*, Cambridge: Cambridge University Press, 1987.

——— , 'Centralisation and Powerlessness: India's democracy in a comparative perspective', in *State power and social forces: Domination and transformation in the third world*, ed. Joel S. Migdal, Atul Kohli, Vivienne Shue, Cambridge: Cambridge University Press, 1994.

Kothari, R. and Rushikesh Maru, 'Federating for Political Interests: The Kshatrias of Gujarat', in *Caste in Indian Politics*, ed. Rajni Kothari, New Delhi: Orient Longman, 1970, pp. 70–101.

Kulkarni, A.G., 'A Study of Political Parties in Maharashtra', Ph.D. thesis, University of Pune, 1968.

Kumar, Girish and Buddhadeb Ghosh, *West Bengal Panchayat Elections, 1993*, Delhi: Institute of Social Sciences and Concept Publishing Company, 1996.

Kumar, Girish, 'Political Empowernment of Women through Panchayats: Evidences from West Bengal and other States', paper prepared for the Friedrich Eburt Stiftungs, Delhi, 1995.

———, 'Bihar Panchayat Elections: Overcoming State's Resistance', *EPW*, vol. XXXVI, no. 20, 19 May 2001, pp. 1681–4.

———, *Constitutionalising Panchayats: The Response of State Legislatures*, New Delhi: CSH Occasional Paper, no. 4, 2002.

Kumar, Sanjay, 'New Phase in Backward Caste Politics in Bihar: Janata Dal on the Decline', *EPW*, vol. XXXIV, no. 26, 21–8 August 1999, pp. 2472–80.

Lele, Jayant, 'Caste, Class and Dominance: Political Mobilisation in Maharashtra', in *Dominance and State Power in Modern India: Decline of Social Order*, vol. II, ed. Francine R. Frankel and M.S. A. Rao, New Delhi: OUP, 1990.

Lieten, G.K., *Continuity and Change in Rural West Bengal*, New Delhi: Sage, 1992.

Louis, Prakash, 'Fractured mandate for social change', *EPW*, vol. XXXIV, no. 49, 4 December 1999, pp. 3417–18.

Maddick, Henry, *Panchayati Raj: A Study of Rural Local Government in India*, London: Orient Longman, 1970.

Mallik, Ross, *Development Policy of a Communist Government*, Cambridge: Cambridge University Press, 1993.

'Maharashtra (1972) From Party to Factions', *EPW*, vol. VII, no. 2, 8 January, pp. 56–7.

'Dividing to Rule' *EPW*, vol. VII, no. 41, 9 September 1972a, pp. 1863–5.

'Battle for Sugar Cooperatives', *EPW*, vol.VIII, no. 49, 8 December 1973, pp. 2163–4.

'Congress Still Supreme', *EPW*, vol. XIV, no. 22, 2 June 1979, pp. 930–1.

'Waiting for final Round', *EPW*, vol. XIV, no. 25, 23 June 1979, pp. 1039–40.

'Employment Guarantee Scheme: An Evaluation', *EPW*, vol. XV, no. 49, 6 December 1980, pp. 2043–5.

MHJ, 'Who Pays for and Who Gains from EGS', *EPW*, vol. XVII, no. 31, 31 July 1982, pp. 1226–8.

Mishra, Surjya Kanta, *An Alternative Approach to Development: Land Reforms and Panchayats*, Calcutta: Government of West Bengal, 1991.

Mukarji, Nirmal and D. Bandyopadhyay, *New Horizons For West Bengal's Panchayats*, Calcutta: Government of West Bengal, 1993.

Mukarji, Nirmal, 'Third Stratum', *The Statesman*, 11–13 May 1993.

Mukharjee, Amitava, ed., *Decentralisation: Panchayats in the Nineties*, New Delhi: Vikas, 1994.

Mukhopadhyay, Apurba, 'The Left in West Bengal: Government and Movement, 1967–82', in *Politics in West Bengal: Institutions, Processes and Problems*, ed. Rakhahari Chatterjee, Calcutta: World Press, 1985.

Mundargi, Tirumal, 'Congress and zamindars, Collaboration and Consultation in Bihar', *EPW*, vol. XXV, no. 22, 2 June 1990, pp. 1217–22.

Nair, Kusum, *Blossoms in the Dust: The Human Element in Indian Development*, London: Gerald Duckworth, 1961.

Namboodiripad, E.M.S., 'Panchayati Raj and Centre-State Relations', *Frontline*, 19–22 September 1995, pp. 118–19.

Pal, Subrata, 'The Issues in West Bengal Panchayat Elections', in *People's Democracy*, 4 June 1978.

Palshikar, Suhas and Rajeshwari Despande, 'Electoral Competition and Structures of Domination in Maharashtra', *EPW*, vol. XXXIV, no. 34, 21–8 August 1999, pp. 2409–22.

Palshikar, Suhas, 'Triangular Competition and Bipolar Politics: Elections to Local Bodies in Maharashtra', *EPW*, vol. XXXVII, no. 13, 30 March 2002, pp. 1273–80.

Pandit, Nalini, 'Caste and Class in Maharashtra', *EPW*, vol. XVI, nos. 7 and 8, 1979, pp. 425–36.

Patel, A.S., 'Oilseeds growers' Cooperatives in Gujarat: The Patidar Factor', in B.S. Baviskar and Donald W. Attwood, *Finding the Middle Path*, New Delhi: Vistaar, 1996, pp. 255–72.

Patel, H., Village-Level Political Leadership: A case Study of Kheda District in Gujarat, Centre for Social Studies, Surat, Mimeo, 1986.

Patel, Pravin J. and Rutten Mario, 'Patels of Central Gujarat in Greater London', *EPW*, 17–24 April 1999, pp. 952–4.

Patel, Priyavadan, 'Sectarian Mobilisation, Factionalism and voting in Gujarat', *EPW*, 21–8 August 1999, pp. 2423–33.

Patel, Sujata, The Anand Pattern: A Socio-historical Analysis of its Origin and Growth, paper submitted to the IDPAD project at the Institute of Social Studies, The Hague, Mimeo, 1984.

People's Democracy, 17 July 1977.

Prasad Pradhan, H., 'Caste and Class in Bihar', *EPW*, Annual Number, 1979.

———, 'Agarian violence in Bihar', *EPW*, 30 May 1987.

Prasad, R.C., 'Bihar Social polarisation and political instability', in *State Politics in India*, ed. Iqbal Narain, Delhi: Meenakshi Prakashan, 1976.

Rajaram, N., 'A Sociological Analysis of Cotton Cooperatives in Baroda district', in B.S. Baviskar and Donald W. Attwood, *Finding the Middle Path*, New Delhi: Vistaar, 1996, pp. 273–89.

———, 'Politics and Cotton Cooperatives in Central Gujarat', *EPW*, vol. XXXIV, no. 24, 24 July 1999, pp. 2095–103.

Rosenthal, Donald B., *The Expansive Elite: District Politics and State Policy-Making in India*, Berkeley: University of California Press, 1977.

———, 'Sources of District Congress Factionalism in Maharashtra', *EPW*, vol. VII, no. 34, 19 August 1972, pp. 1725–46.

Rudolph, Lloyd L. and Susane H. Rudolph, 'Organisational adoption of the Congress under Rajiv Gandhi's leadership', in *Diversity and dominance in Indian politics*, vol. 1, ed. Richard Sission and Ramashray Roy, New Delhi: Sage, 1990.

Sen, Amartya, *Development as Freedom*, New Delhi: Oxford, 1999.

Sengupta, Prasanta, 'The Congress Party in West Bengal: Politics, Patronage and Power, 1947–83', in *Politics in West Bengal*, ed. Rakhahari Chatterjee, Calcutta: World Press, 1985.

Seth, Pravin, 'Gujarat: the Case of Small Majority Politics', in *State Politics in India*, ed. Iqbal Narain, Meerut: Meenakshi Prakashan, 1976.

———, 'Panchayati Raj in Historical Perspective in Gujarat', in *Panchayati Raj in Gujarat: A Study*, ed. Ghanshyam Shah, New Delhi: Institute for Social Science, Mimeo, 1996.

Shah, B.C., 'Political Profile of a Village Panchayat in Gujarat', in *Revival of Panchayati Raj: Trends and Problems*, ed. B.C. Shah and J.N. Pandya, Vallabh Vidyanagar: Sardar Patel University, 1989.

Shah, Ghanshyam, 'The upsurge in Gujarat', *EPW*, vol. IX, Special Number, August 1974.

———, 'The 1975 Gujarat Assembly Election in India', *Asian Survey*, vol. XVI, no. 3, March 1975.

———, 'Caste Sentiments, Class Formation and Dominance in Guajarat', in *Dominance and State Power in Modern India: Decline of Social Order*, vol. II, ed. Francine R. Frankel and M.S.A. Rao, New Delhi: OUP, 1990.

———, 'Decentralisation and Weaker Sections', paper presented in Western Regional Workshop on Panchayats, 23–5 February, CSS, Surat, sponsored by Rajiv Gandhi Foundation, New Delhi, 1994.

———, 'Democratic Decentralisation and Social Transformation', in *Panchayati Raj in Gujarat: A Study*, ed. Ghanshyam Shah, New Delhi: Institute of Social Science, Mimeo, 1996(a).

———, 'BJP's Rise to Power', *EPW*, 13–20 January, 1996(b).

Shrader, L.L. and Ram Joshi, 'Zila Parishad Elections in Maharashtra and the District Political Elite', *Asian Survey*, vol. III, no. 3, California, 1963, pp. 143–56.

Sinha, Arun, 'Politics of panchayat elections', *EPW*, vol. XIII, no. 24, 17 June 1978, pp. 982–3.

Sinha, Indu, 'Bihar: Change of course indicated for RJD', *EPW*, vol. XXXIV, no. 49, 4 December 1999, pp. 3417–18.

Siriskar, V.M., 'Maharashtra: Politics of Linkage Elites', in *State Politics in India*, ed. Iqbal Narain, Meerut: Meenakshi Prakashan, 1976.

Vakil, F.D., 'Gujarat', in *Patterns of Panchayati Raj in India*, ed. G. Ram Reddy, New Delhi: Macmillan, 1977.

Vora, Rajendera, 'Shift of Power from Rural to Urban Sector', *EPW*, vol. XXXI, nos. 2 and 3, 13–20 January 1996, pp. 171–3.

Weiner, Myron, *Party Building in a New Nation: The Indian National Congress*, Chicago: University of Chicago Press, 1967.

Williams, Glyn, 'Panchayati Raj and Changing Micro Politics of West Bengal', in *Sonar Bangla: Agricultural Growth and Agrarian Change in West Bengal and Bangladesh*, ed. Ben Rogaly, Barbara Harris-White and Sugata Bose, New Delhi: Sage, 1999.

Zelliot, E., 'Learning the use of Political Means: The Mahars of Maharashtra', in *Caste in Indian Politics*, ed. Rajni Kothari, New Delhi: Orient Longman, 1970, pp. 29–69.

Index